Transdisciplinary Professional Learning and Practice

Paul Gibbs
Editor

Transdisciplinary Professional Learning and Practice

 Springer

Editor
Paul Gibbs
Middlesex University
London
United Kingdom

ISBN 978-3-319-11589-4   ISBN 978-3-319-11590-0 (eBook)
DOI 10.1007/978-3-319-11590-0
Springer Cham Heidelberg New York Dordrecht London

Library of Congress Control Number: 2014952585

Printed on acid-free paper

Springer is part of Springer Science+Business Media (www.springer.com)

Foreword

Knowledge creation, recognition and use is widely held to be a key concern, not just of universities but of all work organizations in the age of "the knowledge economy". The quest to understand the nature of knowledge preoccupied the ancients and in the West the shadow of Aristotle and the all-pervasive narrative of the Enlightenment still looms large over how we construct and evaluate claims to knowledge. Individual knowledge forms the basis for communication of information to others who will then make sense of it in the light of their own personal knowledge. For individual knowledge to be effective at work it must be shared and accepted by others. This may be problematic as individual knowledge is often unrecognized, not only by the organization but often by the individual holding the knowledge; in such cases the knowledge is "tacit" and its use within the organisation is limited. In a complex global world we are desperately in need of a different paradigm to make sense of real life problems that do not neatly fit into our traditional concepts of single-subject disciplines or multidisciplinary approaches. In contrast to the structured certainty of subject disciplinary knowledge, transdisciplinary knowledge is rooted in the messy problems of real life and is thus primarily emergent, complex and embodied. Transdisciplinarity offers us new ways to understand the modern world.

Although transdisciplinarity can be traced back to the early 1970s it has often been at the margins, is highly contested as a approach to knowledge creation within academia and has yet to make a major impact outside the confines of the university. This book brings an international perspective to bear on thinking about and through transdisciplinarity on professional development and education. The scope of the book ranges from the idea of transdisciplinarity and its applications in professional practice to considerations of pedagogy and transdisciplinary research. A distinctive feature of the book is consideration of key issues and concepts in the context of the lived experience of transdisciplinarity. The book effectively demonstrates how a transdisciplinary lens on the world can open our eyes to multiple realities and thus suggests how we might better understand the complexities and contradictions of our world. This is a challenging intellectual journey, but one which is very necessary and immensely worthwhile.

Director, Institute for Work Based Learning   Professor Jonathan Garnett
Middlesex University

Contents

Contributors

Valerie A. Brown Fenner School of Environment and Society, Australian National University, Canberra, Australia

Ron Collins IBM Global Business Services, London, UK

Carol Costley Middlesex University, London, UK

Tamara Cumming Research Institute for Professional Practice, Learning and Education, Charles Sturt University, New South Wales, Australia

Annette Fillery-Travis Middlesex University, London, UK

Paul Gibbs Middlesex University, London, UK

John A. Harris Fenner School of Environment and Society, Australian National University, Canberra, Australia

Kate Maguire Middlesex University, London, UK

Sue L. T. McGregor Mount Saint Vincent University, Halifax, NS, Canada

Andreas Muhar University of Natural Resources and Life Sciences, Vienna, Austria

Linda Neuhauser University of California, Berkeley, CA, USA

Marianne Penker University of Natural Resources and Life Sciences, Vienna, Austria

Christian Pohl Swiss Academies of Arts and Sciences, Bern, Switzerland

Andre Vyt Artevelde University College and the Faculty of Medicine and Health Sciences of the University of Ghent, Ghent, Belgium

Sarah Wall University of Alberta, Alberta, Canada

Sandie Wong Research Institute for Professional Practice, Learning and Education, Charles Sturt University, New South Wales, Australia

Raymond Yeung Hong Kong, China

Introduction

Paul Gibbs

Welcome to this book. For a long time it has been difficult to defend disciplinary-based knowledge and education for progressive purposes. The default setting in the field is that disciplinarity is the reactionary position and transdisciplinarity the progressive position. We propose that disciplinarity and transdisciplinarity are complementary aspects of a single, more complex whole: routine scholarly work. On this basis, the relationship between the two is not problematic. This is evident in the scope of interest in this form of inquiry. Topics in ecology, care, finance and gender studies have all embraced the multidisciplinary approach, not in some hegemonic way but as a process that, alongside disciplinary expertise, can render problems solvable. In this way transdisciplinarity is evolving where there are several approaches to understanding, and these are reflected in the chapters of this book.

They owe much to two critical books in the field, *The New Production of Knowledge: The Dynamics of Science and Research in Contemporary Societies* (Gibbons et al. 1994) and *Re-Thinking Science. Knowledge and the Public in an Age of Uncertainty* (Nowotny et al. 2001). Upon release, these books pointed to the need for science and society to change their approach to knowledge production. Since then the response from universities, and in particular the professions educated there, has embraced a wider approach to knowledge production, working across the barriers in society.

It is difficult to settle on a definition of transdisciplinarity and I turn to Klein's (2010) taxonomy of interdisciplinarity to set the book on a broad course. The multidisciplinary–interdisciplinary–transdisciplinary research environment spans a wide range of contexts and Klein's taxonomy relates multidisciplinarity, interdisciplinarity and transdisciplinarity by comparing their salient features to disciplinarity.

- Multidisciplinarity: Juxtaposes the disciplines fostering wider knowledge, information and methods, but they remain separate, retaining their structure of knowledge and identity (Klein 2010, p. 17).

P. Gibbs (✉)
Middlesex University, London, UK
e-mail: paul.gibbs@mdx.ac.uk

© Springer International Publishing Switzerland 2015
P. Gibbs (ed.), *Transdisciplinary Professional Learning and Practice*,
DOI 10.1007/978-3-319-11590-0_1

- Interdisciplinarity: 'When integration and interaction become proactive, the line between multidisciplinary and interdisciplinary is crossed' (*ibid*, p. 18)—a blending, focusing and linking of disciplines.
- Transdisciplinarity: A 'common system of axioms that transcends the narrow scope of disciplinary world views through overarching synthesis' (*ibid*, p. 24).

This is a rather simple rendition of Klein's proposals but it works, I believe, to distinguish, if not to offer a compelling definition of, transdisciplinarity that will help guide the reader of this book.

The book's purpose is to present a range of thinking about and through transdisciplinary and professional development as an educative process. However, given the ambiguity and ambition of transdisciplinarity, it is not surprising that a variety of interpretations abound, and finding an embracing definition involves Deleuzian multiplicity (Pohl and Hadorn 2007; Lawrence 2010; Nicolescu 2010; Klein 2008, 2010, are some of the most quoted authorities). Nevertheless, rather than focusing on a delineation of the approaches offered, an analysis of these contributions points to commonality of problems that benefit from a transdisciplinary perspective. These tend towards the:

- complex and heterogeneous
- specific, local and uncertain
- epistemologically pragmatic, and
- ethically-based practical action.

These attributes suggest transcending, transgressing and transforming that is theoretical, critically integrative and morally liberating. These ideas are enshrined in the Charter of Transdisciplinarity (1994) and require rigour, openness and tolerance in their implementation (Article 14). As Manderson proposes, '(T)ransdisciplinarity examines a particular site or sites of interest without a particular disciplinary strategy in mind' (1998).

For the influential Nowotny, '(T)ransdisciplinarity is therefore about transgressing boundaries' (2006). This poses challenges for the practice of all professionals and is the core issue this book addresses. Within the boundary-spanning definitions of transdisciplinary research that emerge from and are applied to transdisciplinary problems, the attempt to resolve value-laden issues requires judgement of practical alternatives affecting others. These concerns are too important to be hampered by the constraints of disciplines in the forms of knowledge and the veracity that they sanction. The knowledge needed is both the means to solve the problem and the goal of the solution. Transdisciplinary knowledge lies in the liberation of reason from formality and in the multi-realities of the presenting problem. To seek such insights often requires collaboration, contextualization and reflection, leading to reasoning that is a collective, ethical, problem-based 'explanatory' engagement. The issues faced by the global economy have never been so evident or so poorly dealt with. Yet, whilst such changes are happening, in policy arenas the voices of those interested in the philosophical, sociological and theoretical consequences of these changes are seemingly hushed. This book attempts to bring leading thinkers' voices together in one volume in a way that reflects changes necessarily within the transdisciplinary movement. Included are a conceptual chapter on methods and epistemology-driven chapters, reflective observations on professional practice and a contribution from a non-academic practitioner. The authors are drawn from three continents and a range of disciplinary and multidisciplinary backgrounds and practices so as to weave a story of transdisciplinary professionalism that we think provides a compelling narrative.

The book has three sections. The first explores ideas of transdisciplinarity and its application to professional practice. It contains contributions from the philosophical and sociological traditions and considers critical issues of pedagogy and epistemology in the forms of professional practice. In so doing it distinguishes between the derivative disciplines and their application in practice. The second section contributes to the generic area of professional workplace learning to be a transdisciplinary profession. It contains a specific discussion of pedagogy and approaches to transdisciplinary professional research and education at various levels and intensities. The third section takes on the issues and concepts discussed in the earlier sections and contextualizes them in the lived experience of transdisciplinarity.

The book opens with Sue's chapter, powerfully discussing how professional development refers to acquiring new knowledge and skills to inform one's practice. The chapter frames the transdisciplinary enterprise as an educative process by which people become a more complex self as they engage in transdisciplinary work using the transdisciplinary methodology. In turn this complex self, who has experienced a series of inner changes (paradigmatic, intellectual and philosophical), can better contribute to solving the problems of the world using the transdisciplinary methodology.

Tamara and Sandie conclude that, although transdisciplinary practice has been strongly advocated as an effective approach to working with children and families, practitioners continue to experience barriers to changing practice and difficulties in challenging the self. These personal–professional challenges can make transdisciplinarity difficult to sustain. Accordingly, in this chapter we suggest some possibilities for working with research partnerships as a means of changing and sustaining transdisciplinary practice, especially in relation to personal–professional challenges. We discuss some of the benefits and drawbacks of using case study methodologies and the potential of action research methodologies for supporting the sustainability of transdisciplinary practice.

Ron and Annette suggest that, rather than being of limited applicability, transdisciplinary approaches are likely to shed light on the most challenging and interesting business problems of the twenty-first century. They use a recent IBM study of over 1500 chief executives that shows how senior leaders believe monodisciplinary and boundaried approaches to be insufficient to address the complexity of the issues confronting them. The chapter delves into the problems of our current business environment and the difficulties to be managed. The authors argue that more information is available, and situations that require stochastic models without simple deterministic behaviour can and should be tackled.

For Sarah, nursing is both a discipline and profession, and it has a history of struggling to define its unique identity and body of knowledge. This history, coupled with nursing's dynamic contemporary sociopolitical context, now compels a renewed conceptualization of its professional identity and purpose and a redirected sense of its potential to contribute to the health and social problems facing society. Although the concept of transdisciplinarity has been interpreted in various ways, the idea that disciplinary knowledge can be expanded and transcended by the blending of other realms of knowledge is potentially a fruitful one for nursing in its quest for significance.

Andre's chapter focuses on the need for, and the characteristics and positive consequences of, interdisciplinary teamwork in healthcare. He discusses factors that determine the success of teamwork, such as a management that promotes openness and an administrative organization that promotes interdisciplinary consultation. A shared care plan is stressed as an important tool, where joint planning of goals is essential to intervention and care. Healthcare workers with different professional knowledge and background have to harmonize their intervention plan with the competences and goal settings of the other team members.

This section of the book closes with Raymond's reflective account of being a professional. He writes about the issues facing a practising accountant who, in addition to accounting qualifications, has two law degrees. The purpose of his chapter is to share his experience and perspective on how accounting professionals learn from the professionals of other disciplines, to give insight for educators designing professional learning programmes for transdisciplinary learners.

The theme of transdisciplinary pedagogical practice and education is central to the second section. Linda and Christian open by offering a discussion of the benefits and challenges of creating transdisciplinary university education, with examples from the University of California, Berkeley (USA) and ETH Zurich (Switzerland). In their chapter they discuss the nature and importance of transdisciplinary research and action, considering the general goals of integrating trandisciplinarity into higher education, and make recommendations for integrating transdisciplinarity into university education.

Carol's chapter follows this in the UK context. She begins by making the case that transdisciplinarity features in programmes of study in universities as well as in the construction of research projects. It is present in the curriculum area of professional and occupational practice as a field of study and educational knowledge that, she argues, is mainly transdisciplinary in nature.

Marianne and Andreas close the section by looking at the merits of researching and teaching transdisciplinarity, on top of doing it. International and cross-disciplinary exchanges can address crucial questions of group size and group compositions, adequate funding conditions and methods that help to deal with powerful interest groups and thus contribute to high quality, legitimate and effective societal outcomes. By publishing and teaching on transdisciplinarity, we make specific concepts and approaches accessible to the critique of others. Thus, we can benefit from the academic principle of scepticism that is a key for quality management and effective innovation processes.

In the final section, the set of contributions discusses new ways of exploring transdisciplinarity and how these might reveal new ways of being. For Paul, professional practices are undertaken in the workplace, known to be a social system that confounds simple analysis and where things change and turn messy. There are many disciplinary approaches (e.g. anthropological, psychological and sociological), but attempts to determine what, and why, things happen within professional practice prove difficult from any single disciplinary and epistemological perspective. His chapter suggests that a transdisciplinary approach could be helpful, and that this is perhaps implicit in successful professional agency when dealing with emergent problems. These issues need to be taken at their face value, informed by a range of knowledge and resolved with the constraints of the sociopolitical context that, in many cases, created them.

Valerie and John take us towards a new reconceptualization of what transdisciplinarity might be like by moving us into the new operating and learning age of the Anthropocene, a term being applied to our current era, marked by significant effects of human ideas and actions on the planet's natural and social environments. The authors explore the emergence of a collective mind that reframes opposites as relationships and asks introspective, physical, social, ethical, creative, sympathetic and reflective questions of complex issues in times of transformational change. The reflective seventh question challenges whether, after many generations of specialization, we can still find ways to combine diverse answers into a meaningful whole that throws light on the complex issues of our age.

All the authors are grateful to Professor Helga Nowotny, President of the European Research Council, for her considered views of the book. Her work continues to influence debate, discussion and application of transdisciplinarity in a wide range of sectors.

Finally, we hope you enjoy reading it, either in its entirety, by section or by chapter.

References

Charter of Transdisciplinarity. (1994). http://basarab.nicolescu.perso.sfr.fr/ciret/english/charten htm. Accessed 12 June 2012.

Gibbons, M., Limoges, C., Nowotny, H., Schwartzman, S., Scott, P., & Trow, M. (1994). *The new production of knowledge: The dynamics of science and research in contemporary societies.* London: Sage.

Klein, J. T. (2008). Evaluation of interdisciplinary and transdisciplinary research: A literature review. *American Journal of Preventive Medicine, 35*(2S), S116–S123.

Klein, J. T. (2010). A taxonomy of interdisciplinary knowledge. In R. Frodeman, J. T. Klein, & C. Mitcham (Eds.), *The Oxford handbook of interdisciplinarity* (pp. 15–30). Oxford: Oxford University Press.

Lawrence, R. J. (2010). Beyond disciplinary confinement to imaginative transdisciplinarity. In V. A. Brown, J. A. Harris, & J. Y. Russell (Eds.), *Tackling wicked problems* (pp. 16–30). Washington: Earthscan.

Manderson, D. (1998). Some considerations about transdisciplinarity: A new metaphysics? In *Transdisciplinarity: Stimulating synergies, integrating knowledge.* UNESCO. http://unesdoc unesco.org/images/0011/001146/114694eo.pdf (npn). Accessed 12 June 2012.

Nicolescu, B. (2010). Methodology of transdisciplinarity-levels of reality, logic of the included middle and complexity. *Transdisciplinary Journal of Engineering & Science, 1*(1), 19–38.

Nowotny, H. (2006). The potential of transdisciplinary interdisciplines. http://www.interdisciplines. org. Accessed 1 July 2014.

Nowotny, H., Scott, P., & Gibbons, M. (2001). *Rethinking science: Knowledge in an age of uncertainty*. Cambridge: Polity Press.

Pohl, C., & Hadorn, G. H. (2007). *Principles for designing transdisciplinary research* (trans: A. B. Zimmerman). Munich: OEKOM.

Paul Gibbs is Professor of Education at Middlesex University. His interests and publications span higher education marketing, philosophy, professional practice and time. He is Series Editor of Educational Thinker for Springer, holds positions on a number the editorial board of a number of international journal and has participated in a number of European projects. His elective interests find a conceptual home in transdisciplinarity.

Part I
Section One

Transdisciplinary Knowledge Creation

Sue L. T. McGregor

Introduction

The focus of this book is thinking about and through transdisciplinarity and professional development *as* an educative process. These three ideas are not normally brought together. Professional development refers to acquiring new knowledge and skills to inform *one's practice* (Jasper 2006). Transdisciplinarity is concerned with creating new, integrative knowledge to address the complex problems of *the world* (Nicolescu 2002). "The educative process is *a series of inner changes* through which an individual is *transformed* from an immature personality to a mature personality. . . .[He or she] is a developing personality which responds to all the external conditions and through his [or her] responses grows into a new and progressively more *complex self*" (Judd et al. 1923, p. 33, emphasis added).

In more detail, through the educative process (series of inner changes), people may experience global changes to their concept of themselves. Indeed, some people recognize and attribute the educative process as the catalyst for their transformative change. The process by which people change while engaged in learning (i.e., the educative process) presupposes the possibility that people might have belief problems (philosophical and pragmatic) that shape their judgement of self. Not surprisingly, the educative process is interpreted by each person based on their own experiences; that is, what and how did they learn and how did that change them (Campbell-Higgins 2000).

This chapter frames the transdisciplinary enterprise as an educative process by which people become a more complex self as they engage in transdisciplinary work using the transdisciplinary methodology. In turn, this complex self, who has experienced a series of inner changes (paradigmatic, intellectual and philosophical), can better contribute to solving the problems of the world using the transdisciplinary methodology.

S. L. T. McGregor (✉)
Mount Saint Vincent University, Halifax, NS, Canada
e-mail: sue.mcgregor@msvu.ca

© Springer International Publishing Switzerland 2015
P. Gibbs (ed.), *Transdisciplinary Professional Learning and Practice,*
DOI 10.1007/978-3-319-11590-0_2

To begin to weave these three ideas together, note that professional development is considered to be a process of *personal* growth through programs, services and activities designed to enable people, individually or collectively, to enhance their professional and disciplinary practice (Jasper 2006); it is an educative process. From a non-transdisciplinary perspective, Jasper (2006) explains that "the main ways we develop professionally... are through the practice of *our* profession [and discipline] itself, and the stimulation from the practice world that makes us continually build on *our* existing knowledge, *seek out* new knowledge and skills, make connections between *our* knowledge base *and* the challenges we encounter in *our* practice, and learn from *our* experiences" (p. 2, emphasis added). Professional development from this perspective is a very personal and private experience.

In contrast, from a Nicolescuian transdisciplinary perspective, professional development would expand to include developing professionally through the practice of one's profession and discipline *in concert with* others, instead of alone. Instead of just become a more learned person, people from a myriad of professions, disciplines and societal sectors would collaboratively work to address complex problems. They would creatively co-generate new knowledge by integrating multiple perspectives using an inclusive logic (to be discussed shortly). Concurrently, people would grow personally and develop professionally (possibly couched within their discipline) through this transdisciplinary enterprise.

To echo Judd et al.'s (1923, p. 33) definition of the educative process, transdisciplinary knowledge creation would help participants "grow into new and progressively more complex" global selves and into collaborative, complex problem solvers. To develop this idea, this chapter introduces the concepts of *transdisciplinary self* and *transdisciplinary maturity* (reflecting Judd et al.'s conception of the educative process). The genesis of transdisciplinarity is briefly discussed, followed with a detailed overview of Basarab Nicolescu's transdisciplinary methodology.

The Genesis of Transdisciplinarity

Transdisciplinarity was introduced to the world in 1972 at a Parisian seminar held by the Organization for Economic Cooperation and Development (OECD). Conceived as a concept in the early seventies (Apostel et al. 1972; Jantsch 1972; Kocklemans 1979; McGregor 2010), it has only just recently gained momentum and grudging acceptance as a necessary paradigmatic, methodological and intellectual innovation. Transdisciplinarity is a relatively new, nascent approach to knowledge creation, competing with longstanding multi- and interdisciplinarity (Du Plessis et al. 2013). Transdisciplinarity remains "a rather elusive concept" that continues to evolve (Jahn et al. 2012, p. 1).

Recognizing that there are two dominant transdisciplinarity camps (Augsburg 2014; Klein 2004), this chapter showcases the approach championed by physicist Basarab Nicolescu (and philosopher Edgar Morin); hence, the moniker *Nicolescuian transdisciplinarity*. They view transdisciplinarity as *a new methodology* to create knowledge, with attendant axioms for what counts as reality, logic, and knowledge (to be discussed shortly). The other camp (frequently referred to as the Swiss, Zurich or German school) emerged from an *International Transdisciplinary Conference* held in Zurich in 2000 (see proceedings at Klein et al. 2001). The Zurich camp conceptualizes transdisciplinarity as a *new type of research*, called Mode 2 research (see Gibbons et al. 1994), informed by the post-normal science perspective (see also Nowotny 2003). New knowledge is not the express intent, nor does it advocate axioms for knowledge generation, as does the Nicolescuian methodological approach.

Regarding the Nicolescuian approach, an editorial committee at the *First World Congress of Transdisciplinarity* (Portugal, in 1994) drafted a *Charter of Transdisciplinarity* (de Freitas et al. 1994). This charter contains 14 articles referring to the notions of multiple realities, different types of logic, the complexity of the world, and the need for a *transdisciplinary attitude* for those engaged in complex problem solving between and beyond disciplines. Nicolescu (2002) further develops these ideas in his book titled *Manifesto of Transdisciplinarity*. In the spirit of a manifesto, it promotes a new idea (i.e., transdisciplinarity) with prescriptive notions for carrying out the changes he felt should be made in knowledge creation; that is, a new methodology in its own right.

In more detail, drawing from quantum physics (and other aligned sciences), Nicolescu (2002) describes transdisciplinarity as multidimensional and supported by the following three pillars (philosophical axioms) : (a) knowledge as complex and emergent (epistemology); (b) Multiple Levels of Reality mediated by the Hidden Third (ontology); and, (c) the Logic of the Included Middle, which contrasts with Classical exclusive logic (Nicolescu 2008). Although Nicolescu eschews the addition of a fourth axiom dealing with values (i.e., axiology) (see Nicolescu 2011a, p. 37), others believe it should be included (see Du Plessis et al. 2013) and Cicovacki (2009) and McGregor (2011) who have developed arguments for its inclusion in the transdisciplinary (methodology). This chapter will focus on Nicolescu's three axioms.

Three Axioms of Nicolescuian Transdisciplinarity

The basic premise of this chapter is that professional development (emerging into a new complex self) can happen through the transdisciplinary practice of one's profession and discipline *in concert with* divergent others who are co-generating new knowledge. Conversely, transdisciplinary knowledge creation would help participants grow into new and progressively more complex global selves and collaborative, complex problem solvers. This rich, reciprocal relationship necessitates being open to very different notions of longstanding approaches to the axioms of knowledge, logic and reality. Without this *methodological openness*, people will not be able to engage in transdisciplinarity and will remain relegated to their particular disciplines. This *methodological segregation* will affect the educative process, compromising the ability to become a more complex intellectual self, and by association, one's ability to engage in transdisciplinary problem solving.

For clarification, conventional approaches to knowledge creation include empirical, interpretive and critical methodologies, which are inspired by Habermas' (1984) theory of communicative action and what constitutes knowledge (i.e., empirical, interpretive and critical lines of inquiry). These approaches fall within the positivistic/post-positivistic and quantitative/qualitative methodological camps. In particular, scientific, empirical approaches tend to be framed as positivistic and quantitative. Interpretive and critical fall more into the post-positivistic and qualitative camps, although one can engage in positivistic qualitative work if numerical measurements are involved (McGregor and Murnane 2010). Table 1 summarizes the main differences between how these three methodologies conceive reality, knowledge and logic, juxtaposed against Nicolescuian transdisciplinarity. It is evident that the transdisciplinary methodology goes far beyond the other methodologies, yet it depends upon them and complements them as well (de Freitas et al. 1994). The rest of the paper spells out the nuances of Nicolescu's three pillars (axioms) of transdisciplinarity (see primer in the right-hand column of Table 1).

Ontology—Multiple Levels of Reality Mediated by the Hidden Third

The development of more complex, transdisciplinary selves, who could engage in jointly addressing complex problems, would involve profound changes in the way people view reality. They would have to first acknowledge how they *do* view reality and then let that go for a more progressive and radical approach. Because of the power of the Western, positivistic, empirical world view (Du Plessis et al. 2013), most people align with reality as understood by positivism and empiricism (see Table 1). They assume there is *one single reality* that people cannot see, yet believe is *out there*. It is made up of discrete elements that have been in existence since the beginning of time. This approach presumes the building blocks for everything (for life) *already* exist, and are just waiting for someone to *reconfigure them*. When all of these elements are found through the scientific method, a full picture of reality will exist. This view of the world also presumes that reality follows a predetermined path. The principle of determinism (aiding predictability) holds that any event is completely determined by previous events (linear cause and effect). This principle rids people of any agency or free will (i.e., purposeful actions or conscious participation). Also, it is assumed reality is external to our consciousness; it is not a product of our minds (Bullard 2011; Heylighten 2006).

Nicolescuian transdisciplinarity evokes a profoundly different notion of reality, one that better accommodates the complexity, diversity and contradictions in perspectives in the world. Rather than just one reality, transdisciplinarity holds there are multiple levels of realities, with interaction and movement amongst them mediated by, what Nicolescu (2002) calls, the Hidden Third.

In a major push back against Newtonian dualism and the singular notion of matter-based reality, Nicolescu proposes that transdisciplinary (TD) ontology encompasses

Table 1 Comparison of methodological axioms

	Empirical	Interpretive	Critical	Transdisciplinary
Reality (Ontology)	The *one reality is out there*, a single reality that people cannot see	Reality is *conditional* upon human experiences	Reality is *of the world*, not imagined, and never fully understood	Multiple realities (upwards of 10) evident along three levels (internal, external and the Hidden Third)
	It is made up of discrete elements; when we find them all through the scientific method, we will have a full picture of reality	Reality is socially and collectively constructed via the lived experiences of people	Reality is *here and now*, shaped by politics, social, gender, values and culture, and deeply mediated by power relations	Reality is *plastic* and always *in flux*, always *moving*
	Reality is external to our consciousness (not a product of our minds)	Reality can be a product of a person's mind OR a product of interactions with others or one's context	Reality is constructed within an oppressive context and reconstructed after challenging the status quo	Interaction amongst the internal and external levels happens in the quantum vacuum (not empty but ripe with potentials)
				Interaction in this fecund vacuum is lubricated by the Hidden Third, creating a zone of non-resistance to others' views on reality (where multiple and contradictory perspectives can be integrated; what appears to be contradictory can temporarily be joined)
Knowledge (Epistemology)	The *one truth* is out there waiting to be discovered	Truth is *created* and there is more than one truth (perspectives)	Truth is grounded in the context, in social, political and historical practices	Knowledge is based on cross-fertilization; that is, it is co-created through an emergent, iterative process amongst those from the academy and civil society
	Knowledge is discovered using the scientific method	There are many ways of knowing aside from the scientific method	Knowledge is created through critically questioning the way things "have always been done"	Resultant knowledge is characterized by complexity, emergence, (re)organization and embodiment (rather than complicated, static and discipline-bound)
	knowledge is objective (bias free)	knowledge is constructed by people	knowledge is transformative, consensual and normative (dialectic)	knowledge is alive; it is 'in-formation', created from intellectual fusion and integrative synergies

Table 1 (continued)

	Empirical	Interpretive	Critical	Transdisciplinary
	Knowledge is viewed through the lens of reductionism, determinism, disjunction (separation), predictability, and linear causality	Knowledge is subjective and value ladened		Knowledge is transcendent in that those involved give up sovereignty of their domain to create a temporary fecund space for the emergence of new knowledge
Logic	Deductive, rational, formal logic	Inductive logic	Inductive logic (more inclusive than empirical)	Inclusive logic (Logic of the Included Middle)
	Clear distinction between facts and values	Concerned with discerning how people understand and make sense of their world by observing them in their world	Inductive logic is used to *induce*; that is, to persuade or lead people to reveal new insights, especially to reveal ideologies and power relationships that are keeping them oppressed	Accommodates the eventual, possible, creation of new, integrative knowledge that does not *yet* exist
	Exclusive logic, which involves cause and effect, linear thinking, reductionism, and either/or approaches (dualism) with no room for contradictions	Inductive logic *suggests* truth but does not ensure it		This logic enables people to imagine that the space between things is alive, dynamic, in flux, moving, perpetually changing and full of potential and eventualities
		The truth generated using inductive logic is *probable* (not certain, as with deductive), based upon the given evidence (there is a chance it can be proven false)		Inclusive logic is used to move through the different types of reality in the zone of non-resistance, leading to unlikely integration of realities and perspectives
				Tensions between people are assumed to hold things together as they emerge through synergistic chaos

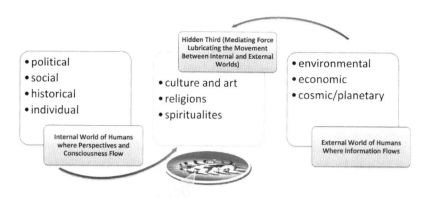

Fig. 1 Transdisciplinary knowledge creation

at least 10 different Realities (disciplinary and sectoral perspectives and view points), aside from just the physical, material reality. Per his convention, this chapter capitalizes the word Reality when referring to his approach. These 10 Realities are organized along three levels. Level one is the internal world of humans, where *consciousness* and *perspectives* flow—the TD-Subject (comprising four Realties: political, social, historical, and individual). Level two is the external world of humans where *information* flows—the TD-Object (comprising three different Realities: environmental, economic, and cosmic/planetary). Interaction and movement amongst the previous two levels are mediated by the Hidden Third level. Peoples' experiences, intuitions, interpretations, descriptions, representations, images, and formulas meet on this third level. As well, three additional Realities exist in this intuitive zone of non-resistance to others' ideas, this mediated interface: culture and art, religions, and spiritualities (Nicolescu 1985, 2002), see Fig. 1.

Of deep significance to Nicolescu's approach to transdisciplinarity is that while each of the 10 Realities is characterized by its incompleteness, in *unity*, they generate new, infinite transdisciplinary knowledge (Nicolescu 2005). This approach to Reality (ontology) is profoundly different from the Newtonian notion of *one* level of reality, the empirical (physical) reality, materialism, predicated on the notion of *matter.* TD transreality includes matter *as well as* consciousness, perspectives, emotions and various approaches to what counts as knowledge and ways of knowing (far beyond Newtonian exclusionary dualism and disciplinarianism).

More about the Hidden Third. Nicolescu needed a concept to accommodate people resisting other people's world views, and a way to allow for the integration of these world views to create new knowledge. Being a quantum physicist, he was inspired by the quantum vacuum, which is actually *not* empty, it is just at its lowest energy point, ready for emergence and potential. With this inspiration, he coined the term the Hidden Third. The word 'hidden' obviously means it is invisible. The word 'third' typically refers to someone playing a mediating role between two entities. Succinctly, Nicolescu (2011a) suggests that the Hidden Third (the quantum vacuum) refers to a zone of non-resistance to others' views on Reality that plays the mediating role of a third between information and consciousness and perceptions. It acts like a *secretly included* middle agent that allows for temporary unification of, what are normally, contradictory ideas (Nicolescu 2005).

Still inspired by the quantum vacuum, Nicolescu (1985, 2011a) posits that the Hidden Third is a way to conceive of people moving to a place where they become open to others' perspectives, ideologies, value premises and belief systems, inherently letting go of aspects of how they currently *know* the world. To that end, he assumed Reality is always in flux, that it is plastic (Cillier and Nicolescu 2012; Nicolescu 2011b), meaning it is malleable and pliable. Transdisciplinarity is deeply concerned with the dynamics created by the simultaneous action of several Levels of Reality; that is, the *movement* of Reality, facilitated by the lubricating role of the Hidden Third (Nicolescu 1999). The result of this *transmovement* is the emergence of new transdisciplinary knowledge, possible because people's eyes and minds have been opened to other points of view, which can be integrated using the Logic of the Included Middle.

Inclusive Logic of the Included Middle

Per Table 1, positivistic, empirical approaches rely on deductive, formal logic. And, "[d]espite the limitations of classical, binary logic that have been laid bare by modern physics, contemporary scientific and western cultural thinking is still dominated by the Aristotelian tradition of *exclusive*... logic" (Cole 2006, p. 11, emphasis added). It is called exclusive because it *negates* the possibility of co-existing contradictions, striving instead for consistency. Classical deductive logic holds that something is consistent if it does not have contradictions (see more below). Presuming that contradictions compromise both regularity and consistency negates (pun intended) the possibility of connecting diverse ideas to create necessary complexity, this exclusive logic precludes inclusive solutions to humanity's complex problems.

In more detail, Classic linear logic (Newtonian exclusive logic) is based on three fundamental axioms (i.e., self-evident truths, not susceptible to proof or disproof): (a) the axiom of identity: A is A; (b) the axiom of non contradiction: A is not non-A; and, (c) the axiom of the excluded middle, meaning there is no third term **T** (Latin *tiers*), which is simultaneously A and non-A. Classical, exclusive logic says A and non-A cannot exist at the same time; classical scholars call this idea *consistency*. In classical logic, a *contradiction* exists when people try to say A (he is brave) and non-A (he is not brave) *exist at the same time*. In simple language, there is no *third* possibility of, for example, being brave and not brave, at the same time (Cole 2006; Nicolescu 1985). Suggesting such a thing is *illogical*; he is either brave or he isn't. Something is either true or it isn't. We all know of people who are brave in some situations and not in others, but exclusive logic denies this possibility of co-existing contradictions. Exclusive logic assumes that ideas that are antagonistic cannot be connected (Brenner 2005, 2008).

Brenner (2005) coined the term *transconsistent logic* to accommodate the inclusive nature of transdisciplinary logic. If Classical science is predicated on consistency, transdisciplinarity must expand to include *transconsistency*. Brenner understood this to mean the "realm beyond the consistent" (2008, p. 161), where new knowledge can emerge because potential was released and acted upon. He explains that when A is *actualized* (exists in fact), non-A is *potentialized* (has the capacity to exist in the future) and vice versa, alternately, without either ever disappearing completely (Brenner 2005, 2008). Both the scientist and the indigenous elder retain their identity while a new insight is gained from their interaction. "[T]hat which appears to be disunited is united, and that which appears to be contradictory is perceived as noncontradictory" (Nicolescu 2008, p. 7). "Opposing aspects of a phenomenon that are generally considered independent can thus be understood as being in dynamic relationship" (Brenner 2005, p. 3).

Brenner, explains that "the law of the excluded middle [is] a limiting case... only instantiated in *simple* situations" (2005, p. 3), and also introduces the idea of *logic in reality* (LIR) (Brenner 2011). He purposely intends LIR to reflect complexity, and views it as a "logical principle of dynamic opposition, an antagonistic duality inherent in... all real physical and non-physical phenomena" (Brenner 2011 p. 3). Nicolescu (1985) refers to the logic required for emergent, complex situations as the *Logic of the Included Middle*. Inclusive logic accommodates the eventual, possible, creation of new integrative knowledge that does not yet exist. It does so by permitting each of (a) empty domains, (b) worlds that do not exist, and (c) worlds that might eventually exist (Nolt 2010). To exclude any of these domains, realities or worlds negates complex solutions to transdisciplinary problems.

In more detail, realizing that in order to address the complex problems facing humanity, there *had* to be way to reconcile the co-existing (a) certainty of consistencies and (b) possibilities opened up with contradictions, Nicolescu (1985, 2011b) proposes a change to the third classical linear logic axiom, submitting that a third term **T** *can* exist, which is simultaneously A and non-A. The Logic of the Included Middle informs the third "T", which stands for *tiers inclus*, the included third (Nicolescu 1985), that which can co-exist in contradiction.

In these instances (for example in the contentious social, economic and political spheres), topics, ideas and people that should logically be excluded or antagonistic *can* be connected (Brenner 2008). Transdisciplinary quantum logic assumes that when A and non-A *do* co-exist at the same time, when a third temporary state *does* emerge, a *contradiction* is resolved at a higher level of reality or complexity. This new state represents the result of two contradictory things interacting and coming to a temporary resolution (Ramadier 2004) (e.g., the scientist accepting insights gained from a narrative reflecting an indigenous wisdom tradition).

Brenner (2011) actually proposes the term *included emergent middle* for these sorts of reality, explaining that the "logic of an *included* middle consist[s] of axioms and rules for determining the state of the three dynamic terms involved in a phenomenon" (Brenner 2005, p. 3); that is, A, non A and an emergent, more complex, temporary Third state. This inclusive logic best describes a transdisciplinary picture of reality, where solutions emerge in the fecund middle, the vacuum. In conclusion, the existence of this inclusive logic and related principles, and the ontology based on them (what counts as reality), bears directly on the problem of the unity of knowledge.

Knowledge as Complex, Emergent, Embodied and Cross-fertilized

The third basic tenet of Nicolescuian transdisciplinarity is complexity. In some documents, he actually refers to *the epistemology axiom* (e.g., 2010), but he usually calls it the *Complexity Axiom: The Universal Interdependence* (see Nicolescu 2011a, p. 36). He believes that complexity is a modern form of the ancient principle of universal interdependence, in that "everything is dependent on everything else, everything is connected, nothing is separate" (Nicolescu 2004, p. 48). Morin (2006) concurs, referring to the "generalized interdependence of everything and everyone" (p. 21). Nicolescu recently recognized the need for a "future detailed study of *transcomplexity*" but he did not define the term except for saying it "unifies different types of complexity" (2010, p. 8). In particular, he commented on horizontal, vertical, transversal and restricted complexity. He has elected to use Morin's notion of *generalized complexity* (1999, 2005, 2006), claiming it comes the closest to what is needed to deal with transdisciplinary problems. This is likely because Morin (2006) views complexity through an *epistemological lens* that respects chaos, disorder, uncertainty, (re)organization, and emergence, rather than within the epistemology of classical science (see left column in Table 1).

Disciplinary science isolates disciplines from each other and isolates them from their environments. The breaking up of knowledge into separate disciplines "prevents [knowledge] from linking and contextualizing" (Morin 2006, p. 14). To offset this effect, he urges us to "recognize the inseparability of the separable" (p. 16). That is, even though disciplines *can* be separated, if we hope to address the complex problems of the world, they have to be re-conceived as inseparable. Morin explains that "everything that is separated is *at the same time* inseparable" (p. 16, emphasis added). This premise is especially true from the Nicolescuian transdisciplinary perspective, which holds that the academy and the rest of the world are inseparable, and their disparate viewpoints must be voiced and integrated to solve complex human problems. But Morin (2006) also realizes that "our aptitude for connecting is underdeveloped and our aptitude for separating is overdeveloped. . . .[O]ur atrophy of the capacity to connect is increasingly serious in a globalized world" (p. 21).

So, it goes without saying that creating transdisciplinary knowledge is all about connecting, all about complexity, emergence and the intellectual fusion of disparate world views into new integral knowledge (McGregor 2004). Complex transdisciplinary knowledge is created in the fertile middle ground between the mediated Multiple Levels of Reality, using inclusive logic. Professional development is a *cognitive* process, pertaining to knowledge (Jasper 2006). This means those engaged in transdisciplinary work must learn to embrace complexity thinking as part of their cognitive personal growth. Complexity is based on a collection of powerful assumptions: (a) people and systems can adapt and reorganize, (b) complex behaviour can emerge from a few simple rules applied locally, (c) order can emerge without central control, (d) small changes can leverage big effects, (e) events are unpredictable meaning people must trust that things will emerge, and (f) co-evolution of life proceeds through constant tension, chaos and balance (McGregor 2012). Indeed, Nicolescu (2010) describes the totality of all of the levels of Reality as a *complex structure*, which necessitates a non-classical understanding of the terms complexity and knowledge.

Pre-empting the discussion of transdisciplinarity epistemology, consider that, based on Newtonian thinking, positivism assumes that everything that exists now (i.e., all matter) has existed since the beginning of time and will continue to exist, just in different configurations (due to humans exerting forces and repositioning the matter in time and space). Discovery of new knowledge is therefore not a creative process; it is merely an *uncovering* of distinctions that were waiting to be observed. The premise that knowledge is out there, waiting to be discovered, leaves little room for novelty or creation when solving complex problems (Bullard 2011; Heylighten 2006). Morin (2006) recounts two examples of unintended negative consequences when people solved complex problems using a techno-economic mindset, which is predicated on classical science notions of what counts as knowledge (separate, fragmented, disconnected, static; the damming of the Nile river and the deviation of rivers in Siberia).

To reiterate, transdisciplinary knowledge is emergent, complex, embodied and cross-fertilized. Emergence refers to novel qualities, properties, patterns and structures that appear from relatively simple interactions among people, qualities that did not exist when presented in isolation. These new qualities are layered in arrangements of increased complexity (Morin 2005; Nicolescu 2008). In fact, the process of emergence manifests when people pass through the zone of non-resistance (accepting there are many Realities) and enter the fertile, temporary *middle ground* to problem solve using inclusive logic. The resultant transdisciplinary knowledge is characterized as embodied, a part of everyone who co-created it, rather than discipline-bound or sector-bound.

McGregor uses a lava lamp metaphor to express this idea. Inclusive logic enables people to imagine that the space between things is alive, dynamic, in flux, moving, perpetually changing and full of potential and eventualities (like a lava lamp). When people from different disciplines and sectors come in contact with each other and are motivated, an energizing force is generated—a synergy is created. This synergy leads to the generation of *embodied knowledge* created from the energy emanating from *intellectual fusion*. Everyone involved now *owns* the new knowledge because it was co-created (McGregor 2004, 2009). Horlick-Jones and Sime (2004) coined the phrase *border-work* to refer to the intellectual work that occurs when people living on the borders of the academy (university disciplines) and other sectors (civil society, industry, government) engage in knowledge generation to address wicked problems. This new knowledge is open and alive because the wicked problems the knowledge addresses are alive, emerging from the life world (Nicolescu 2005).

Finally, cross-fertilization of transdisciplinary knowledge results from the iterative convergence of different actors and their fuzzy-edged balls of knowing, shaped by their respective disciplinary or sectoral expertise (McGregor 2004). Cross-fertilized knowledge emerges through the process of *transintegration*, understood to mean opening things up to all disciplines and to civil society- and other sector-knowing so that something new can be created via synthesis and the harmonization of ideas and perspectives (Nicolescu 1997). Cross-fertilized knowledge is also *transcendent* in that those involved temporarily give up sovereignty of their domain to create a fecund space for the emergence of new knowledge (Somerville and Rapport 2002). Cross-fertilization (transcending disciplines and embracing sectoral knowledge) can lead to an enlarged vision of the issue at hand, the fusion of ideas from different sources, and innovative and inclusive solutions.

Summary and Conclusion

This chapter conceived transdisciplinary problem solving as an educative process that affects professional development whereby, while engaged in transdisciplinary work, individuals are transformed from immature to mature co-participants. In this case, the focus is on people's maturity vis-à-vis the transdisciplinary methodology. To move toward *transdisciplinary maturity*, people must be willing to engage with non-classical approaches to creating knowledge (including reframing what constitutes reality and logic). This chapter showcased Nicolescuian transdisciplinarity (see also Table 1).

As an overview, Nicolescuian transdisciplinarity holds that actors and agents would crisscross disciplinary and sectoral boundaries with the intent to change, remove, or go beyond the borders while integrating perspectives and practices emanating from this intellectual and pragmatic migration. People would recognize that transdisciplinary problem solving for humanity happens in the fertile *middle ground*, encompassing border crossing *within* higher education (disciplines) *and among* higher education, civil society and other sectors. These transdisciplinary border activities are informed by the logic of inclusion and the mediated interaction amongst Multiple Levels of Reality. People would find new respect for tension and chaos, especially as they manage the value-laden transdisciplinary dialogue inherent in intellectual fusion and perspective integration. People would appreciate that resultant transdisciplinary knowledge is complex, emergent, cross-fertilized and embodied.

Drawing on Judd et al.'s (1923) definition of the educative process, we can also suggest that the *transdisciplinary educative process* is profoundly shaped by external factors as well as the degree of a person's transdisciplinary maturity. The external factors are the deep, complex problems being addressed *and* their contexts (local, regional, national and global). Judd et al.'s (1923) theory helps us suggest that, through people's responses to the multidimensional contextual factors, they grow into a new, and possibly more complex, version of themselves. We could say that the transdisciplinary educative process is the catalyst for the emergence of a new, more mature *transdisciplinary self,* couched in the transdisciplinary methodology.

Notions of reality, logic and knowledge would continually morph and emerge for a *maturing transdisciplinary self.* People would (re)organize their personal growth until they became comfortable with, and competent at, integrating diverse, seemingly contradictory, perspectives using inclusive logic while interacting in the fecund middle ground. This transdynamic process leads to knowledge that is emergent, complex, embodied and cross-fertilized. As far as professional development goes (the focus of this book), I conclude that embracing transdisciplinary maturity in the Nicolescuian methodology greatly informs the process of people's *personal* growth, thereby enhancing their professional and disciplinary practice and, by association, better ensuring sustainable, tenable solutions to humanity's complex problems.

References

Apostel, L., Berger, S., Briggs, A., & Machaud, G. (Eds.). (1972). *Interdisciplinarity, problems of teaching and research in universities.* Paris: OECD, CERI.

Augsburg, T. (2014). Becoming transdisciplinary: The emergence of the transdisciplinary individual. *World Futures, 70*(3/4), 233–247.

Brenner, J. E. (2005, September 19–22). *Knowledge as systems: A logic of epistemology. Paper presented at 6th European Systems Science Congress.* Paris: French Association of Systems Science. http://www.ressystemica.org/afscet/resSystemica/Paris05/brenner.pdf. Accessed 25 Jan 2014.

Brenner, J. E. (2008). The logic of transdisciplinarity. In B. Nicolescu (Ed.), *Transdisciplinary theory and practice* (pp. 155–163). Creskill: Hampton Press.

Brenner, J. E. (2011). *Essay: The transdisciplinary logic of transdisciplinarity.* New York: Metanexus Institute. http://www.metanexus.net/essay/transdisciplinary-logic-transdisciplinarity. Accessed 25 Jan 2014.

Bullard, T. (2011). The problems with Newtonian thinking. *A video presentation at the International Alchemy Conference.* Long Beach, CA. http://www.theresabullard.com/IAC_Part3. Accessed 1 Oct 2014.

Campbell-Higgins, C. (2000). *The educative process as a contributor to self-efficacy in adult education graduate students* (Unpublished doctoral dissertation). University of Toronto, Ontario. https://tspace.library.utoronto.ca/bitstream/1807/14548/1/NQ49806.pdf. Accessed 25 Jan 2014.

Cicovacki, P. (2009). Transdisciplinarity as an interactive method. *Integral Leadership Review, 9*(5). http://integralleadershipreview.com/4549-feature-articletransdisciplinarity-as-an-interactive-method-a-critical-reflection-on-the-three-pillars-of-transdisciplinarity/. Accessed 25 Jan 2014.

Cillier, P., & Nicolescu, B. (2012). Complexity and transdisciplinarity: Discontinuity, levels of reality and the hidden third. *Futures, 44*(8), 711–718.

Cole, A. (2006). *Motueka Catchment futures, trandiscinplinarity, a local sustainability problématique and the Achilles-heel of Western science.* Paper presented at the 5th Australasian Conference on Social and Environmental Accounting Research. Wellington, NZ.

http://icm.landcareresearch.co.nz/knowledgebase/publications/public/cole_anthony_17rfc_v2 pdf. Accessed 25 Jan 2014.

Du Plessis, H., Sehume, J., & Martin, L. (2013). *The concept and application of transdisciplinarity in intellectual discourse and research*. Johannesburg: Real African Publishers.

de Freitas, L., Morin, E., & Nicolescu, B. (1994). Charter of transdisciplinarity. In G. Tanzella-Nitti (Ed.), *Interdisciplinary encyclopedia of religion and science*. Rome, Italy. http://www.inters.org/Freitas-Morin-Nicolescu-Transdisciplinarity. Accessed 25 Jan 2014.

Gibbons, M., Limoges, C., Nowotny, H., Schwartzman, S., Scott, P., & Trow, M. (1994). *The new production of knowledge*. London: Sage.

Habermas, J. (1984). *The theory of communicative action* (trans: T. McCarthy). Boston: Beacon.

Heylighen, F. (2006). The Newtonian world view. In F. Heylighen, C. Joslyn, & V. Turchin (Eds.), *Principia cybernetica web*. Brussels: Principia Cybernetica. http://pespmc1.vub.ac.be/NEWTONWV.html. Accessed 25 Jan 2014.

Horlick-Jones, T., & Sime, J. (2004). Living on the border: Knowledge, risk and transdisciplinarity. *Futures, 36*(4), 441–456.

Jahn, T., Bergmann, M., & Keil, F. (2012). Transdisciplinarity: Between mainstreaming and marginalization. *Ecological Economics, 79*(July), 1–10.

Jantsch, E. (1972). Towards interdisciplinarity and transdisciplinarity in education and innovation. In L. Apostel, S. Berger, A. Briggs, & G. Machaud (Eds.), *Interdisciplinarity problems of teaching and research in universities* (pp. 97–121). Paris: OECD, CERI.

Jasper, N. (2006). *Reflection, decision making and professional development*. Oxford: Blackwell.

Judd, C., Bagley, W., Kilpatrick, W., Moore, E., & Chassell, J. (1923). What is the educative process? *Religious Education, 18*(1), 33–51.

Klein, J.-T. (2004). Prospects for transdisciplinarity. *Futures, 36*(4), 515–526.

Klein, J.-T., Grossenbacher-Mansuy, W., Häberli, R., Bill, A., Scholz, R., & Welti, M. (Eds.). (2001). *Transdisciplinarity: Joint problem solving among science, technology, and society*. Berlin: Birkhäuser Verlag.

Kocklemans, J. (1979). Why interdisciplinarity? In J. Kocklemans (Ed.), *Interdisciplinarity and higher education* (pp. 123–160). University Park: Pennsylvania State University Press.

McGregor, S. L. T. (2004). *The nature of transdisciplinary research and practice*. Kappa Omicron Nu Human Sciences Working Paper Series. http://www.kon.org/hswp/archive/transdiscipl.html. Accessed 25 Jan 2014.

McGregor, S. L. T. (2009). Integral leadership's potential to position poverty within transdisciplinarity. *Integral Leadership Review, 9*(2). http://integralleadershipreview.com/4758-feature-article-integral-leadership%E2%80%99s-potential-to-position-poverty-within-transdisciplinarity1. Accessed 25 Jan 2014.

McGregor, S. L. T. (2010). Historical notions of transdisciplinarity in home economics. *KON FORUM, 16*(2). http://www.kon.org/archives/forum/16–2/mcgregor.html. Accessed 25 Jan 2014.

McGregor, S. L. T. (2011). Transdisciplinary axiology: To be or not to be. *Integral Leadership Review, 11*(3). http://integralleadershipreview.com/2011/08/transdisciplinary-axiology-to-be-or-not-to-be. Accessed 25 Jan 2014.

McGregor, S. L. T. (2012). Complexity economics, wicked problems and consumer education. *International Journal of Consumer Studies, 36*(1), 61–69.

McGregor, S. L. T., & Murnane, J. (2010). Paradigm, methodology and method: Intellectual integrity in consumer scholarship. *International Journal of Consumer Studies, 34*(4), 419–427.

Morin, E. (1999). *Seven complex lessons in education for the future*. Paris, France: UNESCO. http://unesdoc.unesco.org/images/0011/001177/117740eo.pdf. Accessed 25 Jan 2014.

Morin, E. (2005). Restricted complexity, general complexity. In C. Gershenson, D. Aerts, & B. Edmonds (Eds.), *Worldviews, science and us: Philosophy and complexity* (pp. 5–29). London: World Scientific Publishing. E-chapter http://www.worldscientific.com/doi/pdf/10.1142/9789812707420_0002. Accessed 25 Jan 2014.

Morin, E. (2006). *Restricted complexity, general complexity* (trans: C. Gerhenson). Paper presented at the Intelligence de la complexité: Épistémologie et pragmatique colloquium. Cerisy-La-Salle, France. http://cogprints.org/5217/1/Morin.pdf. Accessed 25 Jan 2014.

Nicolescu, B. (1985). *Nous, la particule et le monde [We, the particle and the world]*. Paris: Le Mail.

Nicolescu, B. (1997). *The transdisciplinary evolution of the university condition for sustainable development*. Paper presented at the International Congress of the International Association of Universities. Bangkok, Thailand: Chulalongkorn University. http://ciret-transdisciplinarity.org//bulletin/b12c8.php. Accessed 25 Jan 2014.

Nicolescu, B. (1999). *The transdisciplinary evolution of learning*. Paper presented at the American Educational Research Association conference. Montreal, Quebec. http://www.learndev.org/dl/nicolescu_f.pdf. Accessed 25 Jan 2014.

Nicolescu, B. (2002). *Manifesto of transdisciplinarity* (trans: K.-C.Voss). Albany: State University of New York Press.

Nicolescu, B. (2004). Gurdjieff's philosophy of nature. In J. Needleman & G. Baker (Eds.), *Gurdjieff* (pp. 37–69). New York: The Continuum International Publishing Group.

Nicolescu, B. (2005, June 4–8). *Towards transdisciplinary education and learning*. Paper presented at the Metanexus Institute conference on Science and religion: Global perspectives. Philadelphia, PA. http://www.metanexus.net/archive/conference2005/pdf/nicolescu.pdf. Accessed 25 Jan 2014.

Nicolescu, B. (Ed.). (2008). *Transdisciplinary theory and practice*. Creskill: Hampton Press.

Nicolescu, B. (2010). *Disciplinary boundaries—What are they and how they can be transgressed?* Paper prepared for the International Symposium on Research Across Boundaries. Luxembourg: University of Luxembourg. http://basarab-nicolescu.fr/Docs_articles/Disciplinary_Boundaries.htm. Accessed 25 Jan 2014.

Nicolescu, B. (2011a). Methodology of transdisciplinarity-Levels of reality, logic of the included middle and complexity. In A. Ertas (Ed.), *Transdisciplinarity: Bridging science, social sciences, humanities and engineering* (pp. 22–45). Austin: The Atlas Publishing.

Nicolescu, B. (2011b). Transdisciplinarity: The hidden third, between the subject and the object. In I. Chirilă & P. Bud (Eds.), *Şatiinρă, Spiritualitate, Societate [Science, Spirituality, Society]* (pp. 11–34). Eikon, Cluj-Napoca, Romania. http://basarab-nicolescu.fr/Docs_articles/ClujHiddenThird052009Proceedings.pdf. Accessed 25 Jan 2014.

Nolt, J. (2010). Free logic. In E. N. Zalta (Ed.), *Stanford encyclopedia of philosophy*. Stanford: Stanford University. http://plato.stanford.edu/entries/logic-free/. Accessed 25 Jan 2014.

Nowotny, H. (2003). The potential of transdisciplinarity. In *Rethinking interdisciplinarity* (pp. 48–53). Paris: Interdisciplines Project. http://www.helganowotny.eu/downloads/helga_nowotny_b59.pdf. Accessed 25 Jan 2014.

Ramadier, T. (2004). Transdisciplinarity and its challenges: The case of urban studies. *Futures, 36*(4), 423–439.

Somerville, M. A., & Rapport, D. (2002). *Transdisciplinarity: Recreating integrated knowledge*. Montreal: McGill-Queens University Press.

Professor Emerita Sue L. T. McGregor PhD is a Canadian home economist (40 years) with a keen interest in transdisciplinarity, integral studies, moral leadership and transformative practice. Having worked in higher education for 30 years, she is recently retired from the Faculty of Education at Mount Saint Vincent University, Nova Scotia, Canada. She was one of the lead architects for the university's recently launched interuniversity doctoral program in educational studies. She is a *The Atlas Fellow* (transdisciplinarity), was recently appointed Docent in Home Economics at the University of Helsinki, and is the *Marjorie M. Brown Distinguished Professor* (home economics leadership). In 2009, she was awarded the *TOPACE International Award*

(Berlin) for distinguished consumer scholar and educator in recognition of her work on transdisciplinarity. Sue has delivered 35 keynotes and invited talks in 15 countries and published over 150 peer-reviewed publications, 21 book chapters, and 9 monographs. She has published four books: *Creating Home Economics Futures* (2012, co-edited with Donna Pendergast and Kaija Turkki), *Transversity* (2011, with Russ Volckmann), *Consumer Moral Leadership* (2010), and *Transformative Practice* (2006). Dr. McGregor is affiliated with 20 professional journals. She is Interim Editor for the *Journal of Family* and *Consumer Sciences*, Co-Editor of *Integral Leadership Review*, and is Associate Editor of three journals, including the newly launched *Transdisciplinary Journal of Engineering and Science* (2010). She has 20 years experience with consumer policy analysis and development with the Canadian federal government and a burgeoning interest in governance. She is a Principal Consultant for *The McGregor Consulting Group* (founded in 1991) http://www.consultmcgregor.com.

Changing and Sustaining Transdisciplinary Practice Through Research Partnerships

Tamara Cumming and Sandie Wong

Introduction

Although transdisciplinary practice has been strongly advocated as an effective approach to working with children and families, practitioners continue to experience barriers to changing practice, and difficulties challenging the self. These personal-professional challenges can make transdisciplinarity difficult to sustain. Accordingly, in this chapter, we suggest some possibilities for working with research partnerships as a means of changing and sustaining transdisciplinary practice, especially in relation to personal-professional challenges. We discuss some of the benefits and drawbacks of using case study methodologies, and, the potential of action research methodologies for supporting the sustainability of transdisciplinary practice.

Transdisciplinary Practice in Early Years Services

In recent years there have been persistent calls from policy makers, practitioners and researchers alike, for transdisciplinary practice in early years' services to address the 'wicked problems' (Moore 2008) facing contemporary families. In Australia, the term *early years' services* incorporates a wide range of supports available for children from birth to five, and their families. These supports include early education and care services (e.g. pre-school and playgroups, centre-based and home-based childcare), health (e.g. maternal and baby health clinics), and allied health (e.g. speech and language pathology and occupational therapy), early intervention and disability services, and child protection. These services vary considerably, for example, in terms of:

T. Cumming (✉) · S. Wong
Research Institute for Professional Practice,
Learning and Education, Charles Sturt University, New South Wales, Australia
e-mail: tcumming@csu.edu.au

© Springer International Publishing Switzerland 2015

P. Gibbs (ed.), *Transdisciplinary Professional Learning and Practice*,
DOI 10.1007/978-3-319-11590-0_3

- their primary focus—the child or family;
- whether they are universally available or targeted towards particular groups;
- whether the emphasis is on prevention or emergency/crisis care;
- their organisational, auspice, regulatory, legislative and funding and accountability arrangements and requirements (e.g. privately, philanthropically or publically funded); and
- the degree of professional expertise of those delivering the service, from highly qualified (e.g. speech language pathologists), to minimally trained workers (e.g. home-based childcare).

Traditionally, practitioners working in early years' services have tended to work in silos, bounded by their disciplinary and/or epistemological focus (health and early intervention, for example, are typically science based, while education and family support are typically social science based) with little coordination or collaboration across service types, either at the professional or organisational level. This lack of connection and coordination between services has real life implications for the children and families utilising those services. This is especially so for families facing challenging circumstances (such as those with a child with disabilities, or where a parent has substance abuse or mental ill-health issues) who may require the support of multiple services. These families, in particular, have to navigate complex service systems—each with their own rules about accessibility, criteria for funding, and expectations about child and/or parental involvement (Moore 2008). Families also often have to repeat their 'story' multiple times to each professional they meet and negotiate the consistent implementation of these plans across all services that their child accesses. However, over the last decade or so, there has been growing recognition of the complexity of contemporary early years' service delivery and greater recognition of the holistic nature of children's development and well-being. This recognition has led to strong advocacy, internationally, for early years' services and professionals to work in integrated and collaborative ways to provide children and families with a more holistic, coherent experience (Lewis 2010; Nichols and Jurvansuu 2008; Stöbe-Blossey 2013; Uniting Care Burnside 2007).

In the early years' field, inter-professional practice is often conceptualised on a continuum from *multi-disciplinary* (the least integrated), through *inter-disciplinary*, to *transdisciplinary* (the most integrated approach). In this chapter, for consistency with other authors in this volume, we use the term *transdisciplinary practice* to refer to ways of working that are based upon collaborative and cooperative approaches across and between professionals from different disciplinary backgrounds, such as allied health, early childhood education, and family support (Moore 2008). A key characteristic of transdisciplinary approaches is the 'pooling' and exchange of inter-professional knowledge and skills across "disciplinary boundaries, to maximise communication, interaction, and cooperation among the members" (McGonigel et al. 1994, p. 103).

The Complexity of Transdisciplinary Approaches

Despite some cautions (Hughes 2006; Wigfall 2002), an extensive body of international literature (including special editions in at least two journals—*Educational and Child Pschology* (2006) and *Early Years* (2013)) is building a strong argument for the benefits of transdisciplinary work. Not only can the pooling of diverse knowledge and expertise create innovative, and efficacious ways of working with children and families, it can lead to more holistic, cohesive and consistent experiences for children and families (see for example: Burlington 2010; Warmington et al. 2004; Wong and Sumsion 2013).

Despite these benefits, transdisciplinary work is very complex. A number of external, organisational and personal factors as well as issues related to frontline teamwork have been identified as likely contributors to effective transdisciplinary teamwork (Wong et al. 2012). However, to provide a context for findings from our own research, we will focus here on research literature relating to ways that personal-professional factors seem to be implicated in supporting or challenging the sustainability of transdisciplinary approaches. In relation to facets supporting the sustainability of these approaches, existing research has highlighted the importance of team members having a clear understanding of, and ability to articulate their own and others' professional expertise, professional values and motives (Edwards 2009); the capacity to be reflective and reflexive (Atwool 2003); and a willingness to build and maintain relationships within the team (Hudson 2007).

At the same time, evaluations of the use of transdisciplinary approaches in early intervention settings have identified a number of personal-professional challenges, including: teams having unclear definitions or lacking shared understandings of taken-for-granted terms, which can lead to uncertainty among professionals about what is expected, and how to facilitate a transdisciplinary approach (Blue-Banning et al. 2004; Kurrajong Early Intervention Service 2008). In addition, overcoming perceptions of differences in professional 'status' among transdisciplinary team members (Colmer 2008) can pose a major challenge to the effectiveness of these teams. These perceptions can contribute to uncertainty and fear as status and entrenched hierarchies privileging 'scientifically-based' disciplined are challenged in transdisciplinary models (Baxter and Brumfitt 2008).

We now move on to a discussion of the strengths and drawbacks of case study methodologies, then, provide a case study in which research partnerships were used to identify and begin the processes of transdisciplinary practice in early years' services.

Case Study Methodology

Case studies can be of particular value in understanding the complexity of transdisciplinary work., and have been used (for example), in relation to healthcare and social work (Freeth 2001; Hudson 2007, Sengupta et al. 2003), as well as early years' services (Jackson 2013; Payler and Georgeson 2013; Wong et al. 2012). Case study methodologies enable researchers to undertake "deeper examination of a smaller number of participants' 'participation in action'" (Payler and Georgeson 2013, p. 385), and, are useful for "coherently linking applied analysis of [a] project with the broader themes and concerns evident from the existing evidence base" (Sengupta et al. 2003, p. 58). At the same time, case study methodologies have been criticised on the grounds that they are not generalisable, and may lack validity. As Flyvbjerg (2006) argues however, for research that seeks to learn, rather than to prove or add to (what is considered) 'scientific knowledge', case study methodologies have much to recommend them to researchers. In particular, he argues for case studies as a way of generating valuable "concrete, context-dependent knowledge" (p. 224) and relaying powerful examples.

Case Study: A Supported Playgroup Program

Research Context

Our first case study concerns a mobile supported playgroup program. In Australia, supported play groups are considered a financially and substantively effective medium for providing play-based early intervention to specific communities of families and children (Jackson 2013). These communities might include families who are socially isolated and/or disadvantaged, or, where there are mental health and/or disability issues (with either the parent or the child). Supported playgroups are usually initiated and facilitated by a paid coordinator and other professional staff and funded from government sources (Jackson 2013).

The supported playgroup program we discuss here was established in 2004 by SDN Children's Services organisation and the New South Wales Department of Community Services. Its purpose at the time of the case study, was to provide a non-stigmatising, development-enhancing group-play experience to families living in the local area, who had concerns about their child's development. The program model was also designed to assist families to access information and advice about their child's development, along with assessment, diagnosis and therapy options (but, importantly, not to provide therapy itself). In order to facilitate a seamless and coordinated experience for children and their families, and to make the most of limited funding for different professionals, the program was designed according to best practice transdisciplinary models drawn from early intervention literature.

The original team model was made up of two 'qualified' professionals—either an early childhood educator or speech therapist; and/or an occupational therapist. Later, as additional funding became available, a 'play assistant' role was added. The person in this role was usually a student, studying social work, early childhood education or occupational therapy. A maximum of seven families attended per two-hour group session, so that the team could provide effective support and strategies to families. All resources for the groups were transported between the two sites in a specially modified van (hence 'mobile' playgroup). Each team member was jointly responsible for planning the program, implementing practices, talking with and supporting parents, cleaning, unpacking and packing away the play session into the van, and taking part in reflection sessions and any follow-up of information or contacts for families. In addition, a 'play leader' (usually the early childhood-trained professional) was generally responsible for implementing program structures with families (such as organising and documenting goal-setting meetings and exit planning).

Research Design

The purpose of the study of the playgroup program was to explore and document its transdisciplinary approach in practice, with a particular focus upon the role and experiences of early childhood professionals. As in the model informing the playgroup program we discuss here early childhood educators (hereafter referred to as 'educators') are often included in play-based early intervention teams, along with allied health professionals and family support workers. Educators bring particular skills and expertise in relationship-building with families, using group and individual perspectives in relation to children and their development, and offering play experiences that are enjoyable and skill-building (Press et al. 2012). Despite the importance of these abilities to the effective operation of supported playgroups, there is some evidence that the status of educators within the hierarchy of professions involved in early intervention work remains relatively low (Colmer 2008).

To explore and document educators' experiences of the transdisciplinary practice in the supported playgroup program, we used a case study methodology. Data was generated via participant observation of play sessions ($n = 10$), and reflective practice sessions ($n = 4$), along with individual interviews with four past and current team members (an occupational therapist, speech therapist, and two early childhood educators). All participants are female, and had completed their qualifications in Australia. The participants represented diverse cultural backgrounds and ranged in age from early 20s to 50s.

Given the largely exploratory and descriptive nature of the study, our data analysis strategy was based upon simplified principles of grounded theory (Miles and Huberman 2004). Textual data from interviews, transcripts of reflective practice sessions and observations were coded line-by-line, then codes were grouped into a smaller number of thematic categories that represented the combined content of the data. We then interpreted these categories in light of our literature review, highlighting areas of convergence, as well as new findings, in our data. Selected findings relating to personal-professional challenges of transdisciplinary practice are presented here – additional findings can be found in Cumming and Wong (2012).

Findings of Supported Playgroup Case Study

Our intention in this discussion is to briefly illustrate some of the personal-professional challenges of transdisciplinary practice, and to consider how effective our research approach was for assisting the supported playgroup program team to understand their practice. Three key findings relating to personal-professional challenges are discussed—those relating to the value of a common philosophy amongst transdisciplinary team members; those relating to professional roles and boundaries; and the role of discourses of scientific credibility.

Sharing a Common Guiding Philosophy

Findings from interviews, participant observations and reflective practice sessions suggested that members of the supported playgroup team understood that transdisciplinary practice was about: *having different skills that we use together*, and that this approach was valuable because: *you can learn from anyone, no matter who it is*. Team members also perceived that sharing a common purpose in their work helped to create a sense of connection with other team members:

> It's like you share a common goal in a way for the child and the family,whatever it might be... because we have that overlapping philosophy about the respect for the child as a person on their own, it just really helps to know that you're working towards the same things a lot of the time.

These findings confirmed the value of transdisciplinary team members sharing a common guiding philosophy, and a commitment to working respectfully with families and children (Siraj-Blatchford and Siraj-Blatchford 2009). Despite having some shared understandings of what transdisciplinary means, and (what the participant quoted above refers to as an) 'overlapping philosophy' in relation to the focal subjects of transdisciplinary practice (that is, the children and families), there were unspoken, yet markedly different philosophies relating to the key medium of the playgroup—play itself.

The speech and occupational therapists for example, saw the observation of play as useful both for reflecting a child's current development, and as a tool for therapy to develop specific developmental tasks. Play could still be fun and child-directed; however, its main purpose was as a medium through which an observed deficit could be addressed, or a specific skill acquired. Educators on the other hand, whilst also discussing the value of learning about children's abilities by observing their play, looked at the children's interests, strengths and needs, and used this information to better facilitate activities to engage the 'whole' child. This meant creating experiences to facilitate and extend children's abilities, without directing children to play in certain ways to 'fix' a problem, or to do activities that allowed children to practice certain skills.

Although the allied health professional team members seemed to value play as a medium for therapy, there was less value ascribed to those playing with children:

> It's good to have the assistant there to see things that I'm not able to see, the assistant's the one down there playing, and with the children... (Allied health team member 1)
> It's good for [the play assistant] to be there to develop and keep play going while therapists or teachers are busy with parent explanations and issues and modelling techniques... if therapists or teachers are discussing complex issues with parents, you need to know that if

the assistant is free that they can take care of what the children are doing etc. (Allied health team member 2)

In these fragments, play facilitated by the assistant was relegated to the floor, a background activity to be undertaken whilst the professionals conducted 'important conversations' above. Play was also downplayed as unskilled, and presented as a something that 'children do', rather than a meaningful core element of the early intervention setting. These examples of practitioners sharing a broad commitment to families and children, while at the same time having divergent philosophies of play, demonstrates the importance of interrogating taken-for-granted terms that may have vastly different purposes and connotations for professionals from different disciplines. Without ongoing, and carefully facilitated consideration of these difficult yet pivotal concepts, it is easy to see how a transdisciplinary team might never realise the potential of new, integrated knowledge (McGregor, Transdisciplinary knowledge creation).

In addition, this case study highlights a little-explored challenge concerning the place of the non-professional in the transdisciplinary space. Transdisciplinarity assumes professional knowledge, capacity, reward, dispositions and so on, that are not necessarily present, or wanted, in a non-professional team member. Yet, budgetary constraints on early intervention teams (such as the supported playgroup program we have discussed here) may mean that non-professional team members are necessary to the operation of the services. Given the inclusion of non-professional staff in transdisciplinary teams in other early years' services, there is evidently a need to address the effects of unequal power relations (and other barriers) so that the value of the professional and practical wisdom they bring to the team is not diminished.

Professional Territories

Many researchers exploring transdisciplinary practice have highlighted the challenges of overcoming "professional territoriality" (Axelsson and Axelsson 2009, p. 321)—that is, "having 'jurisdiction' over their field of work", and "dominance over other professions within the same field. If the boundaries are unclear or disputed, this may lead to struggles or conflicts between different professional groups." This concept of professional territoriality was evident in our study of the supported playgroup program, where team members continually identified primarily with their own discipline (i.e. speech therapy/early childhood, etc.) rather than as early intervention professionals who were drawing upon the 'pooled' expertise of the team. For example, one educator noted differences in binary terms:

The early childhood practitioner versus the therapist is about having the skills at looking at the big picture of the environment versus the individual. It's holistic versus targeted to their individual interests.

Similarly, one allied health professional team member noted that: It's always good to have different practitioners so parents can have the points of view directly . . . We all have different perspectives, we focus on language, or we focus on building postures and sitting.

Team members were also uneasy and unconfident about applying each other's strategies when they themselves did not have the requisite background knowledge to substantiate it:

> Multidisciplinary relationships are relatively easy, but transdisciplinary is much harder... because you can never know as much about another field as you do about your own.... Being transdisciplinary is about... whatever discipline you are, if the speechie recommends a strategy we all do it, and vice versa. It's hard when you're talking to parents about a strategy, or modelling it, I would prefer [the OT] or [the early childhood teacher] to do it [if it was their strategy] because they know.

In the same way that we argued for the importance of discussing key concepts (in the previous section), the examples of professional territoriality above suggest that without explicit conversations about how discipline-specific knowledge or perspectives are pooled and applied, professionals of different disciplinary background working within the same intervention setting could remain siloed, rather than becoming part of a new transdisciplinary space.

Discourses of Scientific Credibility

A further point relating to the shaping of professional territories is illustrated by the following fragment from an interview with one of the early childhood educators working in the supported playgroup program:

> For families with children with ongoing high support needs or a disability it's very much about diagnosis. The speech therapist gives the team credibility to give valuable information that they [families] will believe. The speechie backs up and supports the play leader and there is a professional understanding about each other, but being a therapist means you have more credibility because you can diagnose. Our credibility as early childhood practitioners is less because we can't diagnose. The strategies might be the same, but the speechie has the credibility of being able to assess a child. It was so important to have the speechie because she could give them [families] real things to do that were valuable to them.

Here, it is evident that professional territories may be structured hierarchically according to discourses of scientific 'credibility', as well as shaped by disciplinary 'boundaries'. In this case, the assumed primacy of speech therapists is reinforced through the educator's assumption that the credibility of her own discipline is less. This positioning of educators as less credible than speech therapists, supports claims that a history of relatively low levels of qualifications coupled with the dominance of 'mothering' discourses, has resulted in the early childhood profession being constructed as a 'common sense' activity rather than a highly skilled professional practice—even amongst early childhood professionals themselves (Osgood 2010; Vincent and Braun 2011).

In addition to highlighting a taken-for-granted hierarchy that positions speech therapists as having the greatest credibility (due to their ability to 'diagnose'), this fragment demonstrates the enculturation of families to professional hierarchies, and the power of 'the diagnosis'. This finding supports calls made in other literature (Worrall-Davies and Cottrell 2009) regarding the importance of including families in efforts to create transdisciplinary space, and to challenge professional territories that families and practitioners may all be implicated in shaping and reinforcing.

The findings from the research study with the supported playgroup program illustrate the usefulness of case studies for identifying facets of the complexity of transdisciplinary approaches in practice. However, case studies are not necessarily useful for transforming and sustaining transdisciplinary practice. We argue that if researchers want to have a greater impact on supporting transdisciplinary ways of working (see Penker and Muhar, What's actually new about transdisciplinarity? Or how scholars from applied studies can contribute and benefit from learning processes on transdisciplinarity), then they have a role to play beyond merely producing research findings, or developing professional development materials. Accordingly, in the following sections, we discuss some of the possibilities for changing and sustaining transdisciplinary practice through research partnerships using collaborative action research approaches.

Developing Research Partnerships

Collaborative action research projects (ARP) involve stakeholders in real-life problem-oriented applied research that is socially, culturally and materially relevant. The purpose of an ARP is to support and empower practitioners, in collective communities of practice, to integrate knowledge from research and practice wisdom into their professional practices, in a continuous cycle of action and critical reflection (Kemmis et al. 2004). Therefore it is through collective, negotiated processes that ARPs bring about change in ways of thinking and practicing. Further, with ongoing commitment and support from team members, as well as their organisations, the community of practice can continue even after the most active phase of involvement with researchers is complete. It is therefore both the research process, and the legacy of a community of practice, that makes collaborative action research projects (arguably) one of the most influential ways that researchers can contribute to sustainable transdisciplinary teams.

Action research methodologies have been used successfully by researchers to support the development of early years' integrated services (for example, see Murdoch Children's Research Institute and The Royal Children's Hospital Centre for Community Child Health 2013). Below, we outline an action research project that aims to sustain transdisciplinary approaches. This project is currently being undertaken by the second author with her colleague Frances Press, and The Infants' Home, in Sydney.

Case Study: The Infants' Home

Research Context

The Infants' Home (TIH) initially opened in Sydney in the late nineteenth century as an orphanage, and is one of Australia's longest established early years' services.

A not-for-profit organisation, TIH currently operates as an integrated early years' service with a particular focus on supporting vulnerable, marginalised and/or disadvantaged children and families. Amongst the services offered by TIH are family day care and centre-based early childhood education and care, early intervention and family support. The Infants' Home is also partnered with a medical centre and other community family support services (such as a women's support group).

The Infants' Home has multiple professionals on staff, including early childhood educators, speech and language therapists, occupational therapists, an art therapist and psychologist. Sandie and Frances have been working with TIH for 3 years, documenting the organisation's 'journey' towards transdisciplinary (see Wong and Press 2013). During this period it has become clear that, although the management and team at TIH were committed to transdisciplinary ways of working and striving to transform their practice, a number of challenges persisted. In particular, challenges relating to professional identity and perceived inequities in working conditions, seemed to be compromising the ability of the TIH team to work in effective and sustainable transdisciplinary ways. In order to mediate these complex dynamics, it seemed that there was a need for someone from 'outside' the transdisciplinary team (and organisation) to become involved. Accordingly, it was agreed with TIH senior management, that in Sandie and Frances' fourth and fifth years of working with the team, a participatory action research methodology would be used to support and document the organisation's continuing journey towards transdisciplinary ways of working.

Research Design

At the time of writing, the action research project involves up to 20 TIH staff members, from the range of professional backgrounds described above, and is led by Sandie and Frances. The project consists of eight half-day workshops with participants (four per year for two years) and ongoing support of staff members' critical reflection on their work towards transdisciplinary practice (e.g. through email contact with researchers). The workshops follow a typical action research cycle of: *planning* (i.e. identifying the problem, analysing the situation, setting goals and planning action); *acting* (i.e. implementing the action); *observing* (i.e. collecting data on outcomes of the action); and *reflecting* (i.e. evaluating and analysing the action) (Kemmis et al. 2004). Whilst the research process is emergent and responsive to the participants' lead, the workshops typically involve the researchers provoking discussion; supporting collegial interrogation of ideas; providing resources and making suggestions for change. In addition, the researchers document the processes and findings of the project to be published in formative and summative reports.

Importantly (and in relation to points made earlier about personal-professional factors), during the workshops the researchers endeavour to manage hierarchies and power imbalances through democratic methods. This is done for example, by: encouraging diverse membership in the small groups investigating issues and ensuring diverse voices are heard; and using transparent processes, such as reporting back to the participants the researchers' reflections on the previous meetings, and inviting feedback on the planning of future workshops.

Findings of The Infants' Home Case Study

Whilst this project is still in its early days, the value of the participatory action research methodology for supporting the sustainability of transdisciplinary practice is already becoming evident. In particular, the mediated approach to working together seems to be valuable for making visible the deeply held, and divergent beliefs and understandings of the team. For example, it has quickly become clear in workshops that discussion of certain aspects of practice—such as 'assessment'—will 'trigger' emotional responses from the participants, and block further dialogue.

For the allied health professionals the term 'assessment' refers to a core aspect of their practice that is central to their professional identity. However, for the early childhood educators, the word 'assessment' carried a negative connotation of 'labelling and measuring children'. The researchers have found it more productive to focus on a single but significant aspect of practice that is not especially emotive or core to the professional's sense of self—for example 'the referral process', and whether referral processes are/should be informal or formal, how the processes work and so on. By focusing on this less emotive, but nonetheless shared 'problem', the participants were better able to listen to others' points of view, and were more open to new ways of thinking and ways of working. These initial successes will provide the basis for bringing to the surface the more difficult aspects of practice at future meetings, so that they may be examined, challenged and worked through.

Through the workshops the researchers have also endeavoured to create a 'safe fecund space' in which staff are able to discuss issues of concern and undertake the work of challenging the self (see McGregor, Transdisciplinary knowledge creation). The effectiveness of the process seems to be facilitated by the absence of senior management at the workshops. Whilst not involving senior management might prove problematic (particularly if the research team identify structural changes that require management support), so far senior management have been open to suggestions emerging from the project—perhaps not least because the team has been able to clearly articulate and argue for the necessity of various changes.

Despite its benefits, participation in the project has placed additional burdens on staff above and beyond their regular duties. In addition, staff members are required by TIH management to participate in the project as part of their ongoing professional development. This requirement poses some tricky issues regarding informed consent and participants' rights. However, this has been negotiated by informing participants that whilst they have to participate in the project, they have the right not to have their words including in the report (to date, no requests have been received). Further, as far as can be discerned, team members seem to enjoy participating in this collaborative critical reflection that supports their shared intent of working in more effective ways with vulnerable, marginalised and disadvantaged children and their families.

Conclusion

Negotiating transdisciplinary practice brings up issues of "identity, power, territory and expertise" (Rose 2011, p. 151), that need to be addressed in order that transdisciplinarity may be sustained. Researchers can play an important role in these processes by using action research methodologies, to mediate unequal power relations and encourage diverse voices and perspectives in ways that support transformation. The brief sketches of action research engagement given above show clearly the complexity (for practitioners and researchers) of negotiating transdisciplinary practice. For example, at The Infants' Home, the shared intent of the team to find ways of working more effectively with children and families appears to be intertwined with their motivation and wiliness to undertake the often difficult work of challenging the self. Yet, this willingness can be quickly shut down or fractured, when 'core' professional values and beliefs are challenged (such as the example of 'assessment' above demonstrates so clearly). At the same time (and as suggested by the case study of the supported playgroup program reported above), if left unspoken and unexplored, core beliefs might act as 'blocks' to transdisciplinary work.

In order to provide more skilled facilitation and support for the sustainability of transdisciplinary practice, researchers may need to build up a specialty in supporting transdisciplinary work over time, and in multiple sites. In addition, researchers themselves need to be aware of the types of professional territories they may build around themselves, and the possible effects on their mediation of unexplored philosophies and values. In the case of TIH, the particular disciplinary expertise of the researchers (in early childhood education) might help support educators to more clearly articulate their practices to other professionals.

Researchers wishing to support and sustain transdisciplinary practices also need to assist professionals to not only integrate the findings from research into their work, but to work collaboratively with professionals to design research projects that aim to address 'real life' problems and transform practice. In short, we agree with (Gibbs, Transdisciplinarity as epistemology, ontology or principles of practical judgement, p. 165) that to support transdisciplinary practice requires researchers to develop "more recursive research design[s] where problems are defined cooperatively" and through collective engagement (McGregor, Transdisciplinary knowledge creation). Participatory action research is a useful methodology in this regard.

While we have explored some of the personal-professional challenges to sustaining transdisciplinary practice, and suggested ways that research partnerships using action research may assist team members, we have not explored the challenge of integrating children and families into transdisciplinary practice, and processes that sustain it. Given the often shared philosophy of socially just opportunities for children and families among staff working in transdisciplinary teams, this remains an important question to be addressed.

References

Atwool, N. (2003). If it's such a good idea, how come it doesn't work: The theory and practice of integrated service delivery. *Childrenz Issues, 7*(2), 31–35.

Axelsson, S. B., & Axelsson, R. (2009). From territoriality to altruism in interprofessional collaboration and leadership. *Journal of Interprofessional Care, 23*(4), 320–330.

Baxter, S. K., & Brumfitt, S. M. (2008). Professional differences in interprofessional working. *Journal of Interprofessional Care, 22*(3), 239–251. doi:10.1080/13561820802054655.

Blue-Banning, M., Summers, J. A., Frankland, H. C., Nelson, L. L., & Beegle, G. (2004). Dimensions of family and professional partnerships: Constructive guidelines for collaboration. *Exceptional Children, 70*(2), 167–184.

Burlington, S. (2010). *Sure start children's centres.* London: Sure Start and Early Intervention Division, Department of Education.

Colmer, K. (2008). Multi disciplinary 'teams' are deliberately constructed. *Reflections Autumn, 31,* 8–10.

Cumming, T., & Wong, S. (2012). Professionals don't play: Challenges for early childhood educators working in a transdisciplinary early intervention team. *Australasian Journal of Early Childhood, 37*(1), 127–135.

Edwards, A. (2009). Relational agency in collaborations for the well-being of children and young people. *Journal of Children's Services, 4*(1), 33–43.

Flyvbjerg, B. (2006). Five misunderstandings about case-study research. *Qualitative Inquiry, 12*(2), 219–245. doi:10.1177/1077800405284363.

Freeth, D. (2001). Sustaining interprofessional collaboration. *Journal of Interprofessional Care, 15*(1), 37–46. doi:10.1080/13561820020022864.

Hudson, B. (2007). Pessimism and optimism in inter-professional working: The Sedgefield integrated team. *Journal of Interprofessional Care, 21*(1), 3–15. doi:10.1080/13561820600991850.

Hughes, M. (2006). Multi-agency teams: Why should working together make everything better? *Educational and Child Pschology, 23*(4), 60–71.

Jackson, D. (2013). Creating a place to 'be': Unpacking the facilitation role in three supported playgroups in Australia. *European Early Childhood Education Research Journal, 21*(1), 77–93. doi:10.1080/1350293X.2012.760345.

Kemmis, S., McTaggart, R., & Retallick, J. (2004). *The action research planner* (2nd ed.rev). Karachi: Aga Kahan University, Institute for Educational Development.

Kurrajong Early Intervention Services. (2008). *Promising practice profiles: Rural beginnings project.* Retrieved from Australian Institute of Family Studies website: http://www.aifs.gov.au/cafca/ppp/profiles/itg_rural_beginnings_team.html. Accessed 22 Nov 2011.

Lewis, J. (2010). From Sure Start to Children's Centres: An analysis of policy change in English early years programmes. *Journal of Social Policy, 40*(01), 71–88. doi: 10.1017/s0047279410000280.

McGonigel, M. J., Woodruff, G., & Roszmann-Millican, M. (1994). The transdisciplinary team: A model for family-centered early intervention. In L. J. Johnson, R. J. Gallagher, M. J. LaMontagne, J. B. Jordan, J. J. Gallagher, P. L. Hutinger, & M. B. Karnes (Eds.), *Meeting early intervention challenges: Issues from birth to three* (2nd ed., pp. 95–131). Baltimore: Paul H. Brookes.

Miles, M. B., & Huberman, A. M. (2004). *Qualitative data analysis: An expanded sourcebook* (2nd ed). Thousand Oaks: Sage.

Moore, T. (2008). *Evaluation of victorian children's centres: Literature review.* Melbourne: Department of Education and Early Childhood Development. http://www.eduweb.vic.gov.au/edulibrary/public/earlychildhood/integratedservice/childcentrereview.pdf. Accessed 22 Nov 2011.

Murdoch Children's Research Institute and The Royal Children's Hospital Centre for Community Child Health. (2013). *The Tasmanian Child and Family Centre action research project: Phase two report*. http://www.earlyyears.org.au/__data/assets/pdf_file/0005/187691/ Phase_Two_ARP_Report.pdf. Accessed 22 Nov 2011.

Nichols, S, & Jurvansuu, S. (2008). Partnership in integrated early childhood services: An analysis of policy framings in education and human services. *Contemporary Issues in Early Childhood, 9*(2), 118–130.

Osgood, J. (2010). Reconstructing professionalism in ECEC: The case for the 'critically reflective emotional professional'. *Early Years, 30*(2), 119–133.

Payler, J., & Georgeson, J. (2013). Multiagency working in the early years: Confidence, competence and context. *Early Years: An International Research Journal, 33*(4), 380–397. doi:10.1080/09575146.2013.841130.

Press, F., Wong, S., & Sumsion, J. (2012). Child-centred, family-centred, decentred: Positioning children as rights-holders in early childhood program collaborations. *Global Studies of Childhood, 2*(1), 26–37.

Rose, J. (2011). Dilemmas of inter-professional collaboration: Can they be resolved? *Children & Society, 25*(2), 151–163. doi:10.1111/j.1099-0860.2009.00268.x.

Sengupta, S., Dobbins, S., & Roberts, J. (2003). Multi-agency training for quality: Reflections and recommendations. *Journal of Interprofessional Care, 17*(1), 57–68. doi:10.1080/1356182021000044157

Siraj-Blatchford, I., & Siraj-Blatchford, J. (2009). *Improving development outcomes for children through effective practice in integrating early years' services*. London: Centre for Excellence and Outcomes in Young People's Services.

Stöbe-Blossey, Sybille. (2013). Implementation of integrated services—the example of family centres in North Rhine-Westphalia. *Early Years, 33*(4), 354–366. doi:10.1080/09575146.2013.849229.

Uniting Care Burnside. (2007). *Integrated child and family services—an innovative approach to early intervention*. http://www.burnside.org.au/content/Integrated%20child%20P20and%20family%20services%20-%20an%20innovative%20approach%20to%20early%20intervention.pdf. Accessed 22 Nov 2011.

Vincent, C., & Braun, A. (2011) "I think a lot of it is common sense . . ." Early years students, professionalism and the development of 'vocational habitus'. *Journal of Education Policy, 26*(6), 771–785. doi:/10.1080/02680939.2010.551143.

Warmington, P., Daniels, H., Edwards, A., Brown, S., Leadbetter, J., Martin, D., & Middleton, D. (2004). *Interagency collaboration: A review of the literature*. Bath: Learning in and for interagency working.

Wigfall, V. (2002). 'One-stop' shopping: Meeting diverse family needs in the inner city? *European Early Childhood Education Research Journal, 10*(1), 111–121. doi:DOI:10.1080/13502930285208881.

Wong, S., & Press, F. (2013). *The art of integration: Attracting and retaining staff in integrated early childhood services*. The Infants' Home Ashfield. http://www.theinfantshome.org.au/site/assets/files/1009/the_art_of_integration_-_may_2013.pdf. Accessed 22 Nov 2011.

Wong, S., & Sumsion, J. (2013). Integrated early years services: A thematic literature review. *Early Years, 33*(4), 341–353. doi:10.1080/09575146.2013.841129.

Wong, S., Sumsion, J., & Press, F. (2012). Early childhood professionals and inter-professional work in integrated early childhood services in Australia. *Australasian Journal of Early Childhood, 37*(1), 81–88.

Worrall-Davies, A., & Cottrell, D. (2009). Outcome research and interagency work with children: What does it tell us about what the CAMHS contribution should look like? *Children & Society, 23*, 336–346. doi:10.1111/j.1099-0860.2009.00241.x.

Tamara Cumming is currently completing her PhD at Charles Sturt University, Australia, where she is also an Associate Lecturer in Early Childhood Education. Her doctoral research focuses upon the sustainability of the early childhood workforce, and the complexity of early childhood practice. Tamara's other research interests include inter-professional working relationships, post structural research strategies, and using research to help facilitate change in integrated and early childhood practice settings.

Sandie Wong is Assistant Director of the Research Institute for Professional Practice, Learning & Education (RIPPLE) at Charles Sturt University, Australia. Sandie's research focuses broadly on the role early childhood education and intervention have in ameliorating disadvantage and reducing marginalisation, both from a contemporary and historical perspective. Her current research, examines integrated early childhood services, collaborative practices and inter-professional working relationships. She has expertise in the evaluation of early childhood programs, and is particularly concerned with utilising collaborative, strengths-based approaches to build and support research capacity in both the academy and the early childhood field.

Transdisciplinary Problems: The Teams Addressing them and their Support Through Team Coaching

Ron Collins and Annette Fillery-Travis

Introduction

The discussion around interdisciplinary, multidisciplinary and transdisciplinary (i-disciplinary) approaches to research and problem solving may seem, at first sight, to be of mainly academic concern and unconnected with the real time problem solving of advanced practitioners in complex organisational settings. As authors representing both these distinct communities- academia and high level consulting practice—we are going to suggest that rather than being of limited applicability transdisciplinary approaches are likely to shed light on the most challenging and interesting business problems in the twenty-first Century.

A recent IBM study of over 1500 CEOs provides some context for this discussion. It showed that senior leaders believe monodisciplinary and boundaried approaches are insufficient to address the complexity of the issues confronting them:

> It is no longer sufficient, or even possible, to view the world within the confines of an industry, or a discipline, or a process, or even a nation. (IBM 2011)

We do not have to go far to identify why this may be so. The business literature is awash with analyses' of the complexity of business environments today. One such example is an analysis by the Center for Creative Leadership (Petrie 2011) that presents several reasons why the business environment of today is difficult to manage. They specify the large number of elements within the environment whose interactions are complex and highly unpredictable. More information is available and situations that require stochastic models without simple deterministic behaviour can now be tackled and need to be tackled. The result is that hindsight can no longer lead to foresight as the constituent elements of the environment are in continual

R. Collins (✉)
IBM Global Business Services, London, UK
e-mail: ronald.collins@uclmail.net

A. Fillery-Travis
Middlesex University, London, UK

© Springer International Publishing Switzerland 2015
P. Gibbs (ed.), *Transdisciplinary Professional Learning and Practice,*
DOI 10.1007/978-3-319-11590-0_4

flux. Alternative approaches to management are being brought into play such as complexity theory (Brown and Eisenhardt 1997) but it is clear that leaders need to be adept at 'adaptive competencies such as learning agility, self-awareness, comfort with ambiguity, and strategic thinking' (Petrie 2011).

Such conclusions are commonplace within major reviews identifying the central themes of interconnectedness and complexity of the system. Clearly the majority of organizational issues will still require mono-disciplinary solutions based upon deterministic models but there are a significant number—the 20 % identified by the Pareto Principle (Koch 2011)—that need alternative and potentially transdisciplinary approaches. Sense making in such an environment requires boundary-spanning (discipline, function and sector) approaches. These transcend the purely disciplinary approaches common to traditional problem solving and require approaches that deliberately encompass alternatively perspectives and bodies of knowledge.

In the Renaissance it was possible for one individual to be cognisant of everything that was known. By the nineteenth century the growth of knowledge meant issues needed to be addressed through working groups whose members each brought their specialisation and expertise to the table. In the twentieth Century innovative systems such as quality circles were being explored as alternative methods of accessing knowledge and creative problem solving. As we move into the twenty-first century the call is for leaders to embrace boundary spanning working methods and problem solving to manage these complex and ambiguous environments. But what are these methods and how can they be brought into service for organisational gain? In this chapter we explore some the i-disciplinary concepts and frameworks being suggested in academic and practitioner arenas and consider what they may have to offer individuals and teams working on such complex issues in current ambiguous business environments.

We start by considering the nature of the issues confronting individuals and organisations and ask when an issue or problem is mono-, multi- or transdisciplinary. We then identify how the working process itself must be adapted to address such issues and become, itself, transdisciplinary and for that we need to consider how groups of people work on the issues. Finally we will consider how these groups can be supported and specifically how coaching of such group must be specifically tuned to deal with them. By necessity given the limited space here this chapter will be merely an overview of the issues to open discussion.

When is an Issue or Problem Monodisciplinary, Multidisciplinary or Transdisciplinary?

When specifically referring to projects, problems or research it is appropriate to first ask whether the i-disciplinarity is a function of the issue itself or the working process to address it. A significant amount of the literature on transdisciplinarity is concerned with investigating the *process* of the enquiry or problem solving to identify if there are specific elements that delineate whether it is mono-, multi- or trans- disciplinary.

In this section the nature of the problem itself is considered by asking what are the criteria or specifications of the problem or project that identify it as a disciplinary, multidisciplinary or transdisciplinary issue?

When considering criteria we can follow the argument of Leavey (2011) and look first at monodisciplinary projects. These are relatively easy to identify as they exist within the boundaries of the body of knowledge for the discipline requiring no knowledge outside of the professional boundary. As such the building, evaluating and disseminating of knowledge within a discipline is regulated by 'disciplinary codes' (Steinmetz 2007) i.e. ritualised and prescribed ways of conducting the work that is specific to the discipline. Members of a discipline share a set of assumptions and use a shared language to describe their knowledge and practice (Klein 1990). This approach has significant benefits in relation to building professional identities and practice and identifying what constitutes a good solution to common professional issues.

However such classification can break down as identified in the oft-quoted comment by Mittelstrass (1992)

> problems seldom do us the favour of letting themselves be defined according to the order of our scientific habits.

He explores how problems commonly found in the working environment will often defy definition in pure disciplinary terms. They can span the boundaries of two or more disciplines requiring knowledge, methodologies and approaches from each in some form of combination or synergy. The question then arises as to whether these boundary-spanning problems are multidisciplinary or transdisciplinary.

Common definitions of multidisciplinarity identify it as a collaboration between two or more disciplines but without integration of the concepts, theories, methods or findings (Hadorn et al. 2008). In effect the process and outcomes are additive and the main challenge for the process is coordination of the discrete working disciplines. Issues that can be addressed in this way can be considered as factorable into discrete units of activity, each of which can be addressed from a disciplinary focus. The most obvious example of this is the Board of a Company. Each member is coming from a specific discipline (HR, Marketing, Finance etc) and responsible for those functions. They work under the leadership of their CEO to address issues that can be factored into these units and the result is a coordinated response to the issue drawing upon each function and discipline.

Knowledge is used within its disciplinary setting as identified in monodisciplinary work and when brought together with knowledge from other disciplines is done so in an additive and linear combinational manner.

In contrast issues requiring a transdisciplinary response cannot be factored neatly into disciplinary work packages. Following the definition of Leavy (2011) for transdisciplinary research:

> . . . [It] is a social justice oriented approach to research in which resources and expertise from multiple disciplines are integrated in order to holistically address a real-world issue or problem. Transdisciplinarity draws on knowledge from disciplines relevant to particular research issues or problems while ultimately transcending disciplinary borders and building a synergistic conceptual and methodological framework that is irreducible to the sum of its constituent parts' l(oc 61 od 3657).

The most critical word here is 'synergistic' i.e. in drawing the knowledge of separate disciplines together they become more that the sum of their parts permanently and 'irreducibly'. In effect a transdisciplinary issue resists factoring into disciplinary 'chunks' of work. This can be due to complexity of the issue where there are a large number of interacting factors contributing to the issue and the interconnectedness of these factors will be:

> non-linear and tightly coupled so small changes can produce disproportionately large effects. (Petrie 2011)

This complexity means potential solutions are more likely to emerge from within the system where the issue resides rather than be developed by imposition from outside. It follows that the solutions generated are less likely to be generalizable i.e. -able to be applied directly to other similar issues.

Alternatively the level of challenge within the issue can also be a critical and defining factor. Where the scope of the goal or solution is beyond current working patterns then it cannot be assumed that the interconnectiveness of the factors will be linear and summative. The use of knowledge within such contexts will also be non-additive and there will be integration of knowledge from a variety of disciplinary perspectives.

In summary such considerations suggest the criteria for i-disciplinarily of an issue can be identified as:

1. monodisciplinarity- all factors impacting upon the issue can be described and predicted within a single discipline.
2. multidisciplinarity—the issue is factorability into discipline 'chunks' that can then be coordinated to give a integrated result.
3. transdisciplinarity—a complex issue with non-linear interconnected elements that resist factoring and may contain a high level of challenge.

If issues and problems can be inherently multidisciplinary or transdisciplinary how does this impact upon how they are addressed by individuals and teams?

How Can We Work With These Issues?

Monodisciplinary and multidisciplinary issues are clearly amicable to being addressed by a single individual or a group of individuals collectively. There is no inherent barrier to solo multidisciplinary work— one person of suitable training can bring a range of disciplinary perspectives to bear on an issue—essentially working as the Renaissance (Wo)man referred to above. There is no intrinsic change required in working patterns or alternative ways of addressing the issue—knowledge, methods etc. from each discipline are applied sequentially to the issue and the results coordinated. Once a group is formed to work on the issue then a range of factors come into play and there is a wealth of literature looking at how groups and teams work together effectively in this mode and these generally assume the issue is mono-or multi- disciplinary (Mathieu et al. 2008). The minimum requirement is that a working group is formed of individuals who can factor up the functions or disciplines, and develop a single action plan. We do not use the term 'team' yet as each individual is working upon their own 'chuck' of work and need only to be coordinated in their action. The leader of the working group fulfils this function through monitoring the work. The classic example of a working group is the Board of a Company where individuals work within specific functions but collaborate to contribute to the company's success. The effectiveness of such teams is generally identified as through the quantity and quality of outputs.

In contrast groups working on transdisciplinary issues have additional criteria for success and that is the development of a shared conceptual framework that integrates and transcends that of the single or multiple disciplines. This type of work has only received significant attention in the last decade. One area of interest has concentrated upon teaming in the heath sector—where a group of professionals comes together to design the treatment plan for an individual with multiple needs. Neonatal care is a classic example where a premature baby can present with multiple problems with lung, intestine and brain for example all requiring different specialisations (King et al. 2009). Although the 'team' that is formed—albeit fleetingly—would probably identify themselves as members of varying disciplines they are used to working within the same context and culture with shared assumptions of the medical model of working.

A team that can have a more diverse demographic is that formed in team science. Since the mid-1950s the natural and behaviour sciences have made a pronounced shift from individually orientated research towards team-based scientific initiatives (Mâsse et al. 2008). This has been in response to the call by funders for research for an integrated response.

Considering the enormous complexity and multifactorial causation of the most vexing social, environmental and public health problems efforts to foster great collaboration among scientists trained in different fields are not only a useful but also an essential strategy for ameliorating these problems (Stokols et al. 2008).

Clearly there has been considerable interest in the factors that enable the transcendence of individual disciplinary perspectives and the integrating of knowledge, concepts and methods drawn from multiple disciplines. A topology of contextual influences has been proposed by Misra et al. (2008b) and identified elements such as diversity of perspectives, social cohesiveness, organisational climate of sharing, attitudes towards sharing and participatory leadership style. Not all were required for all projects but the more transdisciplinary the issue the more factors were necessary. Such elements are highly reminiscent of, and congruent with, the elements required for *true* high performance team (HPT) working as defined by Katzenbach and Smith (2013). Note that we have reserved the term team to denote the small proportion of working groups that display the ability to transcend working as coordinated individuals and instead embrace the synergistic working identified in the definition

A team is a small number of people with complementary skills who are committed to a common purpose, performance goals and approach for which they held themselves mutually accountable. (Katzenbach et al. 1993)

How Can We Understand the Formation and Performance of Transdisciplinary HPT?

In these HPT all members subscribe to the main goal (there is no factoring of the problem) and they are no longer regard themselves as working within and from a single discipline. Each member of the team considers that they own the shared concern or issue. They no longer identify primarily with their discipline or specialisation but with their contribution to the creative group problem solving.

True teams are at the core of transdisciplinary working. Indeed as Katzenbach and Smith (2013) observed in their original work, these teams are unlikely to form successfully unless the challenge of the problem is very significant. This is because the psychological investment required of the members to form the team is substantial and can be avoided if the problem can be successfully addressed by working group methods (i.e. multidisciplinary problems).

Indeed there is a significant risk associated with attempting to form real HPTs from working groups. This risk is the formation of low performing pseudo-teams which deliver an inferior result to conventional working groups. Katzenbach and Smith observed empirically that the team formation process appeared to follow a clear process starting with the formation of a working group, then formation of a low performing pseudo-team often inwardly focused and conflict driven, only then did a real team emerge and performance rise eventually to HPT levels. This observation was not surprising and has strong parallels with the classical model of Tuckman's with its four stages of Forming, Storming, Norming and Performing (Tuckman 1965).

However these empirical observations leave some important questions unanswered. For example what is going on psychologically during the team formation process? Is it possible to predict the extent and probability of the success of team formation from specific working groups, or the eventual level of performance of the team once formed? Is it possible to design selection or intervention strategies that minimise the probability of a stuck low performing pseudo-team or raise the performance of a real team? Is it possible to predict and manage the nature of the problems specific teams are likely to encounter?

Addressing these development questions is something of a transdisciplinary problem in itself requiring bringing together and integrating insights from: classical strategy and management (e.g. Katzenbach and Smith (2013), Tuckman (1965)); team coaching (Hackman and Wageman 2005); facilitation and psychometric and humanistic theories of psychology (Costa and McCrae 1992) (Schutz 1958)).

In understanding both what is going on during team formation and the potential likely "natural" productivity of a specific group it is useful to draw on FIRO (Fundamental Interpersonal Relationship Orientation) theory (Schutz 1992). FIRO theory is concerned with interpersonal needs and the behaviours and feelings that accompany them. Interpersonal needs, as opposed to personal needs, require two or more people to interact in order to satisfy them. So for example a need for order or tidiness in the external environment is a personal need or preference—it can be exercised or satisfied alone on a desert island. By contrast the need to control, or be controlled, by others requires at least two people. The FIRO model suggests that three such needs (Inclusion, Control and Affection (later Openness) are sufficient for understanding basic interpersonal behaviour. When groups and teams form, individuals look to satisfy their interpersonal needs from within the group. The extent to which all members can do so determines the "natural" (i.e. without intervention) productivity of the group or team.

During the pseudo-team phase one of the main psychological processes is the investigation of interpersonal need satisfaction, with the associated formation and potential resolution, or not, of interpersonal need conflicts. So during this phase members determine the extent to which they are "In" or "Out" (Inclusion) and who is in charge "Up" or "Down" (Control) and the extent to which they will be disclose to others "Open" or "Closed". The FIRO model says that the group will undergo successive cycles of ICO need satisfaction resulting in increased mutual trust and performance (norming and performing—a real team emerges).

However most team coaches or facilitators will report this for themselves and if this was all the FIRO theory provided it would not add much to the process. However as part of the theory Schutz developed a psychometric questionnaire- the FIRO-B -that successfully measures the three interpersonal needs across two dimensions (expressed and wanted) and is predictive of group behaviours and the extent and nature of interpersonal conflicts. So not only is it possible to predict potential troubled teams, but to predict the fundamental nature of the conflicts and the members involved. This has important implications for the management and coaching of teams involved in transdisciplinary working as it means that either by selection strategies or by coaching interventions it is possible to minimise the probability of team failure (stuck pseudo-team) and maximise productive behaviours beyond the empirical recipes of Katzenbach and Smith (2013). One of the most powerful applications of the theory is the prediction of apathetic conflict that can often be missed, at least for a while. While everyone would recognise antipathetic conflicts, for example, in control needs i.e. fighting to establish who is "in charge". Spotting the more subtle apathetic conflict where 'I wait for you to take charge and you wait for me to take charge and nothing much happens' is more difficult and a FIRO-B assessment can be most enlightening in these circumstances.

While the work of Schutz and the FIRO theory suggest that interpersonal needs are probably the most important single factor in real (and therefore transdisciplinary) team formation and non-content/knowledge related performance they cannot account for all the variation observed.

The level of challenge and/or the complexity of boundary spanning problems requiring a transdisciplinary approach strongly suggest that personal needs, preferences or values will also play an important part in team functioning and performance. This is where standard psychometric approaches to understanding the structure of individual personality can be helpful. Throughout the twentieth Century ideas about the structure of normal personality were developed and psychometric questionnaires developed alongside. This resulted in both approaches developed from theory such as the Myers-Briggs Type indicator (MBTI) (Bailey 2010; Myers et al. 1998) and those empirically derived from cluster and factor analysis such as Cattell's 16PF

(Cattell and Cattell 1995). What is most interesting is that despite completely differing approaches both kinds of approach strongly suggested a similar top-level five-factor structure. By the 1970's this big five model was being activity studied and developed for example by Costa and McCrae (1992) and resulted in being operationalized as the NEO-PIR inventory (McCrae and Costa 1992). This version of the model describes normal personality in terms of five traits: Openness (to ideas), Conscientiousness, Extroversion, Agreeableness and Neuroticism (negative thoughts and feelings).

While much has been written in general about personality factors and teams there are some particular considerations that apply to teams approaching trans-disciplinary problems as defined here. Firstly the need to integrate knowledge and methods across subject areas to produce a synergistic result puts a strong premium on openness to ideas (not the same as the FIRO openness) and unless this is a feature of a majority of the team, exploratory and creative behaviour may not be sufficiently prominent to solve the transdisciplinary problem at hand. Secondly these problems are "difficult" by definition and require team members to be, and hold each other, accountable for performance. In other words Conscientiousness is a key trait required from the members. Also while a certain level of Neuroticism may provide challenge and urgency preventing complacency, too much will disrupt team performance. Finally team and group work is preferred behaviour for extroverts, while reflection is a standard for introverts. This suggests that a balance of extrovert and introvert behaviour is probably ideal for transdisciplinary working. While these are not hard quantitative guidelines for team composition it is clear that the use of quantitative tools such as the 16PF or qualitative tools such as the MBTI have a useful place in predicting both likely success and trouble spots for trans-disciplinary teams and for developing suitable facilitation and coaching strategies for them.

Finally while we have concentrated upon team formation and process, if the input knowledge and skills required to solve the transdisciplinary problem to hand are not present within, or accessible to, the team then the team will not be able to succeed. This places some requirements on the skills base of people participating in trans-disciplinary problem solving and implementation. Firstly as an HPT is the ideal vehicle it must be small. It cannot, unlike a working group tackling a classical multi-disciplinary problem, be large and highly structured. This implies a level of breadth in the team members, breadth that should span, to some extent at least, the discipline areas involved. This does not necessarily mean that all members need to be classically "T" shaped professionals (Bailey 2010). However it does probably mean that "I" shaped narrow or specialist experts are unsuitable within the team itself although they will probably need to be available for the team members to consult if needed. Similarly broad generalists (combshaped) individuals are probably not suitable unless the number of discipline areas spanned by the problem is small and the deep knowledge required can be covered by other team members.

Supporting Teams Working in a Transdisciplinary Way

Finally we consider the support and development of teams working in a transdisciplinary way. It is not straightforward and draws upon a range of tools and techniques and we will focus here on team coaching as an emerging practice that is growing in use and perceived effectiveness. How it differs from other group interventions is well described from the work of Peters and Carr (2013). They differentiate between the modes of group working in an adaptation of the work of Hawkins and Smith (2006)

Process	Description/Identifying Factors
Group Coaching	Coaching of individuals within a group context
	Individuals take turns being the focus
	The team members are not part of a defined team nor focused on working together on a common goal or to create a common deliverable
	The group members themselves are seen as additional coaching resources available to the other group members
Team Training	Training done as a team to build skills and/or general capabilities
Team Building/Development	Often social and/or challenging team bonding activities
	Process carried out by the team to develop its capacity to work well together on a joint task
Facilitation	To provide external, objective meeting and/or process management to help the team reach complex or difficult decisions
	Frees up the team members to focus on the task, not the process
Team Coaching	"Helping the team improve performance, and the processes by which performance is achieved, through reflection and dialogue" (Clutterbuck 2007, p. 77)
	"Enabling a team to function at more than the sum of its parts, by clarifying its mission and improving its external and internal relationships" (Hawkins and Smith 2006)
	"Direct interaction with a team intended to help members make coordinated and task-appropriate use of their collective resources in accomplishing the team's work" (Wageman et al. 2005, p. 269)

Again the identification of Team Coaching is distinct from Group Coaching and the concept of 'more than the sum of its parts' comes to the fore. Coaching in this instance can be defined as

Effective team coaching addresses the task related behaviour of the team with the intent of helping it develop and sustain three things: (1) high levels of motivation for the team's collaborative work, (2) effective collective approaches to team tasks, and (3) the ability to identify and deploy all the considerable talent that team members bring to the table. High quality team coaching is about the work that members must accomplish together. Behaviour on the part of members that supports or impedes the three work processes just identified is fair game for a coaching intervention, whether the intervention corrects ineffective behaviour or reinforces good team work. (Wageman (1997), p. 163)

There are some specific coaching skills that are at a premium for supporting trans-disciplinary teams. For example coaching the group through the pseudo-team transition stage. Clearly this does not arise with coaching working groups as the only requirement is to avoid this stage entirely. However, this does become critical for any coach working with HPT whether they are transdisciplinary or not.

Some broad guidelines can be given for coaching transdisciplinary teams:

- Firstly the coach should be engaged early and involved if possible at the selection stage. In real life the choice of personnel for the team might be highly restricted but if there is any scope to optimise at the selection stage it should be made. At group formation as much assessment as is possible and ethically allowable should be undertaken, to attempt to predict likely issues and problems and to facilitate the drawing up of a strong and relevant initial team coaching plan.
- Planned effort should be frontloaded, it is getting the team to the point where they become a real team that defines the work of the coach. Once the team is heading for HPT status they effectively become self-coaching and only a light touch should be required thereafter.
- Individual coaching may be required for specific team members or pairs. Again this is not different in kind or methods from individual coaching of for example a manager with some challenging behaviours.

The difference between coaching transdisciplinary teams and other forms of team coaching is not one of nature but of degree and intensity to ensure strong real team formation and performance. This is not true transdisciplinary working in and of itself but rather the focused application of the generic team coaching knowledge base and skill set.

In Conclusion

This has been, of necessity, a brief resume of the challenges posed in the formation and support of high performing teams focused on transdisciplinary issues. The requirement for true team working and not working groups is paramount and although T shaped professionals were not the only option for team membership the individuals within the team need to be able to transcend their disciplinary perspective and be able to contribute to the integration of knowledge, concepts and methods drawn from multiple disciplines. This strongly implied a critical openness to learning and ideas as well as the conscientiousness to hold themselves accountable to the aims of the team. Supporting such teams through team coaching can be effective but it needs to concentrate upon team formation/consolidation processes to avoid being stuck with the pseudo-team.

These considerations have started to bring into focus how using an i-disciplinary framework to examine both issues and working processes allows for better choice of the methods and techniques needed in their solution and design.

References

Bailey, Mark. (2010). Working at the edges. *Networks, 11,* 42–45.

Brown, S. L., & Eisenhardt, K. M. (1997). The art of continuous change: Linking complexity theory and time-paced evolution in relentlessly shifting organizations. *Administrative science quarterly* 1–34.

Cattell, R. B., & Cattell, H. E. P. (1995). Personality structure and the new fifth edition of the 16PF. *Educational and Psychological Measurement, 55*(6), 926–937.

Costa, P. T., & McCrae, R. R. (1992). Normal personality assessment in clinical practice: The NEO Personality Inventory. *Psychological Assessment, 4*(1):5–13. doi:10.1037/1040-3590.4.1.5.

Hackman, J. G., & Wageman, R. (2005). A theory of team Coaching. *Academy of Management Review, 30*(2):269–287.

Hadorn, G. H., Biber-Klemm, S., Grossenbacher-Mansuy, W., Hoffmann-Riem, H., Joye, D., Pohl, C., Wiesmann, U., & Zemp, E. (2008). The emergence of transdisciplinarity as a form of research. In G. H. Hadorn, H. Hoffmann-Riem, S. Biber-Klemm, W. Grossenbacher-Mansuy, D. Joye, C. Pohl, U. Wiesmann, & Elisabeth Zemp (eds), *Handbook of transdisciplinary research* (pp. 19–39). Netherlands: Springer.

Hawkins, P., & Smith, N. (2006). *Coaching, mentoring and organizational consultancy: Supervision and development.* Maidenhead: Open University Press.

IBM. (2011). Capitailising on complexity: Insights from the Global Chief Executive Officier Study. http://public.dhe.ibm.com/common/ssi/ecm/en/gbe03297usen/GBE03297USEN.PDF. Accessed 13 Feb. 2014.

Katzenbach, J. R., & Smith, D. K. (2013). *The wisdom of teams: Creating the high-performance organization.* Boston: Harvard Business Review Press.

King, Gillian, Strachan, D., Tucker, M., Duwyn, B., Desserud, S., & Shillington, M. (2009). The application of a transdisciplinary model for early intervention services. *Infants & Young Children, 22*(3), 211–223. (210.1097/IYC.1090b1013e3181abe1091c1093).

Koch, R. (2011). *The 80/20 principle: The secret to achieving more with less.* LLC: Random House.

Leavy, P. (2011). *Essentials of transdisicplinary research: Using problem-centred methodologies.* Califormia: Left Coast Press.

Mâsse, L. C., Moser, R. P., Stokols, D., Taylor, B. K., Marcus, S. E., Morgan, G. D., Hall, K. L., Croyle, R. T., & Trochim, W. M. (2008). Measuring collaboration and transdisciplinary integration in team science. *American journal of preventive medicine, 35*(2), S151–S160.

Mathieu, John, Maynard, M. T., Rapp, T., & Gilson, L. (2008). Team effectiveness 1997–2007: A review of recent advancements and a Glimpse into the future. *Journal of Management, 34*(3), 410–476. doi:10.1177/0149206308316061.

McCrae, R. R., & Costa, P. T. (1992). Discriminant validity of NEO-PIR facet scales. *Educational and Psychological Measurement, 52*(1), 229–237.

Myers, I. B., McCaulley, M. H., Quenk, N. L., & Hammer A. L. (1998). *MBTI manual: A guide to the development and use of the Myers-Briggs type indicator.* Palo Alto: Consulting Psychologists Press.

Peters, J., & Carr, C. (2013). Team coaching. DProf Report, Institute for Work Based Leaning, Middlesex University, UK.

Petrie, N. (2011). Furture trends in leadership development: Center for creative leadership. New Jersey: Wiley.

Schutz, Will. (1992). Beyond firo-B-three new theory-derived measures-element B: behavior, element F: feelings, element S: self. *Psychological Reports, 70*(3), 915–937.

Steinmetz, G. (2007). Transdisciplinarity as a nonimperial encounter: For an open sociology. *Thesis Eleven, 91*(1), 48–65. doi:10.1177/0725513607082002.

Stokols, D., Hall, K. L., Taylor, B. K., & Moser, R. P. (2008). The science of team science: Overview of the field and introduction to the supplement. *American journal of preventive medicine, 35*(2), S77–S89.

Tuckman, B. W. (1965). Developmental sequence in small groups. *Psychological Bulletin, 63*(6), 384–399. doi:10.1037/h0022100.

Wageman, R. (1997). Critical success factors for creating superb self-managing teams. *Organisational Dynamics, 26*(1), 49–61.

Ron Collins is currently an Executive Partner in IBMGlobal Business Services. Where he leads large complex Business Analytics and Optimisation projects for major multi-national clients. His programmes are intrinsically trans-disciplinary in nature both within the supplier and client teams relying on closely integrated team work for the delivery of optimum business value. He has been in management consulting for more than 18 years, focussing on: Business Processes, Information Management, Decision Making, Analytics and Operational Research. He has previously held several Partner and equivalent positions in KPMG, EDS and HP. By background he is a physical scientist, a Chartered Chemist and spent much of his early career as a defence scientist working in leading edge R&D projects and programmes.

Annette Fillery-Travis is currently Programme Coordinator for the M/DProf at Middlesex University where she is a senior coach educator, researcher and author Within her first career Annette was a senior scientist and developed an extensive research publication list with over 60 peer reviewed journal publications. She continues to be a Fellow of the Royal Society of Chemistry and was the first female Chair of The Food Group from 2002–2005 and Visiting Professor in Colloid Science at the Sante Fe Institute, Argentina in 2000–2004.

After obtaining a Masters in Professional Development and Science Management, Annette began a second career with the Professional Development Foundation (a not-for-profit research trust) as Programme Director and then as CEO. She has designed leadership programmes (as internal programmes and part of an external Masters degree) for public sector managers and school leaders, and manager coach training programmes across a range of sectors. On secondment to the Centre for Educational Leadership at the University of Manchester in 2008 she was responsible for the overhaul of the Masters in Educational Leadership, an advanced CPD offer for Senior Managers and Head Teachers in Secondary Education. At PDF she was Programme Director for the Master degree programme accredited since 2002 by Middlesex University with specialist titles in leadership development and coaching. In 2010 Annette moved full time to Middlesex University where she is part of the faculty for the Professional Doctorate at the Institute of Work Based Learning. Her research interests include the role of doctorate supervisor/advisor as coach.

Transdisciplinarity and Nursing Education: Expanding Nursing's Professional Identity and Potential

Sarah Wall

Nursing, as both a discipline and profession, has a history of struggling to define its unique identity and body of knowledge. This history, coupled with nursing's dynamic contemporary sociopolitical context, now compels a renewed conceptualization of nursing's professional identity and purpose and a redirected sense of its potential to contribute to the health and social problems facing society. Although the concept of transdisciplinarity has been interpreted in various ways, the idea that disciplinary knowledge can be expanded and transcended by the blending of other realms of knowledge is a potentially fruitful one for nursing, in its quest for significance. This chapter will review the history of nursing's conceptualizations of its knowledge and identity, consider the contemporary forces that necessitate a reimagining of nursing's current collective professional identity, and explore the ways in which transdisciplinarity in nursing professional education might, somewhat ironically, allow nursing to find its unique professional pathway by incorporating a transcendent range of disciplinary knowledges.

A Brief History of Knowledge, Education, and Professional Identity in Nursing

Over the years, nursing's professional identity and status have been strongly linked to the knowledge upon which its practice is based. Ideologically-based decisions about what constitutes nursing knowledge are translated into nursing education, which becomes the practical avenue for the development of nurses' professional identity and sense of social significance. In its early years, nursing as an occupation did not have strong foundation of formalized disciplinary knowledge and education. Nursing education at the turn of the twentieth century was more about "appropriate" gender-based character development than it was about the acquisition of knowledge (Larsen

S. Wall (✉)
University of Alberta, Alberta, Canada
e-mail: swall@ualberta.ca

© Springer International Publishing Switzerland 2015
P. Gibbs (ed.), *Transdisciplinary Professional Learning and Practice,*
DOI 10.1007/978-3-319-11590-0_5

and Baumgart 1992). Thus, during the early 1900s, nurses in Canada were mainly untrained women whose work resembled domestic labor (Brannon 1994; Coburn 1988). Those training in hospitals were unpaid apprentices, more exploited than educated (Coburn 1988). Formal definitions of nursing knowledge were largely non-existent. Traditionally, the nursing curriculum was dominated by biomedicine and nurses were dependent upon doctors for their education and training (Allen 2001; Cooke 1993a).

Professional education in nursing moved through a period of increasing formal-ization in the mid twentieth century, as nursing education moved into hospital schools of nursing and eventually universities. An important feature of the increasing for-malization of nursing education was the development of and reliance upon nursing theories and concepts (Larsen and Baumgart 1992) as nursing intensified its attempts to differentiate its knowledge from medical (physician) knowledge. Ironically, how-ever, it has been noted that early nursing theory was in fact organized around the medical model (Rutty 1998; Yeo 2004), which involved a body systems view of the person and an interventionist approach to care. Nursing's understanding of its own knowledge at this point was focused in large part on its role in illness intervention. At any rate, the development of nursing theories represented the beginnings of the movement to defining the unique professional knowledge of nursing.

Interestingly, despite considerable formalization of nursing education and the knowledge upon which it is based, some commentators have observed that nurses continue to lack a clear description of their work that differentiates it from medicine or mothering, which is reflective of its gendered history and close association with medicine and which prevents employers and society from valuing nursing work or defining nursing as professional in conventional terms (Bolton 2000; Daiski 2004; England and Folbre 1999; Nelson and Gordon 2009; Rutty 1998). Since the 1980s, the discipline of nursing has continued on its quest to define its knowledge by focusing on the fundamental concepts of health and caring (Newman et al. 2004). New nursing theories and models identify a distinct nursing territory, shifting focus from the biomedical model toward caring, holism, and ethical expertise (Fawcett and Swoyer 2008; Goodrick and Reay 2010; Maben and Griffiths 2008; Nelson and Gordon 2006). In fact, Newman and colleagues (2004) purport that "a body of knowledge that does not include caring and human health experience is not nursing knowledge," (p. 21). Such an assertion clearly has the effect of narrowing the scope of nursing knowledge and making it possible to justify why nursing should ignore a whole host of disciplinary perspectives that do not have an obvious connection to caring.

Although there has been considerable evolution in the ways in which nursing defines its knowledge and, hence, professional identity, and how it imparts these perspectives through nursing education, there has been an ironic lack of progress in terms of carving out a distinct body of knowledge upon which to build the profes-sional work of nurses. Florence Nightingale observed in her time, the late 1800s, that the elements of nursing were unknown and many commentators have noted that this remains true today (Royal College of Nursing (RCN) 2007). Over the years, nursing has primarily concerned itself with debating the extent to which it should align itself with medical knowledge. At this point, nursing has virtually come full circle, having returned to a focus on potentially very gendered virtues such as caring, while overlooking the concrete knowledge that nurses have and its possible sources (Nelson and Gordon 2006). For some time, nursing has acknowledged that its ways of knowing include scientific, relational, and ethical dimensions (Carper 1978; Newman et al. 2004; RCN 2007) and that its domains of practice include patient care, teaching, research, and administration (Canadian Nurses Association (CNA) 2006; RCN 2007). With such a broad epistemological range and such a breadth of areas in which this knowing is applied, it would seem to be beneficial for nursing to consider the role that other disciplinary perspectives could play in nursing's knowledge development and self-understanding. Nursing's uptake of the concepts of cross-disciplinarity has, however, been quite limited.

In health care, the terms multidisciplinary, interdisciplinary, and transdisciplinary are used interchangeably but, overall, these terms generally refer to levels of teamwork among the various health professions working together in a particular setting and interprofessional collaboration in patient care (Dyer 2003; Fauchald and Smith 2005; Ray 1998). Which of these terms is selected to define a team is based on the level of communication among team members, the integration of the team members' knowledge, and the coordination of service delivery and planning. Curricular implications for cross-disciplinary practice focus on promoting positive group dynamics, exposing students to the perspectives of each health discipline/profession, and developing collaboration skills (Dyer 2003; Freshwater et al. 2013). Developing transdisciplinary work in nursing has been difficult and, in some cases, threatening, both within nursing and the health care realm (Grey and Connolly 2008). "True" transdisciplinarity is poorly defined in nursing but it is said to involve the creation of new frameworks that break down traditional boundaries between disciplines (various health professions) for the purpose of improving clinical outcomes (Dyer 2003; Mitchell 2005). There is little awareness of the transcendence of transciplinarity and the ways in which it might "expand referential fields, open new lines of possibility, allow selves to mutate, autodevelop and redevelop" (Genosko 2003).

Contemporary Forces and the Role of Nursing

In order to understand the potential and importance of transdisciplinarity for nursing, it is first necessary to understand the contemporary forces that impact upon nursing and the ways in which these forces make demands for a re-thinking of the nature of nursing knowledge. For at least the last three decades, there has been a movement toward university-based professional nursing education. Several years into the twenty-first century, nursing jurisdictions across Canada have now implemented the requirement that nurses be educationally prepared at the baccalaureate level; many other Western countries have or are about to introduce this minimum educational standard (Global Knowledge Exchange Network (GKEN) 2009). Interestingly, however, although the baccalaureate entry to practice policy is intended to prepare nurses for the complexities of contemporary life, the policy has actually been divisive among nurses and a great deal of energy has been expended over the years in debating where nurses should be educated rather than how they should be educated (Larsen and Baumgart 1992; Nelson 2002).

As mentioned, the rationale behind this higher standard of education is that nurses need more education in order to "cope with a changing world and to contribute in a thoughtful way to changing patterns of nursing practice" (Larsen and Baumgart 1992, p. 392). As expansive and forward-thinking as this rationale may sound, the justification for increased educational requirements for nursing has emphasized competence and quality of care and has been based upon evidence that university-educated nurses provide safer care in hospitals (GKEN 2009; Larsen and Baumgart 1992). Nurses work in a health care system that, despite ongoing change, continues to privilege biomedical technology and physician-driven services (Campbell 2000). The long-standing association of nurses with physicians and hospital care is taken for granted as a defining feature of nursing and continues to shape nursing's self-identity and its understandings of the disciplinary content and goal of nursing education. To illustrate, Scott et al. (2013) explored the "nature of nursing and the function of the nurse within a twenty-first century health care system" (p. 23). In doing so, they stressed the holistic perspective of nurses and the role they play in attending not only to the physical needs of patients but also the psycho-social aspects of their care and they called for adequate resourcing for "the humane, compassionate treatment of patients" by nurses (p. 31). What is interesting about this is that, despite the promise of considering the possibilities for nursing today, they work within a narrow view of nursing's role as providing care for hospitalized patients within a complex health care system. If this is all that is possible for the nurses of this century, then a continuing focus on the medical model of care, albeit with an emphasis on compassion and virtue, is all that is required of nursing education and an insular and limited disciplinary perspective is sufficient.

It is important to note, however, that contemporary trends and needs in health and health care compel a much broader vision and provide an opening to a much more unique, independent, influential, and effective identity and role for nursing, which requires an expanded and innovative approach to nursing education. If nursing were to embrace an expanded range of transdisciplinary knowledge, nurses could contribute to society's health, in the broadest sense of the term, in new and unique ways. Global health crises, issues in addressing the social determinants of health, advances in medical science and technology, and health care reform, present numerous pathways for nurses to pursue in order to secure a more certain professional identity. Responding effectively and creatively to these issues demands an extensive repertoire of transdisciplinary knowledge.

Many of the world's most challenging health issues have a significant socio-political component, which necessitates an understanding of the social sciences in order to assess and respond to health needs of this nature. According to the World Health Organization (http://www.who.int/features/factfiles/global_burden/en/), several of the most pressing global health problems are amenable to simple and cost-effective care, including vaccinations; clear water and sanitation; medication availability and administration; maternal/child care including breastfeeding support and pregnancy care; health promotion activities related to diet, exercise, smoking, and lifestyle; and health assessment, counseling, and education. Other trends that are shaping society and health care in Canada and internationally include the global HIV/AIDS pandemic, the rise and rapid spread of communicable diseases, rising rates of mental health problems such as anxiety, depression, and fear, aging populations, increasing global migration, climate change and other environmental health issues, and ongoing wars and terrorism around the world (Villeneuve 2010). Few, if any, of these trends and issues require the biomedical approach to illness care that is so familiar in the West.

It has been established for some time that health is largely socially determined (CNA 2005; Mikkonen and Raphael 2010). Social structures and power relationships in society can have a significant impact on overall health and well-being and can have much stronger effects than the typically emphasized individual level lifestyle and behavioural factors (Mikkonen and Raphael 2010). The key social determinants of health include: income (poverty), education, employment status, working conditions, and job security, early childhood development, housing, food security, social inclusion, gender, race, disability, and the presence of a social safety net (Mikkonen and Raphael 2010). The Canadian Nurses Association (2005) notes that, to date, however, despite considerable evidence, there has been only slow progress in addressing the social determinants of health within a context that favours medicalized, reactive care and that there has been an emphasis on individual level interventions and a tendency to attribute blame to individuals living in sub-optimal social situations, rather than viewing the issues at a structural level. In their recommendations to professional nurses across Canada, the CNA (2005) suggests a range of strategies that nurses can implement to attend more deeply to the social issues that influence health, such as assessing patients' social needs and incorporating them into plans of care, advocating for a view of health that includes the social determinants of health, and promoting health-focused social policy. Given that improving social health requires "think[ing] about health and its determinants in a more sophisticated manner than has been the case to date" (Mikkonen and Raphael 2010, p. 8), a new approach to nursing education that incorporates critical, structural level theory, might be in order.

In addition to the social and public health issues now facing the world, there are many concerns about the nature and sustainability of western health care systems. Western health care systems are highly complex and most countries have been dissatisfied for some time with their health care systems (Ben-Zur et al. 1999). Despite many calls over the years for health system reform, change efforts have been mainly directed at improving efficiencies in hospital care. There has not been a comprehensive and committed plan to address the social determinants of health, primary health services remain underdeveloped, the implementation of medical technology has yielded to unrealistic and irrational societal expectations, and the majority of nurses continue to work in hospitals where their autonomy is limited and their professional values are challenged (Storch 2010). Ultimately, despite ongoing chaotic change, what we now see in Canada's health care system is "less of the same or worse" (Armstrong and Armstrong 2003, p. 87). In their visionary document, *Toward 2020: Visions for Nursing*, The Canadian Nurses Association (2006) asserted that Canada's medically driven, "1960s style system" (p. 12) remains essentially intact and noted an unwillingness or inability across health care professionals to talk about issues of power and other dynamics that limit the creation of new structures and ways of behaving. Quite possibly, this is because of limited cross-disciplinary perspectives in professional nursing education that would equip nurses to have these kinds of conversations. The CNA, in this document, envisioned nursing in the future as much more independent and directly accessible to the public. In support of this shift in role for future nurses, the CNA foresaw revolutionary changes to nursing education as part of a shift away from the illness care model to a focus on wellness, although they lamented the deeply entrenched lack of real change in the system. Eight years later, little progress has been made in this regard.

Changes in the health care system have had a profound impact of the professional experiences of nurses. There has been very little uptake of expanded roles for nurses (Armstrong and Armstrong 2003). Rather than contributing to innovation in health care, nurses have had to comply with the efficiency agenda, which has undermined their capacity to provide the patient care they judge appropriate (Rankin and Campbell 2006). System restructuring has led to significant job change for nurses (Aiken et al. 2001; Daiski 2004; Laschinger et al. 2001; Rankin and Campbell 2006; Wynne 2003). They have experienced increased workloads, job uncertainty, disrupted professional relationships, and significant work related stress, along with systemically-produced moral distress and compassion fatigue (Aiken et al. 2001; Austin 2011; Austin et al. 2005, 2009; Daiski 2004; Ingersoll et al. 2001; Laschinger et al. 2001; Shannon and French 2005). Most "nurses have acquiesced to this punishing system" (Sullivan 2002, p. 183) and have been "sublimely unaware of most of [the] flaws" in the system (Carter 2007, p. 270). Thus, they have been party to the devaluing and rationalization of their work, and uncritical or unaware of the issues they face, thus helping to perpetuate a model of care that is at odds with their professional ethics (Austin 2011; Carter 2007; Rudge 2011). Nurses resist and lack the theoretical tools, mainly those from critical social science, that might help them to better assert their place and role in the health care system.

In addition to responding to the changing nature of care and work in today's health care system, nurses are required to manage the ongoing rapid growth of new scientific and technological knowledge and applications in medical care (Maloney 1992). The Canadian Nurses Association points out that "nursing practice will be driven increasingly by the way technology and science change human health and illness care" (CNA 2006, p. 80). Technological advances in surgery, anesthesia, drugs, and medical treatments will change the way care is delivered and technology in general will change communication patterns, jobs, and education (CNA 2006). In the world of advancing science, nurses are and will increasingly be required to learn to use new technologies and develop competence in determining the applications and limitations of new treatment modalities (Maloney 1992; CNA 2007). They will also be called upon to make balanced decisions about how technology interfaces with advances in holistic care and complementary therapies, low-tech primary, community, and social care, human need and experience in health care situations, and how it impacts their own jobs (CNA 2006; Maloney 1992; Villeneuve 2010).

Bowen et al. (2000) acknowledge that, as nursing educators attempt to respond to change within the complex health care system, they will inevitably experience the tensions that accompany politically-charged change. However, they stress that "any program that ignores the sociopolitical forces in the external environment will do a disservice to its graduates" and state that "one of the most important skills that educators can impart to their students is the ability to manipulate their environments to come change agents creating new and more healthy systems" (p. 32). They suggest that nursing curricula must now include instruction in communication, legislative and policy awareness, and leadership skills, which they note are not always present in professional nursing educational programs.

Global health issues, concerns about the social determinants of health, and the care decisions that are forced by the possibilities that accompany advanced science and technology compel the need for new ways to understand and respond to ethical issues in nursing practice. Nursing has a history of commitment to social justice, although most nurses today are scarcely involved in sociopolitical activities. As well, giving attention to the social determinants of health requires that nurses rethink their perspectives about individuals in poverty (CNA 2005, 2006). Even when nurses embrace ideals of social justice in theory, "ethical practice in relation to social structures and marginalizing processes may have limited uptake or be constrained in practice" (Pauly 2013, p. 438). Although scientific advances have led to important gains in health across the world, significant disparities persist and it is time for a re-emphasis on the moral foundations of health improvement activities (Ruger 2004). In the acute care context, which is increasingly technological, nurses must find ways to balance care with technology and to question the values that underpin the application of science and technology (Timmins 2011). Brown and Allison (2013) point out that "the complexity of contemporary nursing practice demands that nurse educators continually engage in. . . educative moments" that will contribute to ethical, reflexive, critical, and transformative nursing practice (p. 302). Such an endeavour must draw upon as yet untapped knowledges.

All of these trends point to a necessary evolution in the responsibilities and roles of registered nurses, which in turn means that nurses of the future will require new knowledge gleaned from fundamentally reconsidered educational curricula (Villeneuve 2010). For real change to occur, nurses will require the knowledge and skills that allow them to question pervasive ideologies about health, professions, and individualism (to name a few), understand the complexities of social life and its inherent power dynamics, have the professional confidence and competence to advocate for and take a leadership role in health system change, and, more practically speaking, work within a different scope of practice (set of responsibilities) and across a range of non-hospital practice settings. Clearly, there would be a benefit to incorporating a greatly expanded range of disciplinary knowledges to inform a new perspective for nursing in the future.

Perspectives on Disciplinary Knowledge in Nursing

Nursing is conflicted about the kinds of knowledge that have legitimacy for the profession and its practice. In 1997, Trnobranski argued that nursing has lacked clarity and cohesion in the definition of its knowledge base and noted that it has diminished the potential contribution of other disciplines in its educational curricula. This lack of clarity and definition is complicated by nursing's long history of affiliation with biomedical knowledge and exposure to value systems that confer power and prestige on scientific knowledge (Cooke 1993a; Rutty 1998). Although there has been much discussion about the value of various kinds of knowledge for nursing practice, the fundamental assumption that remains is that the "'hard' sciences are not contestable and are therefore more relevant for the [nursing] students" (Aranda and Law 2006, p. 562) than is knowledge from the social sciences. Interestingly, the debates that raged in the 1990s about the kinds of knowledge that are important for nursing practice have cooled off to some extent, in favour of pedagogical discussions that focus on process of teaching and learning rather than its content and the acquisition thereof (Holland 2004), leaving nursing with important unresolved questions about what the scope of its professional knowledge should be. The value of theory (of any sort) for nursing has been questioned (Sharp 1994). There is an anti-academic and anti-intellectual bias in nursing (Aranda and Law 2006; Rutty 1998) that perpetuates what is referred to as a theory-practice gap (Stevenson 2005). There is a tension in nursing between "knowing how" and "knowing that," which refers to the distinction between an ability to perform the work competently and theoretical knowledge of what the work is (Sharp 1996). In general, nurses rarely engage in discussions of the ontological or epistemological premises of their knowledge base and are reluctant to question familiar expectations and assumptions, not just about the care they give but also about their own work situations (Cooke 1993a; Sharp 1994). Even though nursing education has moved into universities, it has reverted to or continued with a training/apprenticeship model rather than adopting an educative model that takes advantage of the range of knowledge available in a university setting (Aranda and Law 2006).

The work of nurses deals, in part, with biophysical need and, given that the majority of nurses continue to work in hospitals, the assumption that nursing knowledge is biomedical knowledge has been easily sustained. However, although nurses do value immediately useful scientific knowledge (Jordan 1994), the discipline of nursing has had a certain ambivalence toward including the sciences in nursing education, particularly since nursing has moved toward viewing its knowledge as based upon caring and holism (Jordan et al. 1999; Trnobranski 1997). Dissatisfaction with the biomedical model of care and the dominance of physicians in the health care hierarchy prompted earlier commentators to suggest that nursing reduce or eliminate any attention to the sciences in the nursing curriculum (Jordan 1994). Nursing may have devalued bioscientific knowledge to its detriment in an effort to distance itself from subservience to the medical profession; nursing theories have developed without reference to the biological basis of nursing (Jordan 1994). Nevertheless, it has also been acknowledged that scientific knowledge does not belong to any particular discipline (namely medicine) and that the value of this type of knowledge for human welfare may have been reduced by a lack of application of this knowledge by other disciplines (namely nursing) (Jordan 1994).

Research has shown that nurses tend to lack the knowledge and confidence needed to understand and communicate basic biological processes that underlie common patient conditions and treatments (Clancy et al. 2000). As nurses continue to seek professional autonomy and a place of significance in the health care endeavour, the application of scientific knowledge by nurses to contemporary individual and population health concerns may be of increasing importance (Jordan et al. 1999), which has implications for the disciplinary richness of nursing education. Going forward, nursing can establish its own legitimate claims to scientific knowledge (rather than attempting to separate itself from it) by incorporating it into nursing education, scholarship, and theory, thus reframing the physical problems of patients not as medical problems but as nursing problems that can be addressed through interventions that are associated with nursing knowledge and values (Jordan 1994). For example, nurses with strong scientific knowledge would be able to see a condition such as edema (swelling) of the legs as a condition amenable to changes in diet, exercise, and rest rather than as one requiring pharmacological intervention (Jordan 1994). Further, nurses who understand the behavioural sciences can be reflexive about their own attitudes toward their patients and can promote positive behavioural change from a perspective that acknowledges the social psychological factors that influence health, such as habit, the need to belong, embarrassment avoidance, and the contextual factors that influence choice (Mowforth et al. 2005; Thirsk and Clark 2014).

Perhaps ironically, despite the "hard" or concrete nature of scientific knowledge, nurses continue to question the relevance of scientific knowledge for practice and have difficulty applying it in practice. However, nursing's confusion about the value of scientific knowledge pales in comparison to its assessment of the importance of the social sciences, particularly sociology, to its purposes. Nurses can be especially hostile to theory that takes a critical view (Wall 2007). Even when sociology is incorporated into nursing professional education, these perspectives can be misappropriated and twisted to fit into nursing's prevailing ideological system and to serve nursing's own purposes (Cooke 1993a). Cooke (1993a) argued that nursing has used micro-sociological knowledge to support nursing's values around holistic care and as a way of understanding social factors as properties of individuals rather than society. She also noted that nurses have failed to draw upon the sociological perspective in an analysis of its own occupational circumstances. Edgley et al. (2009) found that nursing students who had taken sociology courses had poor recall of the content and simplified sociological understandings of clinical situations. They also found that students shifted in and out of various sets of knowledge—back and forth between biomedical and sociological knowledge—depending on the situation, rather than drawing upon an integrated foundation of knowledge. Research by Aranda and Law (2006) also revealed "a lack of understanding of the very nature of sociology" on the part of both students and teachers of nursing.

Nursing education sustains nursing's epistemological premises; nurses are often taught in an unquestioned and straightforward manner and success in the acquisition of these perspectives is evaluated on the basis of right or wrong (Sharp 1994). Ultimately, nurses are, in general, focused on the one-to-one care of individuals and they seek workable solutions to the practical demands of patient care (Sharp 1994), without allowing the critiques and complexity of issues that sociology imposes to interfere with their professional identity and perceived purpose. A strong opponent of the inclusion of sociology in the nursing curriculum, Keith Sharp, once argued that it is not even desirable for a nurse to be acquainted with sociology since its theoretical orientation is irrelevant to nurses' practice orientation. He also expressed concern that nurses should gain an understanding of social forces on their work and an ability to imagine new possibilities for nursing, lest it "stir student nurses to some form of revolutionary praxis" (1995, p. 54).

Despite dissention, numerous other nursing authors have articulated a role for sociology in the nursing curriculum because it allows for "the development of a new way of looking at the world—one which calls into question much that we have taken for granted" (Cooke 1993a). Sociology can make a positive contribution to nursing education (and thus professional socialization) through its ability to produce an increased critical awareness and understanding of the social influences on health and illness and an expanded base of knowledge for considering a multi-causal model of health and illness, as opposed to a biomedical model (Pinikahana 2003). Porter (1998) argued that nurses need to understand the influences of sociocultural factors on health and illness and described how some of the major social theories have relevance for nursing practice. As well, sociology can contribute to nursing through its emancipatory aims. This has relevance on micro- and macro- levels, with regard for both patient need and nursing as an occupation. Cooke (1993a) pointed out that sociology can provide a framework for linking personal or individual experiences and needs with social and political contexts by showing us "that existing social relations are not fixed an immutable" and by "expand[ing] our consciousness of the different possibilities for the future" (p. 215). This has relevance for global health issues that are matters of social need, for addressing the social determinants of health, both at home and abroad, and for rethinking the future of nursing as a profession (Cooke 1993a). The incorporation of sociology in nursing can also make possible a critique of the technical rationalism that nursing has turned to for professional legitimation and help develop nurses who are able to work within the messy, confusing world of practice within a constantly changing organizational environment (Williamson 1999). Finally, sociology may be able to provide a new approach to considering moral questions facing the nursing profession that would move away from medico-legal approaches to ethical reasoning toward a more situated and relational understanding of professional ethics (Johnson 1990; Bergum and Dossetor 2005) and an "understanding of how moral values and ethical behaviours are embodied and lived by social agents" (Lopez 2004, p. 878).

Nursing has drawn upon knowledge from other disciplines throughout its development as a profession and discipline. However, because of its primary association with medicine, nursing's attempts to differentiate itself as a discipline have largely centered around distancing itself from biomedical knowledge. Thus, "in the latter half of the twentieth century, nursing has emerged as an academic discipline which is intent upon inculcating its novitiates with its own world view" (Cooke 1993b, p. 1990). Some analysts see nursing as "a composite interdisciplinary area of study derived from a range of primary epistemes" but many more seem to "reject nursing's dependency on other disciplinary knowledge" (Allen 2001, p. 388). Donaldson and Crowley (2004) observed that the breadth of knowledge development in nursing appears to be global but they strongly asserted that "by definition... a discipline is not global" (p. 293). Fawcett (2000 cited in Allen 2001) strongly argued for a perspective of nursing knowledge that is based on discipline-specific theories and research, claiming that knowledge advancement that is said to be nursing but is accomplished within the intellectual traditions of other disciplines is a "great danger to the advancement of nursing science and the survival of the discipline" (p. 388). Clearly, an insular world view such as this has had "a profound effect on [nursing's] relationships with other academic subjects" (Cooke 1993b, p. 1990).

Transdisciplinarity: Possibilities for Nursing

The creation of academic subjects involves boundary work, which involves decisions about what knowledge has legitimacy for each discipline (Cooke 1993b). Perhaps in its attempts to draw the boundary around its professional scope, nursing has fallen prey to the assumption that knowledge belongs to one or another discipline and so must be excluded from nursing in order to avoid contaminating the purity of nursing knowledge. When drawing on a range of disciplinary knowledge, nurses tend to shift in an out of various perspectives, perceiving different forms of knowledge as discrete and distinct, and applying pieces of knowledge to particular situations. They also appear to operate according to a hierarchy of knowledge that privileges knowledge that is seen to be objective and unchanging (such as science) rather than that which is seen as fluid and dynamic (such as sociology), which all too easily "reassert[s] the biomedical model of nurse intervention" (Edgley et al. 2009, p. 20). Sharp conceives of nurses as doers rather than thinkers and suggests that knowledge that cannot be held to be true or that requires reflexivity and skepticism is not appropriate or even comprehensible for nurses (1994, 1995). These ways of conceptualizing knowledge for nursing practice are antithetical to the notion of transdisciplinarity in professional education and to the development of an innovative and expansive professional identity.

In short, the knowledge that is said to be useful for nursing practice is inward-looking, fragmented, and mired by traditional conceptions of nursing's professional identity and purpose. Notions of transdisciplinarity in nursing education and practice seem elusive. As we have seen, the nursing and health literature about cross-disciplinary work is limited to a focus on teamwork among health care professionals for the sake of efficient patient care. However, despite these limitations, the small body of literature on transdisciplinarity in nursing alludes to some of the possibilities inherent in taking a transdisciplinary approach. It is noted that transdisciplinarity in health care can merge concepts from various disciplines in order to create new frameworks for thinking, give birth to new disciplines that are more analytically sophisticated (Mitchell 2005), allow professionals to work on problems that are not typically within their set of responsibilities (Ray 1998), pool expertise in order to address complex problems, and allow for a broader scope of knowledge dissemination (Fauchald and Smith 2005).

Hadorn and colleagues (2008) explain that transdisciplinarity is needed now more than ever as researchers "step into problem fields" (p. 3) and engage with real life people who face complex problems such as poverty, sickness, crime, and environmental issues, spanning the local to global, all the while bearing in mind the established technologies, practices, and power relations within a field. Real movement toward transdisciplinarity requires a certain set of conditions that must be met by a discipline: an ability to question how a given discipline is able to understand its global context, a humble attitude toward the immensity of knowledge, and a commitment to its own specialization while also pursuing heterogenous fields of dialogue (Genosko 2003). Transdisciplinary work and learning can break down the "generalising, decontextualizing and reductionist tendencies of discipline-based inquiry" that is capable of "capturing only part of the situation in question" (Horlick-Jones and Sime 2004, pp. 442, 445).

It is true that disciplines provide us with a social identity (Giri 200) and they frame the boundaries of a web of knowledge that cannot be easily assimilated into another disciplines ways of knowing (McMurtry 2006). Transdisciplinarity requires time, patience, constant communication, and a commitment to respect for the complexity of other disciplines (Fry 2001; McMurtry 2006; Mitchell 2005). However, disciplinary transcendence does not mean that professionals become poorly trained or that they lose their grounding in their own discipline (Rosenfield 1992; Giri 2002). Rather, it means that they are intellectual risk takers who are authentically embedded in their own discipline and expert and confident enough to work with the conceptual frameworks and paradigms of others (Rosenfield 1992; Giri 2002). The crossing of disciplinary borders does not constitute heresy (Genosko 2003). It is "an act of creation rather than one of violation" (Giri 2002, p. 104). A transdisciplinary education can allow a professional to annex new knowledge and, thus, be able to act from a dual point of view based on competencies from various disciplines that are interwoven in daily practice (Hagoel and Kalekin-Fishman 2002).

Transdisciplinarity holds promise for the discipline and profession of nursing. Grey and Connolly (2008) argue that the time is past for nurses to debate the definition of nursing science and that nurses now must begin instead to focus on the real problems facing individuals and groups in clinical and community settings. From their point of view, it is clear that the nurses of the future must embrace transdisciplinarity because of the complexity of human disease. Rosenfield (1992) sees transdisciplinarity as an approach that can provide the theoretical frameworks for considering the social, economic, political, environmental, and institutional factors that influence health and well-being. Certainly the integration of various disciplinary knowledges within the nursing curriculum is complex and requires exploration and clarification (Mowforth et al. 2005). It may be, however, the critical step in re-imagining nursing's identity and purpose into the future.

References

Aiken, L. H., Clarke, S. P., Sloane, D. M., & Sochalski, J. A. (2001). An international perspective on hospital nurses' work environments: The case for reform. *Policy, Politics, & Nursing Practice, 2*(4), 255–263.

Allen, D. (2001). Nursing and sociology: An uneasy marriage? *Sociology of Health & Illness, 23*(3), 386–396.

Aranda, K., & Law, K. (2006). Tales of sociology and the nursing curriculum: Revisiting the debates. *Nurse Education Today, 27*, 561–567.

Armstrong, P., & Armstrong, H. (2003). *Wasting away: The undermining of Canadian healthcare.* Oxford: Oxford University Press.

Austin, W. (2011). The incommensurability of nursing as a practice and the customer service model: An evolutionary threat to the discipline. *Nursing Philosophy, 12*(3), 158–166.

Austin, W., Lemermeyer, G., Goldberg, L., Bergum, V., & Johnson, M. S. (2005). Moral distress in healthcare practice: The situation of nurses. *Healthcare Ethics Committee Forum, 17*(1), 33–48.

Austin, W., Goble, E., Leier, B., & Byrne, P. (2009). Compassion fatigue: The experience of nurses. *Ethics and Social Welfare, 3*(2), 195–214.

Ben-Zur, H., Yagil, D., & Spitzer, A. (1999). Evaluation of an innovative curriculum: Nursing education in the next century. *Journal of Advanced Nursing, 30*(6), 1432–1440.

Bergum, V., & Dossetor, J. (2005). *Relational ethics: The full meaning of respect.* Hagerstown: University Publishing Group.

Bolton, S. C. (2000). Who cares? Offering emotion work as a 'gift' in the nursing labour process. *Journal of Advanced Nursing, 32*(3), 580–586.

Bowen, M., Lyons, K. J., & Young, B. E. (2000). Nursing and health care reform: Implications for curriculum development. *Journal of Nursing Education, 39*(1), 27–33.

Brannon, R. L. (1994). *Intensifying care: The hospital industry, professionalization, and the reorganization of the nursing labor process.* Amityville: Baywood.

Brown, H., & Allison, G. (2013). Educative spaces for teaching and learning ethical practice in nursing. In J. L. Storch, P. Rodney, & R. Starzomski (Eds.), *Toward a moral horizon: Nursing ethics for leadership and practice* (pp. 302–314). Toronto: Pearson.

Campbell, M. (2000). Knowledge, gendered subjectivity, and the restructuring of healthcare: The case of the disappearing nurse. In S. M. Neysmith (Ed.), *Restructuring caring labour: Discourse, state practice, and everyday life* (pp. 186–208). Don Mills: Oxford University Press.

Canadian Nurses' Association. (2005). *Backgrounder on social determinants of health and nursing.* Ottawa: Author.

Canadian Nurses' Association. (2006). *Toward 2020: Visions for nursing.* Ottawa: Author.

Canadian Nurses' Association. (2007). *Telehealth: The role of the nurse* [Position Statement]. Ottawa: Author.

Carper, B. (1978). Fundamental patterns of knowing in nursing. *Advances in Nursing Science, 1*(1), 13–23.

Carter, B. (2007). Reformatting nursing: The invidious effects of the growth of managerialism. *Health, 11*(20), 268–272.

Clancy, J., McVicar, A., & Bird, D. (2000). Getting it right? An exploration of issues relating to the biological sciences in nurse education and nursing practice. *Journal of Advanced Nursing, 32*(6), 1522–1532.

Coburn, D. (1988). The development of Canadian nursing: Professionalization and proletarianization. *International Journal of Health Services, 18*, 437–456.

Cooke, H. (1993a). Why teach sociology? *Nurse Education Today, 13*, 210–216.

Cooke, H. (1993b). Boundary work in the nursing curriculum: The case of sociology. *Journal of Advanced Nursing, 18*, 1990–1998.

Daiski, I. (2004). Restructuring: A view from the bedside. Canadian Journal of Nursing Leadership, October, online exclusive. http://www.longwoods.com/product.php?productid=17025 &cat=252. Accessed 3 Nov 2006.

Donaldson, S. K. & Crowley, D. M. (2004). The discipline of nursing. In P. G. Reed, N. C. Shearer, & L. H. Nicoll (Eds.), *Perspectives on nursing theory* (pp. 293–304). Philadelphia: Lippincott, Williams and Wilkins.

Dyer, J. A. (2003). Multidisciplinary, interdisciplinary, and transdisciplinary: Educational models and nursing education. *Nursing Education Perspectives, 24*(4), 186–188.

Edgley, A., Timmons, S., & Crosbie, B. (2009). Desperately seeking sociology: Nursing student perceptions of sociology on nursing courses. *Nurse Education Today, 29,* 16–23.

England, P., & Folbre, N. (1999). The cost of caring. *Annals of the American Academy of Political and Social Science, 561,* 39–51.

Fauchald, S. K., & Smith, D. (2005). Transdisciplinary research partnerships: Making research happen! *Nursing Economics, 23*(3), 131–135.

Fawcett, J., & Swoyer, B. (2008). Evolution and use of nursing knowledge. In R. Kearney-Nunnery (Ed.), *Advancing your career: Concepts of professional nursing* (pp. 50–81). Philadelphia: F.A. Davis Company.

Freshwater, D., Cahill, J., & Essen, C. (2013). Discourses of collaborative failure: Identity, role, and discourse in an interdisciplinary world. *Nursing Inquiry, 21*(1), 59–68.

Fry, G. L. A. 2001. Multifunctional landscapes—towards transdisciplinary research. *Landscape and Urban Planning, 57,* 159–168.

Genosko, G. (2003). Felix Guattari: Towards a transdisciplinary metamethodology. *Angelaki: Journal of the Theoretical Humanities, 8*(1), 129–140.

Giri, A. K. (2002). The calling of a creative transdisciplinarity. *Futures, 34,* 103–115.

Global Knowledge Exchange Network. (2009). *An overview of education and training requirements for global healthcare professionals.* http://www.gken.org/Docs/Workforce/Nursing%20Educ%20Reqs_FINAL%20102609.pdf. Accessed 29 March 2014.

Goodrick, E., & Reay, T. (2010). Florence Nightingale endures: Legitimizing a new professional role identity. *Journal of Management Studies, 47*(1), 55–84.

Grey, M., & Connolly, C. A. (2008). "Coming together, keeping together, working together": Interdisciplinary to transdisciplinary research and nursing. *Nursing Outlook, 56,* 102–107.

Hadorn, G. H., Hoffman-Riem, H., Biber-Klemm, S., Grossenbacher-Mansury, W., Joye, D., Pohl, C., Wiesmann, U., & Zemp, E. (Eds.). (2008). *Handbook of transdisciplinary research.* Dordrecht: Springer.

Hagoel, L., & Kalekin-Fishman, D. (2002). Crossing borders: Toward a trans-disciplinary scientific identity. *Studies in Higher Education, 27*(3), 297–308.

Holland, K. (2004). Editorial. Sociology and the nursing curriculum. *Nursing Education in Practice, 4,* 81–82.

Horlick-Jones, T., & Sime, J. (2004). Living on the border: Knowledge, risk and transdisciplinarity. *Futures, 36,* 441–456.

Ingersoll, G. L., Fisher, M., Ross, B., Soja, M., & Kidd, N. (2001). Employee response to major organizational redesign. *Applied Nursing Research, 14*(1), 18–28.

Johnson, M. (1990). Natural sociology and moral questions in nursing: Can there be a relationship? *Journal of Advanced Nursing, 15,* 1358–1362.

Jordan, S. (1994). Should nurses be studying bioscience? A discussion paper. *Nurse Education Today, 14,* 417–426.

Jordan, S., Davies, S., & Green, B. (1999). The biosciences in the pre-registration nursing curriculum: Staff and students' perception of difficulties and relevance. *Nurse Education Today, 19,* 215–226.

Larsen, J., & Baumgart, A. J. (1992). Issues in nursing education. In A. J. Baumgart & J. Larsen (Eds.), *Canadian nursing faces the future* (pp. 383–399). St. Louis: Mosby.

Laschinger, H. K. S., Sabiston, J. A., Finegan, J., & Shamian, J. (2001). Voices from the trenches: Nurses' experiences of hospital restructuring in Ontario. *Canadian Journal of Nursing Leadership, 14*(1), 6–13.

Lopez, J. (2004). How sociology can save bioethics...maybe. *Sociology of Health & Illness, 26*(7), 875–896.

Maben, J., & Griffiths, P. (2008). *Nursing in society: Starting the debate*. London: King's College, National Nursing Research Unit.

Maloney, R. (1992). Technological issues. In A. J. Baumgart & J. Larsen (Eds.), *Canadian nursing faces the future* (pp. 293–305). St. Louis: Mosby.

McMurtry, A. (2006). Professional knowledge, complexity and interdisciplinary teams. *Crossing Boundaries: An Interdisciplinary Journal, 1*(2), 35–51.

Mikkonen, J., & Raphael, D. (2010). *Social Determinants of Health: The Canadian Facts*. Toronto: York University School of Health Policy and Management.

Mitchell, P. H. (2005). What's in a name? Multidisciplinary, interdisciplinary, and transdisciplinary. *Journal of Professional Nursing, 21*(6), 332–334.

Mowforth, G., Harrison, J., & Morris, M. (2005). An investigation into adult nursing students' experience of the relevance and application of behavioural sciences (biology, psychology and sociology) across two different curricula. *Nurse Education Today, 25*, 41–48.

Nelson, M. (2002). Education for professional nursing practice: Looking backward into the future. *Online Journal of Issues in Nursing, 7*(3), Manuscript 3.

Nelson, S., & Gordon, S. (2006). Introduction. In S. Nelson & S. Gordon (Eds.), *The complexities of care: Nursing reconsidered* (pp. 1–12). Ithaca: ILR Press.

Nelson, S., & Gordon, S. (2009). The core of nursing: Knowledge and skill. *Nursing Inquiry, 16*(1), 1–2.

Newman, M. A., Sime, A. M., & Corcoran-Perry, S. A. (2004). The focus of the discipline of nursing. In P. G. Reed, N. C. Shearer, & L. H. Nicoll (Eds.), *Perspectives on nursing theory* (pp. 315–320). Philadelphia: Lippincott, Williams and Wilkins.

Pauly, B. (2013). Challenging health inequities: Enacting social justice in nursing practice. In J. L. Storch, P. Rodney, & R. Starzomski (Eds.), *Toward a moral horizon: Nursing ethics for leadership and practice* (pp. 430–447). Toronto: Pearson.

Pinikahana, J. (2003). Role of sociology within the nursing enterprise: Some reflections on the unfinished debate. *Nursing and Health Sciences, 5*, 175–180.

Porter, S. (1998). *Social theory and nursing practice*. New York: Palgrave Macmillan Press.

Rankin, J., & Campbell, M.L. (2006). *Managing to nurse: Inside Canada's healthcare reform*. Toronto: University of Toronto Press.

Ray, M. D. (1998). Shared borders: Achieving the goals of interdisciplinary patient care. *American Journal of Health System Pharmacy, 55*, 1369–1374.

Rosenfield, P. (1992). The potential of transdisciplinary research for sustaining and extending linkages between the health and social sciences. *Social Science and Medicine, 35*(11), 1343–1357.

Royal College of Nursing. (2007). Defining nursing. http://www.rcn.org.uk/__data/assets/pdf_file/0008/78569/001998.pdf. Accessed 29 March 2014.

Rudge, T. (2011). The 'well-run' system and its antimonies. *Nursing Philosophy, 12*, 167–176.

Ruger, J. P. (2004). Health and social justice. *The Lancet, 364*, 1075–1080.

Rutty, J. E. (1998). The nature of philosophy of science, theory and knowledge relating to nursing and professionalism. *Journal of Advanced Nursing, 28*(2), 243–250.

Scott, P. A., Matthews, A., & Kirwan, M. (2013). What is nursing in the 21st century and what does the 21st century health system require of nursing? *Nursing Philosophy, 15*, 23–24.

Shannon, V., & French, S. (2005). The impact of the reengineered world of health-care in Canada on nursing and patient outcomes. *Nursing Inquiry, 12*(3), 231–239.

Sharp, K. (1994). Sociology and the nursing curriculum: A note of caution. *Journal of Advanced Nursing, 20*, 391–395.

Sharp, K. (1995). Why indeed should we teach sociology? A response to Hannah Cooke. *Nurse Education Today, 15*, 52–55.

Sharp, K. (1996). Sociology and the nursing curriculum: A reply to Sam Porter. *Journal of Advanced Nursing, 23*, 1275–1278.

Stevenson, C. (2005). Practical inquiry/theory in nursing. *Journal of Advanced Nursing, 50*(2), 196–203.

Storch, J. L. (2010). Canadian healthcare system. In M. McIntyre & C. McDonald (Eds.), *Realities of Canadian nursing* (pp. 34–55). Philadelphia: Lippincott, Williams & Wilkins.

Sullivan, E. J. (2002). Nursing and feminism: An uneasy alliance. *Journal of Professional Nursing, 18*(4), 183–184.

Thirsk, L., & Clark, A. M. (2014). Editorial. What is the 'self' in chronic disease self-management? *International Journal of Nursing Studies, 51*, 691–693. http://dx.doi.org/10.1016/j.ijnurstu. 2013.10.008. Accessed 26 Sept 2014.

Timmins, F. (2011). Remembering the art of nursing in a technological age. *Nursing in Critical Care, 16*(4), 161–163.

Trnobranski, P. (1997). Power and vested interests—tacit influences on the construction of nursing curricula? *Journal of Advanced Nursing, 25*, 1084–1088.

Villeneuve, M. J. (2010). Looking back, moving forward: Taking nursing toward 2020. In M. McIntyre & C. McDonald (Eds.), *Realities of Canadian nursing* (pp. 470–481). Philadelphia: Lippincott, Williams & Wilkins.

Wall, S. (2007). Nurses' engagement with feminist/poststructuralist theory: (Im)possibility, fear, and hope. *thirdspace: a journal of feminist theory & culture, 7*(1), Essay 1.

Williamson, G. R. (1999). Teaching sociology to nurses: Exploring the debate. *Journal of Clinical Nursing, 8*, 269–274.

Wynne, R. (2003). Clinical nurses' response to an environment of healthcare reform and organizational restructuring. *Journal of Nursing Management, 11*, 98–106.

Yeo, M. (2004). Integration of nursing theory and nursing ethics. In P. G. Reed, N. C. Shearer, & L. H. Nicoll (Eds.), *Perspectives on nursing theory* (pp. 355–364). Philadelphia: Lippincott, Williams and Wilkins.

Interprofessional Education and Collaborative Practice in Health and Social Care: The Need for Transdisciplinary Mindsets, Instruments and Mechanisms

Andre Vyt

Introduction

The human mind provides us with an enormous potential of creativity, but humans are prone to several limitations. One of these is the blindness for own conditions, in organizational psychology also known as organizational blindness. Because we easily adapt to the context we live in, and because our perception is rapidly habituating to recurring contextual elements, we become blind for aspects that are otherwise (by external persons) seen as inappropriate or dysfunctional, and we neglect opportunities for improvement. Another limitation is the proneness to categorize objects, notions and phenomena into distinct classes. Although we know that reality is vastly complex and that nature upholds an infinite continuity, scientists as well as laymen are focused on analyzing elements by putting them into categories.

In such contexts, the described limitations of the human mind work together: stereotyping other professions strengthens the image of the own profession and allows traditional professional identities to endure. We tend to categorize instead of seeing flexible connections. And because we are all busy people and because most politicians focus on day-to-day business instead of on broad and long-term thinking, things remain as they have been for years, even if the profiling of professions is lacking flexibility and cost-effectiveness. Regarding the latter, it is noteworthy, for example, that psychologists become certified in 4 years of study in one country, while in another country for reasons of professional status they need 6 years of study, equaling the duration of a medical education. When it comes to higher education, upholding a pragmatic stance of added value and cost-effectiveness of study programmes would need to involve more flexibility and adaptation of higher education and of institutions to evolutions and needs of modern society. But, in line with the law of Parkinson

A. Vyt (✉)
Artevelde University College and the Faculty of Medicine
and Health Sciences of the University of Ghent, Ghent, Belgium
e-mail: Andre.Vyt@UGent.be

© Springer International Publishing Switzerland 2015
P. Gibbs (ed.), *Transdisciplinary Professional Learning and Practice*,
DOI 10.1007/978-3-319-11590-0_6

(1955) on multiplication of work and bureaucracy, existing mechanisms tend to endure and create conditions to reinforce and legalize their existence.

The Essence of Interprofessional Education (IPE)

Terminology used to denote learning in which different professions are engaged can be confusing. Terms used include 'common learning', 'shared learning', 'multiprofessional learning', 'transdisciplinary education' and 'interprofessional learning'. In the UK, CAIPE defined IPE as "Occasions when two or more professions learn from and about each other to improve collaboration and the quality of care" accentuating that this learning should be interactive, and thus "with, from and about each other" in order to improve collaborative practice. It was stated as clearly different from any other kind of multiprofessional education in which two or more professions or programmes study side by side for whatever reason but which does not necessarily include planned collaboration. This definition is in line with the distinction between multidisciplinary care organized on the basis of parallel but independent contributions based on specific expertise, and interdisciplinary working where close communication and complementary and mutually supportive contributions allow holistic management of the patient's needs (Hall and Weaver 2001). It has been proposed to draw together the notion of interdisciplinarity and transdisciplinarity, indicating that in interprofessional collaboration it may occur that roles and functions overlap in order to provide the best possible care (Gordon and Ward 2005).

IPE has two main elements that can be used to define its core: the nature of the activities (the process) and the expected outcomes of these activities. It is important to distinguish several factors that influence the process, and that can be labelled as presage factors (Freeth and Reeves 2004). These can determine the effectiveness of IPE, but are not essential to define it. Concerning outcomes, one could state that any kind of expected outcome that fosters the quality of interprofessional collaboration would be sufficient to label an educational activity as IPE when these activities take the form of learning with, from and about each other. IP courses can be oriented directly towards improving collaborative practice, or can aim at intermediate goals which in the long term can enhance the quality of collaborative practice. This is the case, for example, for courses that are embedded early in the curriculum, aiming at influencing perceptions and attitudes of participants, or teaching certain skills without integration into a collaborative competence or an immediate implementation in practice. These courses can serve as a basis for IP courses later in the programme, in which learning outcomes are competence-based. Still, from a quality assurance viewpoint one can argue whether those ground-laying courses should be labelled IPE without considering the (quality of the) courses later in the curriculum that build upon these.

As IPE initiatives become more widespread, and as findings of factors determining the effectiveness of IPE become substantial, expectations regarding the essentials for a course to be labelled IPE can be based on more explicit criteria. From the viewpoint of promoting and safeguarding the quality of IPE, a viable suggestion would be to formulate a minimum threshold of learning outcome characteristics. At the end of an IP course, for example, students should be able to demonstrate their collaborative competence. This does not necessarily have to imply that students have to learn or be assessed in clinical practice but that the learning goals are at least at the behavioural level of a demonstrable integration of knowledge, skills and attitudes. In this respect, the competence-based character is included as an essential element for IPE. When a course does not meet this level of formulated outcomes, it can merely be labelled as a preparatory course for IPE. It leaves the option open to structurally embed such preparatory courses in a trajectory ending with a competence-based course, and in this context the trajectory or courses as a whole can be labelled IPE as it results finally in the acquisition of IP competences. IP competences can be manifold. Different projects have proposed sets of IP competences. In the future a consensus may grow on the competences that can be seen as minimal requirements for IP courses in health and social care. The introduction of a competence-based formulation of learning outcomes as a necessary requirement for IPE would be a good first step in that direction.

In this respect, the classification of interprofessional learning outcomes as originally developed by Kirkpatrick (1967) and modified by Barr et al. (2005, see also Hammick et al. 2007) can be useful as a common taxonomy (see Table 1). Level 3, the level of behavioural change, is a crucial one. Here, as in level 2 and 4, one could make a distinction between on the one hand the integration of skills, knowledge and attitudes that can be demonstrated and assessed in simulated situations, and on the other hand the transfer of this integrated behaviour in the professional practice (visible in the spontaneous behaviour at work or during clinical placements). The distinction is largely based on the ability to assess the degree of spontaneous application of the competence in an authentic situation. The assessment is a stronger determining factor here than the learning activity. If, for example, the student has the opportunity to participate in IP activities in clinical placements and can build upon these activities to learn but the competence is assessed in case simulations during practicals or placements, the course is not set at behavioural level 3b. Although learning and coaching activities may allow students to reach that level, in terms of quality assurance the level cannot be set as the standard as long as the behavioural change is not assessed appropriately.

Examinations are the quality check in terms of effective outcomes of the teaching and learning activities and of their goals. Goals may be set at a certain level, and activities may foster the attainment of these goals, but if assessment is not aimed at checking the goals at the right level, the course should not be qualified at this level. A chain is as strong as its weakest element.

Identifying learning activities as being IPE could also be restricted to formal activities and courses as opposed to informal or occasional learning during a course. This does not imply that informal or occasional learning about interprofessional collaboration is to be avoided. But as they are not systematically structured, it is also hard to construct quality assurance mechanisms for them. This stance would restrict

Table 1 Modified version of Kirkpatrick's (1967) outcomes model, as modified by Barr et al. (2005, see also Hammick et al. 2007). Additionally the level of behavioural change could be divided in a level comprising the acquisition of a competence in simulated conditions (3a) and in real practice (3b)

1.	Reaction	Learners' views on the learning experience and its interprofessional nature
2a.	Modification of perceptions and attitudes	Changes in reciprocal attitudes or perceptions between participant groups; changes in perception or attitudes towards the value and/or use of team approaches to caring for a specific client group
2b.	Acquisition of knowledge and skills	Including knowledge and skills linked to interprofessional collaboration
3.	Behavioural change	Identifies individuals' transfer of interprofessional learning to their practice setting and their changed professional practice
4a.	Change in organisational practice	Wider changes in the organization and delivery of care
4b.	Benefits to patients/clients	Improvements in health or wellbeing of patients/clients

the spectrum of IPE drastically. On the other hand, it might stimulate institutions to upgrade existing informal IP learning into formal learning in the curriculum while still valorising the acquisition of competences outside the formal learning. It is perfectly possible and may even be more effective to recognize and validate outcomes of informal learning once formally structured learning paths have been established. The presence of a formal IP learning path in a department entails that the learning goals are well defined, that assessment methods are well structured, and that the necessary competence for (and experience in) assessment is available in the institution. These elements facilitate the recognition and validation of competences acquired by informal learning. In short, in departments where the formal IPE is present and well-structured, the informal acquisition of competences may be better recognized.

Finally, it would be possible to limit IPE qualifications to courses or programmes on the basis of the specific learning goals. Here, the question is not whether the goals are assured to be on the appropriate level—preferably the behavioural level—but whether they include a minimum set of learning goals that are viewed to be essential for interprofessional collaboration. If, for example, the learning goals of a course are only aimed at the ability to assess which health care professions can or should be involved for a specific pathology, or to which health care worker a patient should be referred to, this invokes an important competence at the appropriate behavioural level. It is, however, not aimed at working closely together with other professionals to assess, plan and provide care. In view of the importance of collaborative practice, IP networks may see it as a task to stimulate the incorporation of this element as a direct learning outcome to be achieved in every IPE course. It entails a challenge for many existing IP courses, as the assessment of this achievement is more difficult to organize.

Expectations or minimal requirements regarding outcomes for a course to be qualified as IPE will automatically entail expectations regarding assessment and working methods in teaching and learning. It is hardly conceivable, for example, that a course aimed at developing the ability to construct a patient-centred shared care plan would be highly effective without adopting a case-based approach in teaching and learning. Also collaborative, problem-based or enquiry-based learning can be seen as important elements, in which students develop new knowledge on the basis of experience and discussion.

The Role of the Government for Collaboration Between Institutions

In some European countries, for example UK, governments have taken initiatives in the past 20 years to strengthen interprofessional collaboration. After 10 years of existence of CAIPE, at the end of the last century, its efforts were backed by the renewed UK government policy: it laid emphasis on collaboration as much between organizations as between practicing health care professionals. IPE would be developed in partnership between employers and Higher Education Institutions (HEIs), and integrated in undergraduate programmes instead of after qualification. A shift of emphasis from institutional to community-based services, and calls for a more flexible and more responsive workforce, may have resulted first in role ambiguity and tensions between professions, but were followed by IPE initiatives leading to sustained developments embedded into an increasingly favourable climate.

The workforce strategy spelt out by the UK Department of Health (2000), following the governmental plan of the National Health System, called for education and training to promote teamwork, partnership and collaboration between professions, between agencies and with patients employing a holistic approach. Following extensive consultation with stakeholders, the Quality Assurance Agency developed a set of benchmark statements describing standards of health care study programmes, of which several statements explicitly refer to interprofessional collaboration (QAA 2001, 2002, 2006, see Table 2). The following years were characterized by several projects across the country in which universities collaborated in developing interprofessional learning.

Health care institutions, councils and regulatory and professional bodies progressively have adopted interprofessional collaboration as a core element in systems of auditing or accreditation, although coordination between these bodies is patchy. The Chartered Society of Physiotherapy, for example, has included IPE in their Curriculum framework for qualifying programmes in physiotherapy. Undoubtedly, societies and networks such as the Centre for the Advancement of Interprofessional Education (CAIPE) have given an impetus to IPE in the UK. The Department of Health (England) funded four large scale projects 'common learning sites' in IPE in Higher Education in 2002 and a three year project 2004–7 Creating an Interprofessional Workforce (CIPW 2007). Within UK Higher Education, there has also been funding

Table 2 Benchmarking statements of the UK Quality Assurance Agency with IP implications (QAA 2001; see also appendix in Barr 2002)

Statements for health care referring to collaboration between professions in health care say that each award holder should:

Participate effectively in interprofessional and multi-agency approaches to health and social care where appropriate

Recognize professional scope of practice and make referrals where appropriate

Work, where appropriate, with other health and social care professionals and support staff and patients/clients/carers to maximize healthy outcomes

Draw upon appropriate knowledge and skills in order to make professional judgements, recognizing the limits of his/her practice

Communicate effectively with patients/clients/carers and other relevant parties when providing care

Assist other health care professionals in maximizing health outcomes

Recognize the place and contribution of his/her assessment within the total health care profile/package, through effective communication with other members of the health and social care team

Work with the client/patient (and his/her relatives/carers), group/community/population, to consider the range of activities that are appropriate/feasible/acceptable, including the possibility of referral to other members of the health and social care team and agencies

Plan care within the context of holistic health management and the contribution of others

Have effective skills in communicating information, advice, instruction and professional opinion to colleagues, patients, clients, their relatives and carers; and, where necessary, to groups of colleagues or clients

to promote good practice in IPE through the subject centres of the Higher Education Academy.

The synergy between legislative initiatives, governmental policy and societal context, and collaboration between research and educational institutions provide the most fertile soil for the instalment and advancement of interprofessional practice. Education has to follow important societal trends and needs, and vice versa. Despite signs of synergy there remain resistance and constraints. Monoprofessional education remains the norm, even where IPE has had most support. But the arguments and evidence grow in strength.

In the UK the necessity to implement IPE in higher education is since some years largely driven by governmental policy and more specifically by the Department of Health. Four national leading edge pilot sites for IPE were approved (see Barr 2007, for an overview). Throughout the country, it has resulted in different courses and programmes. One of them is the Combined Universities Interprofessional Learning Unit (CUILU), as a joint initiative between Sheffield Hallam University and the University of Sheffield.

In a survey of interprofessional education in clinical settings in South-East England (Stew 2005) it was found that IPE develops according to a variety of situational factors. Three broad models were identified: student-led sessions (with presentations of patient case studies), clinician-led sessions (with a specialist presenting a topic followed by discussion) and tutor-led sessions aimed at interprofessional debate. IPE was found to be a commonly occurring phenomenon, but the authentic IPE according to the effectiveness criteria (Barr et al. 2005) seems to be absent in many settings. The challenge largely remains to establish an effective blended model of IPE and at the same time setting up mechanisms to assure the quality. One nice example is the Leicester Model of Interprofessional Education (Lennox and Anderson 2007).

Building upon the recommendations of the WHO-report Call upon action (2010) the European Interprofessional Practice & Education Network (EIPEN) has drawn up a Charter for IPE in Europe. Institutions endorse this charter when becoming member of the network. By signing the charter, they subscribe to its recommendations, asking political leaders, decision-makers and institutional managers in health care, professional bodies, governmental agencies, health insurance organizations, patient organizations, and educational institutions, to promote and ensure effective collaborative interprofessional practice in health and social care, following the recommendations of the new framework for interprofessional education and collaborative practice, published under the auspices of the World Health Organization. By the knowledge that interprofessional education can only be fruitful if the necessary changes are implemented in practice, the charter (see www.eipen.eu) asks that

- Professional bodies of health and social care professions explicitly formulate the necessity of competences in interprofessional collaboration being present in graduating students in health and social care professions.
- Educational and clinical institutions formulate interprofessional collaborative work as one of the main values in their mission and in their quality management policy, and support and adhere to bodies and networks that promote and/or supervise interprofessional health and social care.
- Educational institutions comply with this need by ensuring that graduates are competent in interprofessional health and social care and by ensuring that professional body representatives ratify the competence chart of their educational programmes based on the presence of interprofessional competences.
- Clinical institutions comply with this need by ensuring that staff is competent in interprofessional health and social care, by providing continuous training in this, and by allowing patient representatives and/or representatives from patient organizations to take part in the institutional policy.
- Governmental agencies focus on the compliance of clinical and educational institutions with regulations promoting and necessitating interprofessional practice and education, and support the institutions by implementing accreditation and financial mechanisms that foster this practice and education.
- Health insurance bodies, patient organizations, and supportive networks explicitly formulate the need for IPE towards the clinical and educational institutions, as well as towards the governmental agencies.

The Role of the Higher Education Landscape

The European Qualification Framework (EQF) has been developed to provide transparency in levels of education across European countries. If we focus on the EQF levels for which discussions could arise with regard to current practice of IPE, then it would imply a range between level 4 to 7 (level 4 not linked to a cycle in higher education, level 5 for short cycle higher education, level 6 for first cycle or bachelor learning outcomes, and level 7 for second cycle or master). Efforts have to be made to define as specifically as possible potential levels of IP competences or learning outcomes, and allocate these to the appropriate cycle. Students of bachelor and master programmes, and even of vocational training programmes, can share the same IP teaching and learning experiences, and still be oriented towards slightly different levels of IP competences.

In the context of IPE, some things are striking in the EQF. For example, cognitive and practical skills are mentioned explicitly, and practical skills are defined as involving manual dexterity and the use of methods, materials, tools and instruments, while social skills—essential for interprofessional practice—are not mentioned. Also, for level 5, skills are supposed to be used for the development of creative solutions to abstract problems. Problems associated with interprofessional practice usually are not abstract, but can be very complex.

It is clear that it is difficult to write down the dynamics of learning outcomes in a framework which is restricted to one-line characteristics. The use of the EQF will need, therefore, a flexibility and open-mindedness on the part of the user, instead of criticising the incompleteness. As regards IPE, we can put forward that "managing activities in contexts of unpredictable change, and review performance of work" is essential for effective collaborative practice. If we replace the ability to solve "abstract" problems by "problems with a certain degree of complexity", then one could argue to situate a typical IP competence level of a health care worker between level 5 (short cycle) and 6 (first cycle), but arguments can be formulated also to place it between level 6 (first cycle) and 7 (second cycle). It all depends on the specific formulation and the interpretation of the levels in the concrete context.

One could argue that the present EQF is primarily defined from a disciplinary scope, in which interdisciplinary issues are linked to innovation and research. In this way, it is by definition difficult to clearly identify a specific place for interprofessional education as related to clinical practice within this framework. For example, a health care worker surely needs problem-solving skills in order to develop new knowledge and procedures and to integrate knowledge from different fields, but he/she does not primarily use these skills for research and/or innovation. Likewise, a health care worker who is responsible for a team should be able to manage and transform work contexts that are complex, unpredictable and require new strategic approaches, and to take responsibility for contributing to professional knowledge and practice and/or for reviewing the strategic performance of teams. But in essence, these abilities should be present also in some form in health care workers who work in team without being the team leader. This is certainly the case in IP teams where a collaboration exists in the form of case management, in which a health care worker as a team member can assume responsibility for the care planning of a patient, and thus collaborate with others to coordinate care planning activities, while a team leader can focus on general objectives and on the management of the team meetings as such. To put it as a paradox: in some way, in some contexts, the competences with regard to this aspect may be present to a larger extent in team members as case managers than in team managers.

The issue of lifelong learning is of great importance to interprofessional education. If we conceptualize interprofessional learning as involving all kinds of health care professionals, we have to be careful not to limit IPE to the universities and HEIs. Just as students in master and bachelor programmes can interact together, so could students of vocational training programmes be included in interprofessional learning paths installed by HEIs. IP competences also can be acquired through experience in the work setting. One of the major problems, however, is that effective IP collaboration is not always present, and from lack of adequate role models to learn from, or working methods and tools to experiment with, it may be difficult to gather evidence for acquired competences.

From another perspective, it is not only important to find ways to recognize already acquired competences, but also to provide opportunities for health care workers to enrol in post-qualifying courses at graduate or postgraduate level to further develop their IP competences. In light of what I've written about enhancing flexibility in study programmes, one could state that opening doors to individuals to enrol for specific IP courses within existing study programmes may cause problems in administrative handling of the course, but may provide an enrichment for all students enrolled in the course. In clinical practice, health care workers have to deal with heterogeneity and instability in teams and with age differences and differences in the cultural background and belief systems of team members. They also have to deal with conflicts which may be connected with such differences. In order to approach the reality of clinical practice in the learning of IP competences, opening access to IP courses to a wide variety of students should not be seen as a burden but rather as an opportunity to make a course more reality-prone.

Some trends, for example the academic drift in higher education, may lead to disregarding IPE, and overlooking that a synergy of governmental, societal and educational policy is needed to implement and safeguard IPE in HEIs. This may seem to go against the expressed need for institutional autonomy in quality assurance, but it does not. The synergy relates to a legitimate demand to involve relevant stakeholders in defining professional needs for the society, especially in institutions where the core processes tend to be aligned with existing structures around traditional disciplines. An example is given in the list of specific key competences for nursing as defined by the TUNING project: most competences stress discipline-specific aspects as is natural. When it comes to IP competences, graduate nurses have to demonstrate an ability and willingness to function in a multidisciplinary setting. The challenge is to see that IPE is securely embedded in higher education programmes, and it begins with the establishment of the most appropriate objective. In this respect, an "ability to function in a multiprofessional setting" may be regarded as a limited objective for a health and social care study programme.

The Role of Quality Assurance Mechanisms

In the future, a consensus on IP competences in accordance with the EQF, combined with a consensus on good practices in IPE, could lead to the development of quality assurance mechanisms that are complementary to external QA mechanisms. For example, an institution could apply for the certification of an IP course that is run by different academic departments. This certification could then be taken into account for accrediting a degree programme provided that IP competences are recognised as an essential component in all degree programmes in health and social care. These initiatives would fit within a model that seeks a balance between system- or institution-based accreditation and programme-based accreditation, at the same time trying to make external quality assurance mechanisms more lean and efficient.

The complex nature of IPE will demand that extra attention is paid to elements of sustainable quality management, to assure that an IP course can survive conditions that pose a threat or a risk to it. For this, tools can be developed that can be used for self-assessment and auditing purposes. Difficulties in the organization and logistics of courses as well as competing curricula demands, if not solved promptly with management support, can seriously impair the enthusiasm of teachers. From a dynamic systems perspective interaction involves more than three elements of the 3P-model (Freeth and Reeves 2004). Organizational issues may have a direct influence on the effectiveness, and also interact with learner characteristics. For example, in the case of optional IP courses, it could be assumed that the most motivated students would enrol for that course. Enrolment would also depend, however, on the constraints in time and place, and on the perceptions that students have about requirements and benefits. Age, work experience and professional orientation interact in a complex way in influencing students' views about collaborative care (Pollard et al. 2005).

Apart from establishing mechanisms of quality assurance based on the principles of total quality management in a dynamic systems perspective, mechanisms could pay special attention to aspects which have proven to be influential in the effectiveness of IP courses and the examples of good practice related to this. Evaluation studies in the 1990s reported mainly on positive outcomes in student perceptions of other professions, such as the elimination of negative stereotyping (e.g., Parsell and Bligh 1998) or potential effects on students' skills (e.g., Van der Horst et al. 1995). Reviews at the turn of the century argued for more studies of the impact of IPE on interprofessional practice and health outcomes (Zwarenstein et al. 2002) and for methodologically sound evidence to show cause and effect links between IPE and impact on patient care (Freeth et al. 2002).

A growing body of evidence, generated from systematic review work (e.g., Barr et al. 2005) has indicated that IPE can help foster a range of attributes required for effective collaboration. Over the past 10 years evidence has been generated regarding facilitating and pivotal factors as identified in the 3P-model (e.g., Hammick et al. 2007). Published studies and shared knowledge through networks have led to the establishment of generally accepted principles for IPE. Learning is very successful when it is active, interactive, case-based (e.g., Lindquist et al. 2005) and patient centred, placing service users at the centre of learning. Practice-based learning is seen as essential and can take many forms such as observational study and experience on training wards. Practice-based learning offers greater opportunity for experiential learning, suggesting that IPE within practice enables students to develop shared responsibility more effectively (Morison et al. 2003). Teaching methods based on adult learning (Brookfield 1986; Knowles 1984) and experiential learning (Kolb 1984), facilitating students' reflections and exploiting their expectations and their practice, a comfortable learning environment, and viewing mistakes as opportunities to improve promote interprofessional learning. Any differences within an IP student team with regard to their confidence in their professional role or with regard to the mastery of IP competences is to be seen as an opportunity to learn, for example through peer observation. Learning should be very much self-directed, in which the perceived learning needs and learning preferences are in harmony with the desired learning outcomes (Barr et al. 2005).

A persistently debated issue concerns the timing of IPE in study programmes. This is linked to differing views as to whether IPE should be planned before or after uniprofessional identity has been established. On entering higher education students become professionally socialized, and in parallel with this, stereotyping of other professions may take place. Students may develop a more positive image of the role of their own profession in comparison with that of other professions. This can contribute to creating cognitive and social boundaries between professions. Good facilitation of contact between professions can reduce stereotyped perceptions, encourage more positive attitudes between professions and foster a positive attitude to enhance collaborative team working (Barnes et al. 2000).

Besides specific educational methods, elements and tools can be used that enhance the effectiveness of both IP collaborative practice and IP education. Quality assurance of IP programmes thus can depend on the elements used in that programme to reach the learning outcomes. Learning outcomes of students have to include elements of practice that have proven to enhance the quality of this practice. If a method or a tool supports the efficiency of decision-making in IP teams, then this tool—or a similar one—should be used both in practice and in training for practice. A useful tool for enhancing collaboration in care planning is a shared care planning matrix (Vyt 2008; Vyt et al. 2014). Health care workers define shared care goals, identify who is involved for each goal, and define who is responsible for each goal.

Knowledge and the explicit use of conceptual frameworks and theories is an element of good practice. Effective team-based decision-making, for example, may require appreciation of underpinning theories. A shared conceptual framework of illness may enhance dynamic interaction between participants. If a theory of illness as single-cause or sum of causes, is in use then the decision-making process is likely to involve an inventory of these causes. A more complex multiple cause theory of illness would lead to analysis of the complex interplay between factors to determine a good way of intervention. A widely known conceptual model is the ICF framework, put forward by the World Health Organization. In this biopsychosocial model health and functioning is perceived as complex and multidimensional, and a language has been developed that enables communication about health across professional boundaries. The ICF framework is especially suited to establishing a foundation for professionals in interprofessional health care (Allan et al. 2006).

Elements and Tools for Effective Interprofessional Teamwork

To achieve effective interprofessional collaboration, health care workers not only need specific interprofessional competences but also tools and working methods. Efficient communication and information management is a major issue in this. Although modern information technology can bring us great steps forward, it cannot guarantee an efficient collaboration and an open communication. Regular personal contact between team members and team management are essential components to achieve this.

Some characteristics of well-functioning teams can be depicted (McPherson et al. 2001; Mickan and Rodger 2005). A team needs effective leadership stimulating openness and self-reflection. A team should consist of members who take up complementary roles. They should have knowledge of, and respect for, the competences and contributions of other professionals in the team, abandoning stereotyped perceptions. Effective teams can be characterized also by their search for common goals, which everybody can agree upon. They have common frameworks and tools stimulating the sharing of knowledge. Skills in communication and conflict management have to be present in every team member.

Interdisciplinary meetings foster collaboration between different disciplines. Creating opportunities for formal and informal dialogue between health care providers are important in improving interdisciplinary collaboration at least if a safe atmosphere is created for this. A safe atmosphere will for instance stimulate an open and honest communication about difficult ethical issues, hereby allowing health care providers to express their emotions and moral concerns (Ten Have et al. 2013).

When these elements are present, teamwork is well underpinned. The quality of team meetings, being a very important aspect of teamwork, can be enhanced by elements such as the preparation of documents, the presence of key persons, the availability of information, and the management of the meeting process. The team coach should structure the meeting in such a way that enough time is devoted to a shared problem definition, with exploration and analysis, before constructing an intervention strategy. Finally, a meeting should end in a clear follow-up of goals and tasks.

Instruments have been developed to measure behavioural characteristics of groups and individuals in the context of interprofessional collaboration. These instruments can be used for research purposes, and also for monitoring progress during an IP course or for pre/post measurements. An international collection of tools is generated by the US National Centre for Interprofessional Practice and Education (www.nexusipe.org). A recently developed instrument to measure the quality of transdisciplinary team decision making is the Team Decision Making Questionnaire (TDMQ; Batorowicz and Shepherd 2008). TDMQ consists of 19 items grouped into 4 subscales: decision making, team support, learning, and developing quality services. Further validation with larger groups and different clinical fields is still needed.

To measure perceptions with regard to interdisciplinary education two types of questionnaire are in use. The Interdisciplinary Education Perception Scale (IEPS) exists in an original version (Luecht et al. 1990) and in a recently remodelled version (McFadyen et al. 2007). The questionnaire is directed to identifying the perceived characteristics of individuals about their own and other professions. The remodelled version has three subscales: competency and autonomy, the perceived need for cooperation and the perception of actual cooperation. The other questionnaire is the Readiness for Inter-professional learning Scale (RIPLS), in an original version (Parsell and Bligh 1998) and a revised version for use with undergraduate students (McFadyen et al. 2005). In the revised version, 3 of the 4 subscales (teamwork and collaboration, positive professional identity, and roles and responsibilities) show good reliability (McFadyen et al. 2006). In contrast with the IEPS, the RIPLS focuses on the perception and appreciation of collaboration, shared learning and professional roles.

A recent set of questionnaires has been developed in Belgium for use in educational as well as in clinical settings. The Interprofessional Practice and Education Quality Scales (IPEQS Vyt 2014) is to be used with the PROSE Online Diagnostics and Documenting System. A first set includes a team-oriented self-assessment by a validated 60-item questionnaire consisting of three subscales (20 items each) on aspects of interprofessional teamwork. The first subscale covers the conditions for interdisciplinary collaboration. The second covers specific aspects relating to the interdisciplinary work processes, and the third covers the individual interdisciplinary competence and mindset of the health workers. A second set includes a 40-item questionnaire for study and training programmes. Each item is rated on a five-point Likert scale, and optionally respondents can also make comments about the item. The system generates performance indexes based on summations of item scores.

For interprofessional teamwork, we need a collective code of ethics, a shared complementary responsibility, effective team coaching and coordination of care planning, and instruments which scaffold teamwork, such as shared electronic patient files. Effective goal setting and care planning is frequently hindered by a mindset of healthcare workers focused on professional identity and qualifications rather than on common goals for the patient or client system. This mindset also limits the quality of interprofessional collaboration and shared care. To counter this mindset, a planning tool can help, by making a clear differentiation between goals and actions and by clearly identifying shared goals, responsibility, task differentiation and collaboration. Also, therapists and health care workers can follow a stepwise reasoning starting with the personal factors and the context of the patient, identifying strengths and limitations, followed by seeking what we could achieve for and with the patient, and then proposing concrete actions in which different professions can collaborate. This tool which promotes the interprofessional teamwork is the shared care plan (Vyt 2008; Vyt et al. 2014). On a matrix, for each goal the actively contributing health care workers are identified by the team. For each goal, one of the health care workers takes up the responsibility, while one of them can take up the responsibility for coordinating the shared care. The joint use of this matrix is aimed toward better involvement of team members. This method also avoids the pitfall of starting the clinical reasoning on the level of physical functions and then identifying implications on activity and participation level. This pitfall is frequently associated with a linear mode of causal thinking and narrowed vision on physical root factors.

Interprofessional Competences

Interprofessional competences are the core of interprofessional teamwork. They play key roles in several dimensions of health care work, such as corresponding and reporting, consulting, goal setting and intervention planning, care management, referral and follow-up. A framework that systematically analyses components and performance criteria of the competence is necessary for health care education as well as continuing education and training clinical professionals. A clear differentiation between the identification of essential knowledge and skills, and the definition of criteria to assess the behavioural performance of health care workers is crucial.

The umbrella competence of interprofessional collaboration encompasses the communication of ideas from the own disciplinary framework of reference towards other disciplines, the use of expertise of other disciplines and health care workers, and active and effective involvement in teams. It includes the harmonisation of own ideas and activities with those of other health care workers, and the ability to cooperate in the planning, follow-up, and evaluation of the interdisciplinary care. The interdisciplinary focus of a health care worker becomes evident in the way of analyzing situations of health problems, and in drawing up interventions and care provision.

A team member has to be able to plan activities in accordance with those of others and to anticipate problems that may arise for other health care workers. A team member needs a mindset that focuses on the possible role and information of other disciplines, while being careful not to draw conclusions to soon on the basis of partial data. An assessment of this competence is not based on the profoundness of knowledge, but on the way knowledge is used.

Providing students with experiences of interprofessional teamwork is important, but when robust assessment is lacking as a cornerstone, IPE may lead to more negative consequences than positive ones. Failing to assess interprofessional competence could imply that this is less important than other professional competencies, and means that assessment of competence is less robust.

There is a clear distinction between the notion of competences and that of learning outcomes. A multidimensional construct of professional competence has been defined by Epstein and Hundert (2002) as "the habitual and judicious use of communication, knowledge, technical skills, clinical reasoning, emotions, values, and reflection in daily practice for the benefit of the individual and the community being served" (p. 226). One dimension of professional competence involves the ability to integrate multiple aspects of practice. A competence-based assessment approach is opposed to measurement techniques that assess one performance dimension rather than assessing the whole performance of the student.

While competences can generally be conceptualized as integrated clusters of knowledge and insight components, skill components and attitude components, learning outcomes are the conversion of competences into a curriculum whereby components of a competence or a competence as such can be acquired. Learning outcomes can refer to a part of a module, a module, a semester or an academic year.

The conceptualization of competence-based models of interprofessional education began in the mid-1990s. Some focus on competences common to all health care workers. Drawing on a European-wide interprofessional consultation using the Delphi research method, Engel (2001) pointed out the competences to be expected of newly qualified professionals to adapt to and participate in the management of change.

Another way of construing a framework for IP competences, is to analyze the necessary knowledge, skills and attitudes as underlying components, and develop a set of performance criteria in which one or more elements of those components are combined. This is, for example, done in the competence chart of the European Network of Physiotherapy Higher Education (ENPHE, see Ven and Vyt 2007). One competence was explicitly identified as an IP competence. The definition and clarification of the IP competence of collaboration has been formulated as "This competence encompasses the communication of ideas from the own disciplinary perspective (and frameworks of reference) towards other disciplines, making use of expertise of other disciplines and health care workers, and active/effective involvement/participation in task-oriented groups/teams. The central roles are those of health practitioner, but also advisor and colleague. The competence is important for daily collaboration within or between units, in interprofessional consultation by telephone or e-mail, in correspondence in the case of referrals, and in meetings and discussions about and with clients. The interdisciplinary focus of a physiotherapist becomes evident in the way he/she analyzes situations of health problems, interventions and care provision, and also in the way he/she talks with and about other health care workers. The competence includes the alignment of own ideas and activities to those of other health care workers, and the ability to cooperate in the planning, follow-up, and evaluation of the inter-professional care.

The competence is of importance in diverse settings, such as home care and (complex and highly specialized) hospital units. Frequently this work involves stressful and hectic situations which require swift handling, and in which conflicts may arise about the competences required. Competent practice requires attention to process and outcome, with an open attitude and sensitivity towards the perception of others. In meetings, methods for problem analysis, problem solving, and prioritization can be used. Interdisciplinary collaboration is also expressed through active participation in (the formation of) interprofessional networks. A central aspect is also the ability to report and communicate with colleagues and other health care workers in a professional way—orally, in writing and electronically- about the demands of clients, diagnostics data, treatment goals, and data about intervention and prognosis. In situations of consultation, the physiotherapist can take up a leading role."

Because a competence is dynamic and can consist of a combination of many different elements and quality criteria, it is important that a student holds a dynamic view of the competence chart. The listed criteria are also just a limited set of examples. When students are familiar with the aims and constituent parts of a competence they ought to be able to formulate extra relevant assessment criteria. Of course, different components can also be assessed during the education. Each element in the listing can be transformed into evaluation goals.

The precise formulations of components and criteria are important, and make it possible to derive clear objectives. For example, the integration of opinions formulated by other team members, in the process of problem analysis, can be characterized as a cognitive skill which the student can demonstrate when asked. It does not mean that the student does this spontaneously. Therefore orientation towards consulting other health care workers and attending to the ideas of others should be present. And finally the student should have knowledge of working methods and work domains of the different health care professionals in order to choose or contact the appropriate persons for a consultation. This implies that the assessment of those competences in terms of evaluating whether the student shows a spontaneous integration of the knowledge, skills and attitudes, can only be done to its full extent in real-life practice or in case simulations with a high degree of authenticity. In the course, at Artevelde University College and University of Ghent the following 5 key competences were defined:

- Consult and collaborate effectively in IP teams, on the basis of knowledge of competences of health care workers
- Work out patient-centred shared care plans on the basis of information and interaction with other health care workers
- Anticipate, identify, and remediate problems in interprofessional teamwork and shared care planning
- Make appropriate referrals to other health care workers based on the knowledge of competences of health care workers
- Evaluate interprofessional communication, decision making and care planning in terms of efficiency

Also 5 handling dimensions were identified that are applicable to several competences: Consult and collaborate, Involve and stimulate colleagues, Communicate and inform, Learn and reflect, Act and advise. Each of the 5 dimensions were broken down in performance criteria linked to one or more competences. For example, in Consult and collaborate it is essential to formulate intervention goals in such a way that they can be integrated in a shared care plan, to work constructively with others in formulating shared care goals, and to select relevant clinical data in view of shared care planning.

The identification and formulation of IP competences or capabilities has certainly resulted in a major move forward. These frameworks provide an overview of what is essential to achieve and further develop in continuous professional improvement. A teacher, facilitator or assessor can provide very specific feedback on the performance of the student on this basis.

Institutions may still refrain from establishing an IP course based on the argument that IP competences are already integrated in the learning outcomes of different courses in the programme, and that there is no need to run a separate course because of overlap. The embedding of IP competences during the whole curriculum is certainly an asset, providing opportunities for a gradual acquisition of competences and preventing the perception of interprofessional collaboration as an isolated or singular event. On the other hand, it is necessary to have a clear identifiable assessment of these competences, assuring that students have effectively acquired them. A specific course in which students are assessed explicitly on IP competences is a good way to assure this.

Conclusion

Disciplines and professions in health and social care, as in hard sciences, are not absolute but are artificially made by man, and thus bound to cultural and historical context. The science policy of today strengthens a specialisation drift within disciplines. If we put human health in the focus rather than professional identities, then a rethinking of higher education is necessary, in which a dynamic interplay should be possible between disciplines. As long as teenagers are forced to make a choice for a specific profession when enrolling in higher education, and as long as every profession will stick with his own professional code instead of creating a common deontology as a health care worker, it will be hard to overcome the traditional siloing between professions. Following the WHO framework and the European charter of EIPEN, politicians, educational leaders, and clinical institutions need to collaborate on implementing this interprofessional collaboration. A change in mindsets is needed, as well as instruments and mechanisms that underpin the interprofessional and interdisciplinary collaboration, both in science and in clinical interventions. Among these are competence frameworks and tools for assessing and fostering these competences, but also guidelines and standards for clinical paths in which different professions need to collaborate, and tools making this collaboration more effective, such as the shared care planning matrix.

References

Allan, C. M., Campbell, W. N., Guptill, C. A., Stephenson, F. F., & Campbell, K. E. (2006). A conceptual model for interprofessional education: The International Classification of Functioning, Disability and Health (ICF). *Journal of Interprofessional Care, 20,* 235–245.

Barnes, D., Carpenter, J., & Dickinson, C. (2000). Interprofessional education for community mental health teams: attitudes to community care and professional stereotypes. *Social Work Education, 19,* 565–583.

Barr, H. (2002). *Interprofessional education: Today, yesterday and tomorrow.* London: Health Sciences and Practice Network.

Barr, H. (2007). *Piloting interprofessional education: Four English case studies.* London: Higher Education Academy, Health Sciences and Practice Network.

Barr, H., Koppel, I., Reeves, S., Hammick, M., & Freeth, D. (2005). *Effective interprofessional education: Argument, assumption & evidence.* Oxford: Blackwell Publishing.

Batorowicz, B., & Shepherd, T. A. (2008). Measuring the quality of transdisciplinary teams. *Journal of Interprofessional Care, 22,* 612–620.

Brookfield, S. (1986). *Understanding and facilitating adult learning.* San Francisco: Jossey Bass.

CIPW. (2007). *Creating an interprofessional workforce: An education and training framework for health and social care in England.* London: Department of Health & CAIPE.

Engel, C. (2001). *Towards a European approach to the wider education of health professionals in the 21st Century. A European interprofessional consultation.* London: CAIPE.

Epstein, R. M., & Hundert, E. M. (2002). Defining and assessing professional competence. *Journal of the American Medical Association, 287,* 226–235.

Freeth, D., Hammick, M., Koppel, I., Reeves, S., & Barr, H. (2002). *A critical review of evaluations of interprofessional education.* London: Learning and Teaching Support Network for Health Sciences and Practice.

Freeth, D. F., & Reeves, S. (2004). Learning to work together: using the presage, process, product (3P) model to highlight decisions and possibilities. *Journal of Interprofessional Care, 18,* 43–56.

Gordon F., & Ward, K. (2005). Making it real: Interprofessional teaching strategies in practice. *Journal of Integrated Care, 13*(5), 42–47.

Hall, P., & Weaver, L (2001). Interdisciplinary education and teamwork: A long and winding road. *Medical Education, 35,* 867–875.

Hammick, M., Freeth, D., Koppel, I., Reeves, S., & Barr, H. (2007). A best evidence systematic review of interprofessional education. *Medical Teacher, 29,* 735–751.

Kirkpatrick, D. (1967). Evaluation of training. In R. Craig & L. Bittel (Eds.), *Training and development handbook* (pp. 131–167). New York: McGraw-Hill.

Knowles, M. (1984). *Androgogy in action.* London: Jossey Bass.

Kolb, D. A. (1984). *Experiential learning.* Englewood-Cliffs: Prentice-Hall.

Lennox, A., & Anderson, E. (2007). *The Leicester Model of Interprofessional Education. A practical guide for implementation in health and social care.* University of Newcastle: Higher Education Academy Subject Centre for Medicine, Dentistry and Veterinary Medicine.

Lindquist, S., Duncan, A., Shepstone, L., Watts, F., & Pearce, S. (2005). Case-based learning in cross-professional groups—The design, implementation and evaluation of a pre-registration interprofessional learning programme. *Journal of Interprofessional Care, 19,* 509–520.

Luecht, R. M., Madsen, M. K., Taugher, M. P., & Petterson, B. J. (1990). Assessing professional perceptions: Design and validation of an interdisciplinary education perception scale. *Journal of Allied Health, Spring,* 181–191.

McFadyen, A. K., Webster, V., Strachan, K., Figgins, E., Brown, H., & McKechnie, J. (2005). The Readiness for Interprofessional learning Scale: A possible more stable sub-scale model for the original version of RIPLS. *Journal of Interprofessional Care, 19,* 595–603.

McFadyen, A. K., Webster, V. S., & MacLaren, W. M. (2006). The test-retest reliability of a revised version of the Readiness for Interprofessional Learning Scale (RIPLS). *Journal of Interprofessional Care, 20,* 633–639.

McFadyen, A. K., MacLaren, W. M., & Webster, V. S. (2007). The Interdisciplinary Education Perception Scale (IEPS): An alternative remodelled sub-scale structure and its reliability. *Journal of Interprofessional Care, 21,* 433–443.

McPherson K., Headrick, L., & Moss, F. (2001). Working and learning together: Good quality care depends on it, but how can we achieve it? *Quality in Health Care, 10(Suppl II),* 46–53.

Mickan, S. M., & Rodger, S. A. (2005). Effective health care teams: A model of six characteristics developed from shared perceptions. *Journal of Interprofessional Care, 19,* 358–70.

Morison, S., Boohan, M., Jenkins, J., & Moutray, M. (2003). Facilitating undergraduate interprofessional learning in health care: Comparing classroom and clinical learning for nursing and medical students. *Learning in Health and Social Care, 2,* 92–104.

Parkinson, C. N. (1955). Parkinson's law. The Economist, November 9, 1955.

Parsell, G., & Bligh, J. (1998). Interprofessional education. *Postgraduate Medical Journal, 74,* 89–95.

Pollard, K., Miers, M., & Gilchrist, M. (2005). Second year scepticism: Prequalifying health and social care students' midpoint self-assessment, attitudes and perceptions concerning interprofessional learning and working. *Journal of Interprofessional Care, 19,* 251–268.

QAA. (2001). *Nursing: Subject Benchmark Statements.* Gloucester: Quality Assurance Agency for Higher Education.

QAA. (2002). *Medicine: Subject Benchmark Statements.* Gloucester: Quality Assurance Agency for Higher Education.

QAA. (2006). *Statement of common purpose for subject benchmark statements for health and social care professions.* Bristol: Quality Assurance Agency for Higher Education.

Stew, G. (2005). Learning together in practice: A survey of interprofessional education in clinical settings in South-East England. *Journal of Interprofessional Care, 19,* 223–235.

Ten Have, E. C. M., Nap, R. E., & Tulleken, J. E. (2013). Quality of interdisciplinary rounds by leadership training based on essential quality indicators of the Interdisciplinary Rounds Assessment Scale. *Intensive Care Medicine, 39,* 1800–1807.

Van der Horst, M., Turple, I., & Nelson, W. (1995). St. Joseph's Community Centre model of community-based interdisciplinary health care teams' education. *Health and Social Care Community, 3,* 33–42.

Ven, A., & Vyt, A. (2007). *The Competence Chart of the European Network of Physiotherapy in Higher Education.* Antwerp: Garant.

Vyt, A. (2008). Interprofessional and transdisciplinary teamwork in health care. *Diabetes/Metabolism Research and Reviews, 24,* 106–109.

Vyt, A. (2014, in prep). *Interprofessional Practice and Education Quality Scales (IPEQS). A tool for self-assessment using the PROSE Online Diagnostics & Documenting System (PODS 2.0).* Antwerp: Garant.

Vyt, A., Brocatus, N., & Vandaele, B. (2014). A practical framework to enhance collaborative practice: Interprofessional shared care planning through the use of a matrix planning tool and the integrative approach of ICF. Poster presented at the VIIth All Together Better Health Conference, Pittsburgh, 6–8 June 2014.

WHO Study Group on Interprofessional Education and Collaborative Practice. (2010). *Framework for ACTION on interprofessional education and collaborative practice.* Geneva: World Health Organization.

Zwarenstein, M., Reeves, S., Barr, H., Hammick, M., Koppel, I., & Atkins, J. (2002). *Interprofessional education: Effects on professional practice and health care outcomes.* London: The Cochrane Library.

Andre Vyt is associated professor in human behaviour at the Artevelde University College and the Faculty of Medicine and Health Sciences of the University of Ghent, Belgium. He is chairman of the European Interprofessional Practice & Education Network (www.eipen.eu), director of the PROSE Quality Management Network (www.prose.eu) and board member of the World

Coordination Committee on Interprofessional Education and Collaborative Practice "All Together Better Health" (www.atbh.org). During his career Andre Vyt has held positions as researcher, lecturer, board member, student services manager, R&D manager, and quality manager. He is also an expert in teaching & learning in higher education and in e-learning. He has served as an expert in more than 50 visiting audits.

Transdisciplinary Learning in Professional Practice

Raymond Yeung

Introduction

I am a practicing accountant. In addition to accounting qualifications, I have two law degrees. The purpose of this chapter is to share my experience and view of how accounting professionals learn from professionals of other disciplines, in the hope that it would give some insights for educators to design the professional learning programmes for transdisciplinary learners. This chapter is not intended to explore any learning theories or to report an extended research on trans-disciplinary learning. I shall focus on sharing my view on how professionals in different disciplines, especially lawyers and accountants, would learn from each other during their cross-disciplinary collaboration. Fundamentally, this is written from my perspective through my experience and observations, but not based on any extensive literature review or research.

On Characteristics of Professionals

I had been an accountant in industry for 10 years before becoming a practicing accountant 22 years ago. Even though both accountants in industry and accountants in practice are qualified from the same accounting education and certification programme, their training paths are different. Accountants in industry are those who service within an organisation or a group of organisations. They tend to rely on professional services to solve their problems. Accountants in practice are those who provide accounting services to the general public. They rely more on their own to solve problems (not only accounting problems). When this chapter mentions about professionals, I refer to professionals in practice.

R. Yeung (✉)
Hong Kong, China
e-mail: ryeung@rycpa.com.hk

© Springer International Publishing Switzerland 2015
P. Gibbs (ed.), *Transdisciplinary Professional Learning and Practice,*
DOI 10.1007/978-3-319-11590-0_7

From a professional's perspective, I would expect professionals have to possess the skills, knowledge and ethical values of their specific discipline at a level above technicians. In addition, they should have attitudes and ability to learn on their own. As a professional, they have a responsibility to learn, both from their belonging professional body or for their business. They are doomed to be lifelong and self-directed learners. The professional bodies expect their members to continue learning throughout their career through continuing professional education. The International Federation Accountants ("IFAC") sets out a range of competences in the accounting education programme expecting accounting students to have acquired by the end of their studies so that the students would be work-ready to join the profession. The International Education Standard prescribes the mix of professional skills and general education that candidates require to qualify as professional accountants. The professional skills are grouped under 5 main headings: intellectual skills; technical and functional skills; personal skills; interpersonal and communication skills; and orgainisational and business management skills. There include some non-business related studies or generic skills in the requirements. The aim of these generic skills is to develop students into people with skills and qualities that are appropriate for a professional life after graduation; and their ability to continue to develop such skills over a lifetime, i.e. learning to learn skill. Learning to learn skill is important to professionals as they will face a rapidly expanding knowledge base and complex world. It is impossible for them to acquire all the knowledge in their field in the course of their professional education and training. They have to learn how to learn from new sources and colleagues in the same discipline as well as from different disciplines after they are qualified as professional members.

Most professionals have themselves been clients of other professionals. Clients do not require a professional creative, but want a professional that has sufficient knowledge and experience in solving their problems. Clients seek professional advice when they need to deal with complex problems. Accountants may hire lawyers for legal consultation, medical doctor for health problems, surveyors for property valuations, etc. From the perspective of a client, I would first consider one that is professionally qualified to solve my problem with his technical skill and experience. While professionals in the same discipline would more or less have the same qualifications which represent their technical skills and competence, I would further look at the reputation of the professionals especially their working attitude.

Professionals charge clients on a time basis. During my course of practice, I collaborate with lawyers more often than with other professionals. One of the common questions was that clients did not understand the charges on the "research" time. They expected that the professionals possessed the hands-on knowledge to solve their problems without carrying out extensive research. Some knowledgeable clients claimed that they could conduct the research themselves if they knew it in advance. Even though it is not uncommon that some issues are required to conduct some research before providing a professional answer, this reflects that, from the public's perspective, professionals should keep their knowledge current. In this knowledge expanding and complex world, professionals could no longer rely on the knowledge gained in their professional education alone which might have been outdated.

They are required to learn on their own after qualification and to keep their knowledge current and wide. They need to learn from other professionals to widen their knowledge.

From either the perspective of the professional themselves or the public, professionals should possess the characters of a self-directed, lifelong and intentional learner.

On Learning Attitudes

In Chinese, it has a saying that there are three types of people in learning (i) never learn even being taught; (ii) learn after being taught; (iii) learn without being taught. It distinguishes people's learning attitude but not on their intelligence. The attitudes reflect one's willingness to learn which depends on three learning factors i.e. the learning need, the learning contents and learning environment.

The learning attitude of a person is somewhat inborn, but it can also be fostered. The higher level of curiosity one has, the stronger the learning attitude one would be. Professional learning is generally based on some sets of regulations and standards, which are developed into a specific area and discipline. People having the first type of learning attitude hardly want to be professionals because they resist or are reluctant to learn. People having the second type of learning attitude can be trained to be professionals but may be difficult to expect them to learn from other professionals. Their learning is passive but not active. They learn after being taught but not easy to learn how to learn.

The third type of learning attitude likely inherits the characters of professionals. People with this type of learning attitude are usually active and self-directed learners. On the one hand, they are driven to learn by the client's problems. On the other hand, their self-motivated learning character would lead them to connect new knowledge with what they have known, organize facts and rules into concepts and principles. This type of people enjoys learning and continues to learn out of personal and professional interest; and prepares to meet the challenges of the profession in the future. They are likely not satisfied with purely hiring other professional service, but keen to learn from professionals of other disciplines.

On Trans-disciplinary Learning

From my perspective, "disciplinary learning" means some training or education in specific knowledge within the boundary of ethical conducts and regulations. "Interdisciplinary learning" refers to one person who possesses more than one set of disciplinary knowledge. "Multi-disciplinary learning" refers to professionals having different professional disciplines working together but there is no transfer of their discipline-related knowledge between them. These professionals possess different disciplinary knowledge and practice, they may work together in a multidisciplinary hub but one relies on the expertise of the others on a case-by-case basis or on a practice basis. Cross disciplinary learning seldom occurs between them except for partnering skill. "Transdisciplinary learning" refers to the intersection of two or more sets of disciplinary knowledge between professionals through collaboration. The discipline-related knowledge is transferred from one to the other. Only when this happens between different disciplinary professionals, trans-disciplinary learning occurs.

Most of the literal discussions of multi-disciplinary and transdisciplinary practice relate to social, health, childcare, environmental contexts etc. Few literatures respond to transdisciplinary practice of business services. Business problems are not less complex than any of the social, health, childcare or environmental problems. There are a number of variables causing the problems and outcomes. A complex business problem that clients require professional help seldom caused by one single factor. Multi-disciplinary professional may provide one-stop service while transdisciplinary may not only provide service, but it also provides solutions to the clients and the professional team on similar issues that they may come across in the future.

Clients acquiring professional services are expecting solutions for their problems from professionals. Thus, professional practices are in principle problem-based or practice-based. During the course of carrying out problem-based research, it creates learning opportunity. Most of the business issues involve the systematic collaboration of experts from different fields of knowledge and professional backgrounds. Lawyers need accountants and financial experts in dealing with complex commercial cases, accountants need legal professionals to help assess the legal liability of various business transactions which might affect the truth and fairness of their clients' financial statements, etc. The more complex the business case is, the more professionals of different disciplines will be required. Complex investment projects involve lawyers along with accountants, financial specialists and valuation analysts. The professional practices in different disciplines thus change from an autonomous and rather isolated activity to a transdisciplinary venture. The cross disciplinary collaborations provide ample lessons to professionals in their daily practice; all they have to do is to take advantage of the learning opportunities. The contents and environment of professional practice made learning available to professionals. Whether the professionals can learn from the others depends largely on their learning attitudes and their learning needs. Learning would not occur if the professionals do not find any learning need, especially when they solely rely on other's professional service.

Today, most business problems require cross disciplinary knowledge. For instance, it is commonly known that clients go to accountants if they have tax problems. However, tax is law. Accountants may handle some simple tax issues, but it requires tax lawyers in dealing with complex tax issues, especially when the tax issue may finally need to settle in court. During the course of my practice, I need legal practitioners in most civil cases, especially those related to corporate disputes or civil claims. Most of the claims related to complex calculations that lawyers require accountants to quantify the consequence. Synergy therefore arises between cross disciplinary professionals. In some commercial cases that I worked with lawyers, both legal and accounting discipline-related analyses were required to work out reports. If the problem requires different professionals to work together, the solution is likely found from transdisciplinary collaboration and research. The business need generates collaboration between professionals in different disciplines and the learning environment. If the working parties find learning needs, new knowledge may be developed within the practice and between the professions.

Transdisciplinary learning occurs when the parties have a strong learning need and when the other learning factors are available. However, this learning need is not to say that the professional wants to replace the other professional in different disciplines but is mostly arisen from their curiosity and professional's suspicious nature.

On Professional Education

Learning in Chinese is combined with two characters. *"Study"* and *"Practice"*. In the *"On Learning"* of the *Analects of Confucius (Lun Yu)* written more than 2500 years ago, Confucius said, *"is it not a pleasure after all to practice in due time what one has learnt?"* It reflects that learning could not be achieved by studying alone. It must be accompanied with *"practice"* and have to practice in due time too. Before 1906, the examination system of China was mainly for recruiting government officials. The examination was based on the ancient classical texts, which were archaic and extremely concise. They were very different from spoken language. Students had to memorize them, soak themselves in these texts and become versed both in the thoughts and sentiments expressed there as well as in the manner of expressing them. The mechanical part of the training was considered very important. This *"learning by memorizing"* Confucian system has been last for 1000 years. The word *"practice"* actually meant repeating the writing and reading rather than *"work based"*. However, since the main purpose of the education system was to train government officials, the education system was actually professional education for professional officials even though the contents of the education were not too much related to the work nature. After 1905, China ended the Confucian system, but the *"learning by memorizing"* technique has a far reaching impact on the learning method in Chinese. The learning by memorizing method is perhaps a barrier for professional development and transdisciplinary learning since both are emphasized on analytical and partnering skill but learning by memorizing is emphasized on personal effort.

The traditional professional education was originated from apprenticeship. Apprenticeship used a vocational approach to achieve a professional goal. Students learnt technical skills from their masters through continuing practice, and became masters themselves. They were not allowed to be innovative during their apprenticeship. There were not many formalized professional education programmes at universities in early 1900s. The earliest formalized professional education at universities was likely to be legal and medical profession. The purpose of university was to educate people with a cognitive objective, emphasizing analytical, reasoning and learning-to-learn skills.

Accountants in the 1960s hardly had an accounting or business-related degree from universities. My former partner graduated from the University of Hong Kong with a degree in social science, even though the programme contained some accounting subjects. I graduated from a combined degree of Accounting, Finance and Economics in the 1980s which contained little technical knowledge in the programme. Instead, we studied mostly on social science topics such as the impacts of the accounting on motivation, economy, human behaviour etc. I learnt accounting from my work rather than from the university programme. At that time, not many employers complaint that the fresh graduates could not apply their learning at work. However, I have to admit that the university taught me learning skill which was more important than any technical skill for my development. The university education strengthened my problem solving skill that I have applied in my work. That is what education should be, from an academic approach to a professional goal with a cognitive objective.

Both accounting and legal professionals were developed from apprenticeships. They started learning from work, then supported by formalized education when the theories developed in their respective fields. They then returned to work and applied what they learnt from formalized education. This learning process is consistent with the Chinese expression of "Learning"- "*Study*" and "*Practice*". Today, accountants and lawyers start with academic preparation at college, which are supposed to equip the potential professionals with the skills, knowledge, value and attitudes required for success in their professional career paths. Accountants are based on established financial reporting standards, rules and regulations set out by the accounting bodies, while lawyers are based on the established statutes and case laws. Both are somewhat following the rules and regulations established from time to time. Both have to apply their learning to professional practice, adapting what they have learnt to meet new challenges. The approach of their qualification education is in common but the context is different. There is a synergy of trandisciplinary practice among them.

On the Development of Transdisciplinary Learning

Professional practices provide two learning dimensions for transdisciplinary learning i.e. learning contents and learning environment. The market force and disciplinary-dependent generic skill elements within the two learning dimensions foster the learning need for transdisciplinary learning.

Market force generates demands for interdisciplinary professionals. The demand generates business needs for professionals to expand their knowledge in various disciplines and increase collaborations among professionals of various disciplines. The market force will drive the professionals to learn to cope with the rapid changes and complexity of the business world. However, whether professionals in one discipline can learn from professionals of other disciplines depends on their generic skills of learning. Professional knowledge has its disciplinary nature. The concepts of generic skills of this disciplinary-dependent nature may not be lacking in professional education, but it may not be able to connect different disciplines in one curriculum.

The four types of disciplinary learning mentioned earlier should be considered as a process of development, from single disciplinary to interdisciplinary; from interdisciplinary to multidisciplinary; from multidisciplinary to transdisciplinary. From my informal survey over 200 accounting professionals who have worked with me, it indicated that they developed their accounting competencies from work rather than from formal accounting studies. Fresh accounting graduates generally found it difficult to apply what they learnt from university in the real business problems. It is a challenge for them to move from surface learning of accounting rules to deep understanding of accounting principles and to skills in applying knowledge in practice. It is not difficult to imagine the difficulty for professionals who were trained up from a specific discipline to expand their knowledge in the other disciplines without being taught of the discipline-dependent generic skills. For instance, if I did not receive some legal education, I would have difficulty in understanding the legal jargons and contexts. That would discourage me to learn from lawyers. I would tend to rely on their service during joint ventures, rather than taking the opportunity to learn and develop new knowledge for myself or the profession. I hardly learn from a joint healthcare project because I do not possess the generic or fundamental skills of healthcare. I would tend to rely on the healthcare professional's service. No learning would occur as I have no learning need. The business need and my curiosity in knowledge explain why I decided to study law when I was practising in accounting.

Conclusion

Learning is a professional responsibility. Business problems are complex and require cross-disciplinary knowledge to solve. Single-disciplinary professionals might not be able to deal with complex business problems without the help of professionals from other disciplines. Transdisciplinary research may provide solutions to complex problems and build the cross disciplinary knowledge within the practice or the profession. The market force would foster transdisciplinary learning need. However, the overriding objective of professional programmes is to teach students to learn on their own and learn from other disciplines. Like the Chinese expression of "Learning", which combines with the characters of "Study" and "Practice", professional programmes should be a combination of formal study and experiential learning but, among other things, should also expand to include cross disciplinary generic skills to cope with today's cross-disciplinary knowledge required in complex business problems.

Raymond Yeung is visiting professor at the Institute of Work Based Learning, Middlesex University. He is a Certified General Accountant of Canada, Chartered Accountant of Australia, Certified Public Accountant of U.S.A and Hong Kong. He had worked in industry for 10 years before practicing as a public accountant. He has established his own firm in Hong Kong for more than 15 years. He earned his doctoral degree in professional studies (concentrated in economic policy) from Middlesex University. He has been the business director of East Asia Work Based Learning Centre since its inception in 1997. He is a founder of Canadian Certified General Accountants Association of Hong Kong ("CGA-Hong Kong"). CGA-Hong Kong is an affiliate of Certified General Accountants of Canada. He was awarded the honour of 100 CGAs who have made an outstanding contribution to their designation, their communities and the lives of others over the past century since the founding of the CGA designation in 1908. He is a life member of CGA-Hong Kong and a fellow member of CGA-Canada. He has published articles in Financial Post published by THC and newsletters of CGA-Hong Kong.

Part II
Section Two

Integrating Transdisciplinarity and Translational Concepts and Methods into Graduate Education

Linda Neuhauser and Christian Pohl

> *If the world of working and living relies on collaboration, creativity, definition and framing of problems and if it requires dealing with uncertainty, change, and intelligence that is distributed across cultures, disciplines, and tools—then graduate programs should foster transdisciplinary competencies and mindsets that prepare students for having meaningful and productive lives in such a world.*
>
> (Derry and Fischer 2005, p. 4)

Introduction

The so-called "scientific revolution" that emerged in the middle of the 1900s (Kuhn 1962) transformed thinking about reality (ontology) and ways of understanding it (epistemology). As critical realism began to eclipse traditional positivist paradigms, many scholars moved away from the view that the world is knowable and governed by universal laws as it was thought to be in the natural sciences, toward the perspective that reality is complex, contextual, and ever changing (Cook 1985). This evolution/revolution generated two new epistemologies: human (interpretive) sciences and design (artificial) sciences.

Human sciences, including social sciences and the humanities examine "human and historical life" (Dilthey 1988), the difficulties of generalizing about human behavior, and the value of studying it from many perspectives (Cook 1985). Design sciences, including architecture, engineering and informatics focus on human-created ("artificial") objects, services and other phenomena intended to solve problems and meet goals. Design sciences are concerned "not with how things are, but how they might be" (Simon 1996; Gregor 2009). Knowledge is gathered using iterative "build and evaluate loops" (Markus et al. 2002).

L. Neuhauser (✉)
University of California, Berkeley, CA, USA
e-mail: lindan@berkeley.edu

C. Pohl
Swiss Academies of Arts and Sciences, Bern, Switzerland

© Springer International Publishing Switzerland 2015
P. Gibbs (ed.), *Transdisciplinary Professional Learning and Practice*,
DOI 10.1007/978-3-319-11590-0_8

Deleuze and Guattarti (1980) propose an even more radical concept of the scientific challenge to understand reality. They argue that Western thought assumes that the world is characterized by an essential coherence or "whole" of its units, with laws and linear origins. However, in their view, reality is made up of multiple dimensions, (or, "directions in motion") with neither a beginning nor an end. Like the Internet, there is no center, but rather an infinite number of links. Understanding occurs through examining these heterogeneous "multiplicities" as they spread and interact.

According to the emergent thinking, knowledge, therefore, is "collective" and cannot be found through any single discipline (Kahn and Prager 1994). Seeking knowledge requires that multiple investigators and stakeholders gradually study phenomena from as many different perspectives as possible, and by using multiple theoretical frameworks, methods, settings and interpretations of evidence, a concept known as "critical multiplism" (Cook 1985).

Changes in scientific thinking have also been prompted by the realization that narrow disciplinary research carried out under controlled conditions has not been effective in addressing complex problems such as climate change, poverty, or epidemics (Lubchenco 1998). Complex, or "wicked" problems are typically heterogeneous, changeable, contextually localized, value-laden, difficult to define and—obviously—to solve (Rittel and Webber 1973; Brown et al. 2010; Tapio and Huutoniemi 2014; Buchanan 1992). The quest to understand and solve complex problems has generated increasing interest among researchers, practitioners and policymakers to find ways to integrate and apply knowledge across disciplines and societal sectors. These efforts have created rich cross-disciplinary theoretical frameworks and methods and have shown improved outcomes in addressing a variety of problems (Bammer 2013; Stokols 2006; Hirsch Hadorn et al. 2008; Bergmann et al. 2012). "Transdisciplinarity," as discussed below, is an emergent term for highly integrated applied research.

Radical changes in scientific thinking and complex problem solving strategies have resulted in many recommendations for transdisciplinary training in higher education and professional development. This will be hard to achieve because since the Middle Ages, university education has become increasingly fragmented into disciplines and sub-disciplines. In this chapter, we discuss the benefits and challenges of creating transdisciplinary university education, with examples from the University of California, Berkeley (USA), and ETH Zurich (Switzerland).

Our objectives are to: (1) Discuss the nature and importance of transdisciplinary research and action; (2) Describe the scientific foundation of transdisciplinarity; (3) Describe the general goals of integrating transdisciplinarity into higher education; (4) Present two models of transdisciplinary university education; and (5) Provide recommendations for integrating transdisciplinarity into university education.

Crossdisciplinarity

In the "postpositivist/postnormal" view of science, cross-disciplinary approaches to understand reality and knowledge seeking predominate. Cross-disciplinary perspectives include "multidisciplinarity," "interdisciplinarity" and "transdisciplinarity." In general, multidisciplinarity refers research and implementation activities that involve input from multiple disciplines working independently or sequentially (with little interaction) to address a common problem (Rosenfeld 1992; Stokols 2006; Abrams 2006).

Although multidisciplinarity is not viewed as a strong approach to improve scientific thinking or problem solving, the distinction between inter- and transdisciplinarity is less clear. One view of interdisciplinarity is that researchers work jointly, but from their own disciplines to address a common problem, whereas in transdisciplinarity, researchers work together from the outset to develop a shared conceptual framework that integrates and *transcends* discipline-based concepts to create new theories, and/or methods (Rosenfeld 1992; Stokols 2006; Abrams 2006; Wickson et al. 2006). Another distinguishing feature of transdisciplinary approaches is that they usually have a problem focus and emphasize "translating" research findings into actions to address problems. Pohl and Hirsch Hadorn (2007) call these "problems of the life world" and Stokols (2006) calls this process "Transdisciplinary Action Research." Such research requires, besides researchers of different disciplines working jointly, that multiple actors from the private, the public or the administrative sector be involved in the research (Klein et al. 2001)

It is beyond the scope of this chapter to examine differences between concepts of inter- and transdisciplinarity, many of which currently overlap (Froderman et al. 2010; Szostak 2007; Youngblood 2007; Hirsch Haddorn et al. 2010; Klein 2010). We have focused on transdisciplinarity in this chapter because it emphasizes a transcendent and transformative view of research and action. Transdisciplinarity is also "aspirational" and intended to inspire researchers and practitioners to seek high levels of collaboration, disciplinary integration, paradigm expansion, methods creation and real-world problem solving.

Emergence of Transdisciplinarity

Noted philosopher and educator Jean Piaget is credited with introducing the term "transdisciplinarity" (Nicolescu 2002). In 1972, Erich Jantsch first linked transdisciplinarity to education when he recommended that higher education be reshaped via a university-government-industry model of societal planning (Jantsch 1970). He argued that university disciplines should be organized into "goal-oriented" systems to solve societal problems. Since then, scholars, practitioners and decision makers have often called for transdisciplinary education as a pragmatic way to better align university training and societal needs. For example, Hoffman-Riem et al. (2008) comment: "Transdisciplinary orientations to research, education and institutions try to overcome the mismatch between knowledge production in academia and knowledge requests for solving societal problems."

Physicist Basarab Nicolescu, a key champion of transdisciplinarity, emphasizes both its critical ontological/epistemological value *as well as* its utility to solve problems. He considers transdisciplinarity a new methodology to create knowledge and comments that because there are multiple levels of reality governed by different types of logic, reducing complex phenomena to "a single (ontological) level governed by a single form of logic" limits the potential of researchers to successfully address social problems (Nicolescu 2002, 2010; Gehlert and Browne 2013).

A spirited scholarly conversation is underway about ontological, epistemological and practical perspectives related to transdisciplinarity. McGregor (2014) discusses differences between Nicolescuian and other views of transdisciplinarity. In her view, transdisciplinarity is characterized by multiple, constantly changing realities, in which multiple and contradictory perspectives can be "temporarily joined" in the search for knowledge. To do so, people from academia and civil society need co-create knowledge using an emergent, iterative process. Knowledge produced in this way will be "complex, emerging and constantly reorganized, rather than static and discipline-bound." She advises those co-producing such "transcendent" knowledge to "give up sovereignty of their domain, and create a temporary fecund space for the emergence of new knowledge." Likewise, Gibbs (2014) provides a strong ontological and logical rationale for using "abduction" (educated "guessing") during transdisciplinary processes.

Clearly, Transdisciplinarity is profoundly different from Western classical, Aristotelian and Newtonian linear scientific thinking that assumes coherence, precludes logical contradictions, and separates knowledge into isolated disciplinary domains. Transdisciplinary thinking assumes that "everything is dependent on everything else, everything is connected; nothing is separate" (Nicholescu et al. 2004; Deleuze and Guattari 1980).

McGregor comments that engaging in transdisciplinary work involves a process of "synergistic chaos" (McGregor, 2014). Transdisciplinary scholars assert that even though transdisciplinary thinking and its application are highly complex and antithetical to the traditions in which most of us have been educated, they are essential for better science and problem solving.

Translational Research Beginning in the 1990s, some scholars and other stakeholders have advocated for distinguishing transdisciplinary research (integrating knowledge across disciplines) from its application across societal sectors, called "translational research" or "research dissemination." One definition of research translation in the health field is: "an extended process of how research knowledge that is directly or indirectly relevant to health or well-being eventually serves the public" (adapted from Sussman et al. 2006). Translational research has been popularized by the US National Institutes of Health (NIH) that has made major investments in efforts to move from basic and clinical research to application of results to benefit populations. In this model, research happens on a unidirectional continuum, starting at the "basic" level ("T1": laboratory) and moves over time to applied levels ("T2": practice settings and communities) in society.

This concept of translational research has been useful to highlight the importance of "converting knowledge to action." However, just as narrow disciplinary research has been criticized for its weaknesses in producing knowledge, so too is translational research for its weaknesses in applying research. One critique is that such concepts often assume an artificial dichotomy between "basic" and "applied" research. Rubio et al. (2010) comment that the NIH concept and similar perspectives of research translation ignore the importance of involving multiple knowledge sets, methods and stakeholders for research to benefit society.

Likewise, outcomes of linear, limited approaches that separate knowledge production from its application are often disappointing. Balas and Boren (2000) estimate that it may take 17 years to turn 14 % of original basic health research into clinical applications (Balas and Boren 2000), and that it would take even longer for such knowledge to have an impact on a community or population level. For this reason, Woolf (2008) recommends that from the beginning, research include many disciplines, such as psychology, behavioral science, economics and others, so that findings can be used effectively to "improve health and quality of life." As noted below, the current trend is to incorporate "translational" issues into a robust perspective of transdisciplinarity that includes its application.

Defining Transdisciplinarity Since the 1970s, scholars have proposed many definitions of transdisciplinarity (see Pohl and Hirsch Hadorn 2007, pp. 70–95) and its relationship to research, practice and education. Of those, we suggest the following definitions, relevant to higher education and professional development:

Stokols et al. (2013) define transdisciplinary research and practice as:

> An integrative process whereby scholars and practitioners from both academic disciplines and non-academic fields work jointly to develop and use novel conceptual and methodological approaches that synthesize and extend discipline-specific perspectives, theories, methods, and translational strategies to yield innovative solutions to particular scientific and societal problems.

Jahn et al. (2012) propose this definition:

> Transdisciplinarity is a reflexive research approach that addresses societal problems by means of interdisciplinary collaboration as well as the collaboration between researchers and extra-scientific actors. Its aim is to enable mutual learning processes between science and society; integration is the main cognitive challenge of the research process.

Pohl and Hirsch Hadorn's definition (2007) is problem-focused and grounded in components that can be used for competencies in education:

> The starting point for TR is a socially relevant problem field. Within this field, TR identifies, structures, analyses, and deals with specific problems in such a way that it can:
> a) grasp the complexity of problems,
> b) take into account the diversity of life-world and scientific perceptions of problems,
> c) link abstract and case-specific knowledge, and
> d) develop knowledge and practices that promote what is perceived to be the common good.
> Participatory research and collaboration between disciplines are the means of meeting requirements a)–d) in the research process.

We note that in addition to definitions of transdisciplinarity, some scholars and other stakeholders have advocated the use of other terms for similar concepts. For example, Bammer (2013) proposes "Integration and Implementation Sciences (I2S)" to refer to integrated applied research and practice.

Transdisciplinary Models Conceptual frameworks related to transdisciplinary thinking and action have greatly matured since their inception in the 1970s, and especially during this century. Neuhauser et al. (2007) trace the roots of such models relevant to health and social issues with the rapid expansion of integrated biological, social, and ecological perspectives, combined with complexity and systems theories (operations research, learning organizations, etc.). Such models include social epidemiology (Syme 2005), ecological systems (Bronfenbrenner 1979), and social ecological models (Stokols 2000). Another important contribution was the understanding that participatory processes among researchers, practitioners and other stakeholders were a core feature of transdisciplinary research and action (Bammer 2005; King et al. 1998; Stokols 2006; Sussman et al. 2006; Neuhauser 2013). During this century, action research and participatory action research frameworks have helped guide researchers and practitioners to collaborate across disciplines and sectors to co-create knowledge and apply it across sectors (Minkler and Wallerstein 2008; Neuhauser and Kreps 2013; Neuhauser et al. 2013a).

Early models of research and its application for health/social issues tended to be linear (Best et al. 2006). Knowledge was viewed as a product passively transferred from researchers to implementers. The current view focuses on knowledge *integration*, wherein knowledge is viewed as tightly woven within priorities, culture and contexts (Green and Glasgow 2006). Such models highlight the shift from studying phenomena under controlled conditions to those in varied and uncertain real world contexts. Examples of health and social issue-related transdisciplinary models that encompass complexity across time, place, culture and that advocate highly collaborative processes include: Stokols (2006), Sussman et al. (2006), and Bammer (2013).

Transdisciplinarity was introduced early in the development of environmental and sustainability sciences (Mittelstraß 1993). In this area, there are roughly two kinds of models in which the aim of transdisciplinarity has been elaborated over the years. First, are the extensive earth system mathematical models, created as a way to integrate knowledge of multiple disciplines (Schellnhuber 1999). These models serve to identify "syndromes" of global change and to suggest management strategies that—according to the model—would be successful (Lüdeke et al. 2004). These models are very rich in quantifiable scientific insights, but less relevant to the needs of decision makers. Second, are conceptual models of sustainability issues that researchers have developed to describe specific socio-ecological situations (Becker and Jahn 2006). These models are mathematically less elaborate, but are designed to facilitate joint learning processes among decision makers from civil society, and private and public sectors (Kiteme and Wiesmann 2008; Wiesmann et al. 2011).

Integrating Transdisciplinarity into Higher Education

As the critical value of transdisciplinarity has become increasing clear over the past 40 years, there has been a surge of interest and investment in this approach (Stokols et al. 2005). To date, the most intensive research about transdisciplinary processes has been conducted in studies of specific research collaborations. For example, in the US, the National Institutes of Health has invested hundreds of millions of dollars in Transdisciplinary Research Centers. A key finding was that without some formal training—especially at the university level—few scientists have the essential skills to excel at this work (Stokols 2006; Sussman et. al. 2006).

Who will train the next generation of transdisciplinary researcher–practitioners (Nash et al. 2003), or integration and implementation scientists (Bammer 2013)? How can we shift education towards transdisciplinarity in universities that are increasingly fragmented into sub-disciplinary areas and value "new" rather than applied knowledge? How can we create stronger partnerships between researchers and those who integrate knowledge for public benefit?

Because research about transdisciplinary processes and outcomes is still at an early stage, limited evidence exists about specific factors that facilitate or hinder success of this approach. For this reason, there is no comprehensive conceptual framework for such training (Nash et al. 2003) and consequently, no clearly defined competencies, curricula, textbooks, or accreditation criteria (Bammer 2005; Neuhauser et al. 2007). However, during the past four decades, educators and scientists have provided valuable guidance to address this challenge.

As noted earlier, Erich Jantsch (1970) recommended that university education be more problem-oriented and link efforts of collaborators from the university, government and industry domains. Adult educator Ernest Boyer (1990) proposed a "Four Scholarships" model intended to foster a stronger link between research and its translation into action. In Boyer's view, university training should include the scholarships of *discovery* (creating new knowledge), *integration* (synthesizing information from multiple disciplines and perspectives), *engagement* (bidirectional, collaborative approaches to solving important problems), and *teaching* (including student-driven and problem-based learning and *participatory pedagogy* between teachers and students).

Kahn and Prager (1994) proposed "five milestones" for successful transdisciplinary science that are relevant to higher education and professional training: (a) listening across disciplinary gulfs, (b) learning the language and ideas of other disciplines, (c) developing a common language for new conceptual development, (d) jointly developing new methods and measures, and (e) conducting research that reflects disciplinary integration.

Early research findings (Neuhauser et al. 2007) about the effectiveness of transdisciplinary work (within and outside academia) support and add to the above guidance by highlighting the importance of personal skills, processes, and organizational factors related to transdisciplinary education, including:

- Institutional incentives for participation;
- Institutional commitment and flexibility to facilitate this work;
- Leadership skills to facilitate this work across disciplines;

- Expertise in negotiation and conflict resolution skills;
- Expertise in problem-based research and practice;
- Regular face-to-face meetings;
- Close collaboration between researchers and other stakeholders;
- Expertise in multi-method research, and
- Expertise in assessment of the "added value" of this work.

University Transdisciplinary Programs in Public Health and Environmental Science

Although "interdisciplinary" programs combining training and research in several disciplines have existed in universities since the 1970s, programs intended to adhere to the definitions above of "transdisciplinarity" (some are called "interdisciplinary") have just emerged during the past two decades. To date, there are an increasing number of examples, but no comprehensive inventory or evaluation of such programs. Below, we describe issues and examples of transdisciplinary university programs in the fields of public health and environmental science. Both these fields are inherently crossdisciplinary and problem-oriented, and not surprisingly, ones in which early transdisciplinary programs have been created.

Public Health The field of public health intersects a broad range of disciplines in the natural sciences (such as biology, biophysics and vaccinology) social sciences (such as sociology, anthropology, policy and education) and design sciences (such as engineering, bioinformatics and urban planning). There are few disciplines or fields that do not have a connection with health.

As a "professional" field, public health is concerned not only with theory and basic science, but also with solving health problems, many of which would be considered complex or "wicked," such as epidemics, obesity, violence, and developing cost-effective health care systems. Beginning in the 1990s, public health scholars and institutions began to advocate for inter- and transdisciplinary university education (Rosenfeld 1992). In 2004, the US National Academies and the Institute of Medicine gathered recommendations from university faculty, outside research scientists, and leaders from a variety of public and business sectors about the future of public health university training (Committee 2004). The report recommended that undergraduate students gain a strong foundation in one discipline, and learn other disciplinary skills and techniques, and that graduate students work with advisors from multiple disciplines, including in fields outside public health. Researchers and faculty were encouraged to "immerse themselves in the languages, cultures, and knowledge of their collaborators" (Committee 2004; Gehlert and Browne 2013).

Accreditation requirements have been a key factor in the development of cross-disciplinary and transdisciplinary programs. The Council on Education for Public Health (CEPH)—the accrediting agency for US schools of public health and public health programs—requires that public health students be trained in knowledge and practical skills in five core public health disciplines: biostatistics, epidemiology, environmental health sciences, policy and management, and social and behavioral sciences (Council 2011). CEPH-accredited schools and programs must also define competencies (knowledge, skills and behaviors expected of program graduates) for each disciplinary area and for practical skills.

Since the 1970s, the move toward competency-based education (CBE) (May 1979) has generated an important profession-wide conversation about explicit performance goals of graduate education in public health. The Association of Schools of Public Health (ASPH)—the professional association for US schools of public health—has conducted initiatives with academic and practice stakeholders to define core competency models for masters of public health (MPH) and doctor of public health (DrPH) programs (ASPH 2006, 2010). ASPH recommends that MPH students not only be trained in the core disciplines, but also gain competencies in seven cross-cutting areas: public health biology, communication and informatics, diversity and culture, leadership, professionalism, systems thinking and program planning (ASPH 2006). The evolution of public health graduate education has resulted in a greater emphasis on integrated disciplinary knowledge and acquisition of applied skills. However, CEPH requirements and ASPH recommendations do not yet meet the ambitious standard of "transdisciplinarity" as defined in this chapter.

Doctor of Public Health Programs Traditionally, PhD public health degrees have been focused on specialized disciplinary research, and DrPH degrees on "advanced public health leadership" (Calhoun et al. 2012). Prior to this century, many DrPH degree programs had a disciplinary focus, such as maternal and child health or nutrition. However, with the realization that solving complex health problems requires leaders who can work across disciplines and sectors, DrPH programs are being re-examined and transformed. During the past two decades, an increasing number of programs are defining themselves as "transdisciplinary" (Gehlert and Browne 2013; Neuhauser et al. 2007) In 2010, ASPH recommended the DrPH Core Competency Model shown in Fig. 1 (ASPH 2010). According to this model, DrPH students should be trained in the five public health disciplines and in seven crosscutting domains of knowledge and skills. "Leadership" is the area intended to integrate knowledge and skills from the other domains and disciplines.

The currently recommended DrPH model represents an important shift towards integrated applied knowledge and practice, even though, like the MPH model, it does not yet rise to the level of transdisciplinarity as defined it in this chapter. Transforming public health education to be transdisciplinary means that students would be exposed to *transcendent* conceptualizations of health that go far beyond the traditional five public health disciplines—for example: how urban planning affects asthma and diabetes, or how good early childhood education can decrease the risks of poverty and violence in adults. Further, students would gain high-level skills to collaborate with researchers, practitioners and other stakeholders on creating successful interventions. Such transdisciplinary education is needed to "accelerate the pace" of cutting-edge research and practice (Stokols et al. 2013).

Fig. 1 US Association of Schools of Public Health, Doctor of Public Health (DrPH) Core Competency Model, Version 1.3—graphic depiction. (ASPH 2010)

As more public health programs are branded as "transdisciplinary," important efforts are underway to align curricula, competencies and practice experiences with this aspiration. Arnold et al. (2013) propose MPH transdisciplinary competency knowledge and skill areas and recommend processes to vet competencies with stakeholders and integrate them into coursework and practice experiences. Similar efforts are emerging for DrPH programs, as discussed below.

University of California, Berkeley Doctor of Public Health Model

The University of California, Berkeley (California, USA) is richly multidisciplinary and has over 130 academic departments organized into 14 colleges and schools, offers 350 degree programs, and served over 35,000 students in 2012. Berkeley is consistently ranked as the top public university in the US and worldwide. The School of Public Health (SPH) has 12 degree programs (including the DrPH program) that serve about 700 students.

Like other DrPH programs, Berkeley's SPH originally awarded DrPH degrees in specific public health disciplines such as nutrition, epidemiology or maternal and child health. These DrPH degrees (as opposed to PhD degrees) were for students who intended to focus primarily on advanced leadership practice in specific areas, rather than research or teaching. In the 1990s, when national and international scientific and health organizations advocated for inter- and transdisciplinary education, SPH faculty, students and diverse stakeholders began to consider major revisions to its DrPH programs. In addition to the convincing scientific and practical arguments for transdisciplinary education summarized above, community partners and employers—such as directors of health departments—provided valuable input. They wanted graduates who could excel at problem-focused research and practice involving many topical areas in many societal contexts. As the director of a large urban health department explained "We need people who can go to a high poverty area and respectfully work with residents to find out what they need. Often, we get someone with a PhD who prefers to crunch data at their computer."

First transdisciplinary Phase In 1996, four discipline-specific DrPH programs at Berkeley were joined to create the current "school-wide" program, to integrate training among all SPH disciplines. The newly unified program had strong emphasis on creating university-community partnerships for both research and its application. Further, it aimed at developing public health leaders by combining traditional academic education with training in collaboration and other skills. During the first decade of development, the program mission was explicitly redefined to have a focus on "transdisciplinary and translational research and practice." The program revision was partly guided by social ecological frameworks (Green and Potvin 1996; Stokols 2000) and by Boyer's (1990) "four scholarships" of discovery, integration, engagement, and teaching. Another important principle was the commitment to a participatory design process in which faculty, students, staff, and community partners work in an ongoing and collaborative way to improve the program. Since 1998, about 150 students have graduated from the program.

Program Structure During the first phase of development, the DrPH program was led jointly by an academic director and a community co-director to link the academic and the practice worlds. A DrPH Management Committee, consisting of representatives of all disciplines within the school and a Community Advisory Board representing local public health leaders, were established to provide guidance and bridge program knowledge and action. A student-led DrPH Program Committee helped design the curriculum and other program components. Finally, reflecting the program's commitment to community partnerships and to diversity of public health leadership, a field placement supervisor and a diversity director had key staff roles.

Each year, about 10 students were selected for academic excellence in one or more fields, evidence of leadership and professional experience in a health-related field, and commitment to research that can be applied to benefit society. Each cohort was selected to include a mix of students from multiple disciplines both within public health and beyond (such as medicine, nursing, education, policy, business, media, and social work), and with diverse of interests and cultural backgrounds.

Curriculum With the collaboration of students, faculty and community partners, transdisciplinary/translational components were gradually built into the curriculum. In addition to coursework in the five aforementioned disciplines required for CEPH accreditation, program developers integrated information about the goals, history, and theoretical frameworks and methods of transdisciplinary and translational research, advanced leadership training, case-based and problem-based learning, community-based participatory research, and training in methods for conducting mixed quantitative and qualitative research.

In the first phase of the new DrPH program, students were also required to conduct a "DrPH-in-Action" project. For this project, teams of 4–5 students collaborated with a local health department or other agency to identify an area of concern. Some student groups worked in other US states or internationally. For, example, one group worked with the Ministry of Health in Mexico to help develop a new HIV/AIDS policy. Another team worked with local residents in the state of Louisiana after the devastating Hurricane Katrina to co-develop improved emergency preparedness plans. In keeping with the findings of transdisciplinary studies, student teams would report back during face-to-face meetings with faculty and with other teams to deal with problems and share successes from their projects.

In addition, students were required to do a field residency (of about 240 h) in a research or practice organization where they could learn new skills. The residency provided opportunities for students to use transdisciplinary approaches to identify and address problems in community, research and policy environments. In some cases, residencies helped studies jointly identify problems and research needs with their host agency partners and then plan practice-based dissertation research.

A detailed internal and external evaluation in 2005 found increased satisfaction on the part of students, alumni, health department personnel, and other stakeholders (Samuels & Associates 2005). Initial findings showed that about half of the graduates took academic positions and most of the others took senior-level positions in government, community, private, philanthropic, and other sectors. Despite traditional academic barriers, graduates created hybrid positions to link research and practice worlds—such as through adjunct professorships.

Second Transdisciplinary Phase About 10 years after the new transdisciplinary DrPH program began, faculty, students and other stakeholders reexamined the program. On the positive side, students, and the diverse organizations that hired them, embraced the strong theoretical, methodological and translatable aspects of the program. However, they also mentioned important constraints. Because DrPH students were now required to master coursework across multiple disciplines and crosscutting domains, as well as learn transdisciplinary theory and methods, some students needed six years to complete the program. The DrPH-in-Action projects were wonderful transdisciplinary learning opportunities, but also very intensive and took nearly a year to complete. As the costs of university education rapidly increase in the US (and government support decreases), there is pressure to reduce the length of doctoral education. Also, there was great demand for the DrPH "researcher-practitioners" graduating from the program.

After weighing the "lessons learned," the program was revised. The transdisciplinary goals of the program were retained, but the length of the program was reduced to 3–4 years. The DrPH-In-Action projects were eliminated, but the transdisciplinary learning components were strengthened in the curriculum to put greater emphasis on collaborative techniques such as negotiation, communication and other skills. Students were encouraged to take advantage of workshops offered by the school's Center for Public Health Practice. These workshops cover many useful areas, such as risk communication and media skills, social media techniques, policy advocacy, and many other topics important for leadership development. The student selection process was also strengthened to ensure that admitted students already had strong backgrounds and could succeed in an intensive program. Because it proved impractical to have both a community and a university director, currently a faculty member with strong community background is the director. In addition, the many DrPH committees were streamlined into two committees.

As a result of these changes, students now concentrate a lot of transdisciplinary learning in their first year and most select a dissertation topic then. During that summer, they complete their residency. In the second year, students engage in a concentrated and collaborative process to outline their dissertation research and complete a literature review. Most also take their doctoral qualifying exam at the end of that year to advance to candidacy. In the third year, students conduct and write up their dissertation research. In the DrPH seminars that 3rd year, they also explore opportunities for post-doctoral research and a wide variety of job opportunities. Most DrPH students now graduate within about 3.5 years. Although solid data about students' post-graduation outcomes do not yet exist, an increasing number are offered prestigious post-doctoral positions and the vast majority find rewarding employment in research, practice, policy and—often—hybrid situations.

In the current third phase of DrPH program development, further revisions are underway relevant to transdisciplinary education. Students are increasingly encouraged to take coursework and engage in research or projects outside public health. To support this effort, faculty and students have created matrices of courses across campus that could meet core DrPH requirements. Typically, students identify courses in other departments and petition the DrPH committee that they be approved. Such courses might be in business, information, journalism, anthropology, urban planning or other departments. Students have been highly creative in searching out new disciplinary connections and sharing them with their peers. For example, several DrPH students have immersed themselves in design thinking methods originating at the school of engineering and are now teaching workshops at the school of public health in these innovative problem-identification and problem-solving processes.

Another important development is that transdisciplinary competencies are now being defined. Although this work is at an early stage, the competencies are intended to translate the domains of the ASPH DrPH Competency Model into specific knowledge and skill outcomes necessary for transdisciplinary work.

ETH Zurich Model: Teaching Inter- and Transdisciplinarity[1]

The second example we discuss forms part of teaching at ETH Zurich's Department of Environmental System Science (USYS). ETH Zurich is a leading international university focused on natural sciences and technology and serves over 18,000 students from over 110 countries. Since it was founded in 1987, the Department of Environmental System Science has been educating about 100–150 students per year. The emphasis of the curriculum is on natural sciences, but includes courses in social sciences, humanities and engineering. Case studies, in which students analyze, for instance, the restorations of a river or whether or not to build a wind farm, have been the main teaching format for inter- and transdisciplinarity. Interdisciplinarity here stands for integrating knowledge of different disciplines. Transdisciplinarity means to, on top of that, include stakeholders in knowledge production. Both are required to work on real world issues like river restorations or wind parks. Knowledge of different disciplines has to be integrated, and actors beyond academia have to be included, in order to come to a comprehensive understanding and to support societal problem solving on the ground. This understanding of inter- and transdisciplinarity has become increasingly common in European countries since the 1990s (Mittelstraß 1993; Jaeger and Scheringer 1998; Klein et al. 2001).

Over the past several decades, the Department of Environmental System Science has grown from a hand-full of professors to over 40, currently organized in six institutes. The number of professorships grew as environmental sciences diversified into specialized subfields like atmosphere and climate, ecology or biogeochemical cycles. This on-going specialization has been integrated into the curriculum. In their third year, undergraduate (Bachelor) students decide on whether to become specialized in areas such as biochemistry and pollutant dynamics, forest and landscape management or atmosphere and climate when they begin the Masters program. The last revision of the curriculum reflects the ongoing specialization, but there was less emphasis on educating students about inter- and transdisciplinarity and on how to tackle complex sustainability issues. This changed in 2013 when the Department created USYS TdLab mandated to cover inter- and transdisciplinary teaching. Below is a brief summary of the general goals and organization of the USYS TdLab program and especially of the Winterschool "Science meets Practice" component.

Framework The main goal and challenge of USYS TdLab's teaching is to bridge academic knowledge production and societal problem solving. The final goal of bridge building—at an environmental science department—is sustainable development of society. The conceptual framework underlying the curriculum is shown in Fig. 2, juxtaposing the realm of science to the one of practice (Bergmann et al. 2005; Jahn et al. 2012; Pohl and Hirsch Hadorn 2007). The realm of science is where researchers study sustainability issues. The realm of practice is where society

---

[1] The teaching described here was developed by Michael Stauffacher, Pius Krütli and Christian Pohl.

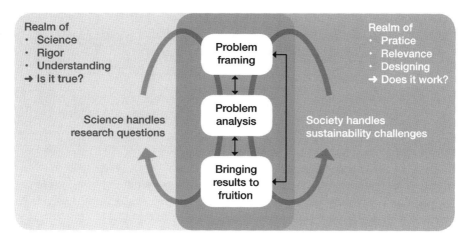

Fig. 2 Transdisciplinary sustainability research links scientific knowledge production and societal problem solving (see Pohl 2014 and www.transdisciplinarity.ch/e/Transdisciplinarity)

handles sustainability issues. Both realms are typically characterized by different rationalities. The search for truth and scientific rigor governs the realm of science. However, the meaning of truth and rigor is relative to the different scientific communities. The realm of practice is governed by relevance and technical, economical, political or socio-cultural feasibility—the concrete meaning of which again depends on a particular sector's or societal subgroup's understanding.

Students advance into the realm of science during their Bachelor and Masters studies in environmental sciences. During Master studies they begin to specialize in a sub-field of environmental sciences and become a member of that field once they complete their PhD thesis. The goal of our teaching in inter- and transdisciplinarity is to link students' work back to the realm of practice. In terms of Fig. 2, the gap between science and practice grows as students advance in their studies and become specialists of a sub-field of environmental sciences. To take account of that situation, process, content and methods of courses are adapted to where students are on their way to specialization.

In their first Bachelor semester, students conduct a case study of an environmental issue. In 2013, the case study involved collaboration with an energy company to examine whether or not a particular wind power station should be built (5ETCS). Besides this case study, students mostly attend basic courses in mathematics, physics, chemistry and biology. As fresh(wo)men, they cannot significantly contribute specific disciplinary knowledge to the case study. Therefore, the methods introduced are of a basic and intuitive nature. For example, systems dynamics models are used in the case example about developing a wind power station. Further, students conduct a basic stakeholder analysis and develop a comprehensive understanding of the situation through analyzing social, legal, economic and environmental aspects related to building or not building the wind power station.

At the Masters level, students specialize in one of seven majors, such as forest and landscape management, animal sciences or biogeochemistry and pollutants. USYS TdLab offers another case study as an elective minor course (10ECTS). Currently, this case study is undergoing a major revision, because for several years it has been tailored to one particular major. Students from all seven majors and faculty are working together to redesign the case study, and are evaluating potential topics. In this way, students from all majors can contribute their specialized knowledge to the case study.

Winterschool "Science meets Practice" One course USYS TdLab offers for PhD students is a two-week intensive Winterschool "Science meets Practice."[2] The Winterschool is organized into two four-day blocks, with a month in between. During the first block, students are introduced to theories, case studies, and methods of different ways in which science meets practice. They learn about story telling, lay summaries, participatory research, and stakeholder engagement. At the end of the first week three groups are set up, each with about eight PhD students. One group is assigned to organize a stakeholder workshop. The coaches introduce the workshop as the first meeting in a virtual project that serves to jointly identify and frame research questions. This year (2014), students were asked to organize a workshop on the topic of "world food systems." During the month until the beginning of the second block of the Winterschool, students had to (1) define the specific topic for the workshop, (2) select and invite relevant participants, and (3) develop a detailed schedule and facilitation plan for the 2-h workshop.

1. Students were intentionally given a broad topic—not a well-defined question. The coaches explicitly asked the students to look for 'hot issues' in the area of world food systems—"hot" in the sense that they are disputed among different stakeholder groups from economy, government, politics or civil society. Students this year decided to run the workshop under the framing of "Local or global food production—do we care?"
2. In order to discuss local or global food production, students invited 11 regional and national stakeholders : The head of a globally active butchery, the director of the Swiss organic farmers associations, the head of environment of the Swiss farmers organization, a citizen of the small remote village that hosts the Winterschool, a national and a regional official from the governmental agency for agriculture, a couple producing olives in Italy, a vegetable farmer from the area who delivers seasonal products directly to regular clients, and two food researchers.
3. In terms of the facilitation process, students placed emphasis on how to introduce stakeholders to each other and how to initiate the discussion of the topic. The invited stakeholders were asked to bring a food item with them. After introductory words and exercises, participants introduced themselves by explaining why they had brought the specific food item. The butcher explaining how his firm is entering the world market with the Swiss sausage "Cervelat;" the village resident brought

---

[2] The stakeholder workshop described here was conceptualized by Patricia Fry and Christian Pohl.

a bread baked by a neighboring farmer; the vegetable producer showed the jute bag used to deliver products to the customers; and the representative from the farmers' association put a potato on the table to remind everybody that a now regional product is originally an import from South Africa. This story telling provided an extremely rich picture of the various aspects of local and/or global food production.

After this story telling exercise and a 1-h group discussion on the challenges of food production and possible solutions, the students closed the workshop with an Apéro and continued discussions and networking in an informal way.

Lessons Learned We found that generally, students greatly appreciated engaging in real world issues through case studies and engaging with stakeholders outside academia. Student comments were reported in evaluations of the Winterschool that we have been holding for the past four years. Some of our observations are:

- PhD students evaluate the second week of the Winterschool, when they actually interact with stakeholders, more positively than the first, which they consider too theoretical. What students particularly appreciate is to self-organize, plan, conduct and evaluate a workshop with 'real' stakeholders from the beginning. One student expressed how valuable the experience was as follows: "Next time my supervisor asks me to run a workshop, I will say 'Yes, I will do it' because I feel ready."
- The everyday experience and the home ground of PhD students is the realm of science. They are far away from practice. A sign of this distance to practice is how eager and curious they are to meet and talk to "real" stakeholders. Another learning is that students underestimate what stakeholders know about an issue. This year, the food story telling made clear how rich stakeholders' knowledge about regional and local food production is and how it complements what scientists know.
- Like many inter- and transdisciplinary efforts, the USYS TdLab has had to struggle against the university's primary focus on science in sub-fields rather than the integration and application of this knowledge to benefit society. For example, the TdLab does not have the formal professorial status of other program areas. However, the enthusiasm of the students for the TdLab approach has increased its importance. Also, because ETH Zurich has recently created a "critical thinking initiative," TdLab's teaching is strongly contributing to that effort.

Discussion and Recommendations

"University" is derived from the Latin word "universitas," or "whole." How far we have come from that universal view to our fragmented silos of knowledge removed from the whole of society.

The renewed focus on what is now called transdisciplinarity is long overdue. As society faces potentially catastrophic environmental, health and other problems, we need better and faster ways to integrate knowledge from all perspectives and use it for a better world. Transdisciplinarity has become a core concept in the scientific revolution of the past 50 years and has gained a critical mass of thinkers and practical experimenters who have come together from many fields.

Transforming university education to be transdisciplinary is definitely challenging, but is a goal of critical global importance. Because of the contributions of many people, there is a strong foundation of theory, methods and empirical findings to inform this work. In our experiences building transdisciplinary programs, we have faced similar barriers of reorienting education in the face of the university system that favors sub-specialization. However, we have found increasing interest among faculty colleagues, highly engaged students and appreciative real-world stakeholders.

With the many "lessons learned" to date from transdisciplinary education, there is valuable guidance to build and support these programs. In our view, it helps to begin programs in areas of the university that are already inherently interdisciplinary, such as in public health and environmental science. We also recommend that these individual efforts be better connected internationally to become strong communities of practice.

References

Abrams, D. B. (2006). Applying transdisciplinary research strategies to understanding and eliminating health disparities. *Health Education and Behavior, 33*(4), 515–531.

Arnold, L. D., Kuhlmann, A. S., Hipp, J. A., & Budd, E. (2013). Competences in transdisciplinary public health. In D. Haire-Joshu & T. D. McBride (Eds.), *Transdisciplinary public health: Research, education and practice*. San Francisco: Jossey-Bass.

Association of Schools of Public Health. (2006). *Core competency development project, version 2.3*. Washington DC: Association of Schools of Public Health.

Association of Schools of Public Health Education Committee Doctor of Public Health (DrPH). (2010). *Core competency model, Version 1.3*. Washington, DC: Association of Schools of Public Health. http://www.asph.org/publication/DrPH_Core_Competency_Model/index.html. Accessed April 2014.

Balas, E. A., & Boren, S. A. (2000). Managing clinical knowledge for health care improvement. In J. H. van Bemmel & A. T. McCray (Eds.), *IMIA Yearbook of Medical Informatics* (pp. 65–70). Stuttgart: Schattauer.

Bammer, G. (2005). Integration and implementation sciences: Building a new specialization. *Ecology and Society, 10*(2), Article 6. http://www.ecologyandsociety.org/vol10/iss2/art6/. Accessed Oct 2014.

Bammer, G. (2013). *Disciplining interdisciplinarity: Integration and implementation sciences for researching complex real-world problems*. Canberra: Australian National University Press. http://epress.anu.edu.au/titles/disciplining-interdisciplinarity/pdf-download. Accessed Oct 2014.

Becker, E., & Jahn, T. (Eds.). (2006). *Soziale Ökologie—Grundzüge einer Wissenschaft von den gesellschaftlichen Naturverhältnissen*. Frankfurt a. M.: Campus.

Bergmann, M., Brohmann, B., Hoffmann, E., Loibl, M. C., Rehaag, R., Schramm, E., & Voß, J. -P. (2005). Quality Criteria for transdisciplinary research. A Guide for the formative evaluation of research projects. In *ISOE Studientexte* 13, 76. Frankfurt am Main: Institute for Social-Ecological Research (ISOE).

Bergmann, M., Jahn, T., Knobloch, T., Krohn, W., Pohl, C., & Schramm, E. (2012). *Methods for transdisciplinary research: A primer for practice*. Frankfurt a. M.: Campus.

Best, A., Hiatt, R. A., & Norman, C. (2006). *The language and logic of research transfer: Finding common ground* [Report]. Working Group on Translational Research and Knowledge Integration, National Cancer Institute of Canada, Toronto, Canada.

Boyer, E. L. (1990). *Scholarship reconsidered: Priorities of the professoriate.* Princeton: Carnegie Foundation for the Advancement of Teaching.

Bronfenbrenner, U. (1979). *The ecology of human development: Experiments by nature and design.* Cambridge: Harvard University Press.

Brown, V. A., Harris, J. A., & Russell, J. Y. (2010). *Tackling wicked problems through the transdisciplinary imagination.* London: Earthscan.

Buchanan, R. (1992). Wicked problems in design thinking. *Design Issues, 8,* 5–21.

Calhoun, J. G., McElligott, J. E., Weist, E. M., & Raczynski, J. M. (2012). Core competencies for doctoral education in public health. *Am J Public Health, 102*(1), 22–29.

Committee on Facilitating Interdisciplinary Research. National Academy of Sciences, National Academy of Engineering, National Institute of Medicine. (2004). *Facilitating interdisciplinary research.* Washington: National Academies Press.

Cook, T. (1985). Postpositivist critical multiplism. In R. Shotland & M. Mark (Eds.), *Social science and social policy* (pp. 25–62). Beverly Hills: Sage.

Council on Education for Public Health. (2011). *Accreditation criteria for schools of public health.* Updated June 2011. http://www.ceph.org/pg_accreditation_criteria.htm. Accessed Oct 2014.

Deleuze, G., & Guattari, F. (1980). *A thousand plateaus* (trans: Brian Massumi). London and New York: Continuum, 2004. Vol. 2 of *Capitalism and Schizophrenia.* 2 vols. 1972–1980 (trans: *Mille Plateaux*). Paris: Les Editions de Minuit.

Derry, S., & Fischer, G. (2005, April). *Toward a model and theory for transdisciplinary graduate education.* Paper presented at the meeting of the American Educational Research Association (AERA), *Symposium on Sociotechnical Design for Lifelong Learning: A Crucial Role for Graduate Education,* Montréal, Canada. http://l3d.cs.colorado.edu/ gerhard/papers/aera-montreal.pdf. Accessed 19 March 2007.

Dilthey, W. (1988). *Introduction to the human sciences.* Detroit: Wayne State University Press.

Froderman, R., Klein, J. T., & Mitcham, C. (Eds.). (2010). *The Oxford handbook of interdisciplinarity.* New York: Oxford University Press.

Gehlert, S., & Browne, B. (2013). Transdisciplinary training and education. In D. Haire-Joshu & T. D. McBride (Eds.), *Transdisciplinary public health: Research, education and practice.* San Francisco: Jossey-Bass.

Gibbs, P. (2014). Towards a transdisciplinary methodology for professional practice featuring abductive reasoning. In P. Gibbs (Ed.) (2014). *A transdisciplinarity study of higher education and professional identity.* New York: Springer.

Green, L. W., & Potvin, R. L. (1996). Ecological foundations of health promotion. *American Journal of Health Promotion, 10*(4), 270–281.

Green, L. W., & Glasgow, R. E. (2006). Evaluating the relevance, generalization, and applicability of research: Issues in external validation and translation methodology. *Evaluation and the Health Professions, 29*(1), 126–153.

Gregor, S. (2009). *Building Theory in the Science of the Artificial,* Proceedings of the 4th International Conference on design science research in information systems and technology. New York: Association for Computing Machinery.

Hirsch Hadorn, G., Hoffmann-Riem, H., Biber-Klemm, S., Grossenbacher-Mansuy, W., Joye, D., Pohl, C., Wiesmann, U., & Zemp, E. (Eds.). (2008). *Handbook of transdisciplinary research.* Dordrecht: Springer.

Hirsch Hadorn, G., Pohl, C., & Bammer, G. (2010). Solving problems through transdisciplinary research. In R. Frodeman, J. Thompson Klein, & C. Mitcham (Eds.), *The Oxford handbook of interdisciplinarity* (pp. 431–452). Oxford: Oxford University Press.

Hoffman-Reim, H., Biber-Klemm, S., Grossenbacher-Mansuy, W., Hadorn, G. H., Joye, D., Pohl, C., et al. (2008). Idea for the handbook. In G. H. Hadorn, H. Hoffman-Reim, S. Biber-Klemm, W. Grossenbacher-Mansuy, G. H. Hadorn, D. Joye, C. Pohl, et al., (Eds.), *Handbook of transdisciplinary research* (pp. 3–18). London: Springer.

Jaeger, J., & Scheringer, M. (1998). Transdisziplinarität. Problemorientierung ohne Methoden-zwang. *GAIA, 7*(1), 10–25.

Jahn, T., Bergmann, M., & Keil, F. (2012). Transdisciplinarity: Between mainstreaming and marginalization. *Ecological Economics, 79,* 1–10.

Jantsch, E. (1970). Interdisciplinary and transdisciplinary university systems approach to education and innovation. *Policy Sciences, 1*(4), 403–428.

Kahn, R. L., & Prager, D. J. (1994, July 11). Interdisciplinary collaborations are a scientific and social imperative. *The Scientist, 17,* 11–12.

King, L., Hawe, P., & Wise, M. (1998). Making dissemination a two-way process. *Health Promotion International, 13*(3), 237–244.

Kiteme, B. P., & Wiesmann, U. (2008). Sustainable river basin management in Kenya: Balancing needs and requirements. In G. H. Hadorn, H. Hoffman-Reim, S. Biber-Klemm, W. Grossenbacher-Mansuy, D. Joye, C. Pohl, U. Wiesmann, & E. Zemp (Eds.), *Handbook of transdisciplinary research* (pp. 63–78). Dordrecht: Springer.

Klein, J. T. (2010). A taxonomy of interdisciplinary knowledge. In R. Frodeman, J. T. Klein, & C. Mitcham (Eds.), *The Oxford handbook of interdisciplinarity* (pp. 15–30). Oxford: Oxford University Press.

Klein, J. T., Grossenbacher-Mansuy, W., Häberli, R., Bill, A., Scholz, R. W., & Welti, M. (Eds.). (2001). *Transdisciplinarity: Joint problem solving among science, technology, and society.* Basel: Birkhäuser.

Kuhn, T. S. (1962). *The Structure of scientific revolutions* (1st ed.). Chicago: University of Chicago Press.

Lubchenco, J. (1998). Entering the century of the environment: A new social contract for science. *Science, 279*(5350), 491–497.

Lüdeke, M. K. B., Petschel-Held, G., & Schellnhuber, H. -J. (2004). Syndromes of global change: The first panoramic view. *GAIA, 13*(1), 42–49.

Markus, M. L., Majchrzak, A. & Gasser, L. (2002). A design theory for systems that support emergent knowledge processes. *Manag Inf Syst Q, 26,* 179–212.

May, B. J. (1979). Competency based education: General concepts. *Journal of Allied Health, 8*(3), 166–171.

McGregor, S. L. (2014). Nicolescuian transdisciplinary as an educative process In P. Gibbs (Ed.) (2014), *A transdisciplinarity study of higher education and professional identity.* New York: Springer.

Minkler, M., & Wallerstein, N. (Eds.). (2008). *Community based participatory research for health: From process to outcomes.* San Francisco: Jossey-Bass.

Mittelstraß, J. (1993). Unity and transdisciplinarity. *Interdisciplinary Science Reviews, 18*(2), 153–157.

Nash, J. M., Collins, B. N., Loughlin, S. E., Solbrig, M., Harvey, R., Krishnan-Sarin, S., et al. (2003). Training the transdisciplinary scientist: A general framework applied to tobacco behavior. *Nicotine and Tobacco Research, 5*(Suppl. 1), S41–S53.

Neuhauser, L. (2013). Integration and Implementation Sciences: How it relates to scientific thinking and public health strategies. In G. Bammer (Ed.). *Disciplining inter-disciplinarity: Integration and Implementation Sciences for researching complex real-world problems* (pp. 461–472). Canberra Australia: Australian National University Press. http://epress.anu.edu.au/titles/disciplining-interdisciplinarity/pdf-download. Accessed Oct 2014.

Neuhauser, L., Richardson, D., Mackenzie, S., & Minkler, M. (2007). Advancing transdisciplinary and translational research practice: Issues and models of doctoral education in public health. *Journal of Research Practice, 3*(2), Article M19. http://jrp.icaap.org/index.php/jrp/article/view/103/97. Accessed Oct 2014.

Neuhauser, L., Kreps, G. L., & Syme, S. L. (2013a). Community participatory design of health communication programs: Methods and case examples from Australia, China, Switzerland and the United States. In D. K. Kim, A. Singhal, & G. L. Kreps (Eds.), *Global health communications strategies in the 21st century: Design, implementation and evaluation*. New York: Peter Lang.

Neuhauser, L., Kreps, G. L., Morrison, K., Athanasoulis, M., Kirienko, N., & Van Brunt, D. (2013b). Using design science and artificial intelligence to improve health communication: ChronologyMD case example. *Patient Education and Counseling, 92*(2), 211–217. Available online 29 May 2013.

Nicolescu, B. (2002). *Manifesto of transdisciplinarity*. Albany: State University of New York Press

Nicolescu, B. (2010). Methodology of transdisciplinarity—levels of reality, logic of the included middle and complexity. *Transdisciplinary Journal of Engineering & Science, 1*(1), 19–38.

Nicolescu, B. (2004). Gurdjieff's philosophy of nature. In J. Needleman & G. Baker (Eds.), *Gurdjieff* (pp. 37–69). New York: The Continuum International Publishing Group.

Pohl, C. (2014). From complexity to solvability: The praxeology of transdisciplinary research. In P. Tapio & K. Huutoniemi (Eds.), *Transdisciplinary sustainability studies: A heuristic Approach*. London: Routledge.

Pohl, C., & Hadorn, G. H. (2007). *Principles for designing transdisciplinary research* (trans: A. B. Zimmerman). Munich: OEKOM.

Rittel, H. W. J., & Webber, M. M. (1973). Dilemmas in a general theory of planning. *Policy Sciences, 4*(2), 155–169.

Rosenfield, P. L. (1992). The potential of transdisciplinary research for sustaining and extending linkages between the health and social sciences. *Social Science and Medicine, 35*(11), 1343–1357.

Rubio, D. M., Schoenbaum, E. E., Lee, L. S., Schteingart, D. E., Marantz, P. R., Anderson, K. E., Platt, L. D., Baez, A., & Esposito, K. (2010). Defining translational research: Implications for training. *Academic Medicine: Journal of the Association of American Medical Colleges, 85*(3), 470–475.

Samuels & Associates. (2005). *University of California, Berkeley DrPH program evaluation report*. Oakland: Samuels & Associates.

Schellnhuber, H. J. (1999). "Earth system"analysis and the second Copernican Revolution. *Nature, 402*(Suppl. 2), C19–C23.

Simon, H. (1996). *The Sciences of the Artificial, 3 Ed.* Cambridge: MIT Press.

Stokols, D. (2000). Social ecology and behavioral medicine: Implications for training, practice, and policy. *Behavioral Medicine, 26,* 129–138.

Stokols, D. (2006). Toward a science of transdisciplinary research. *American Journal of Community Psychology, 38,* 63–77.

Stokols, D., Harvey, R., Gress, J., Fuqua, J., & Phillips, K. (2005). In vivo studies of transdisciplinary scientific collaboration: Lessons learned and implications for active living research. *American Journal of Preventive Medicine, 28*(2), 202–213.

Stokols, D., Hall, K. L., & Vogel, A. L. (2013). Transdisciplinary public health: definitions, core characteristics and strategies for success. In D. Haire-Joshu & T. D. McBride. (Eds.), *Transdisciplinary public health: research, education and practice*. San Francisco: Jossey-Bass.

Sussman, S., Valente, T. W., Rohrbach, L. A., Skara, S., & Pentz, M. A. (2006). Translation in the health professions: Converting science into action. *Evaluation and the Health Professions, 29*(1), 7–32.

Szostak, R. (2007). How and why to teach interdisciplinary research practice. *Journal of Research Practice, 3*(2), Article M17. http://jrp.icaap.org/index.php/jrp/article/view/92/89. Accessed Oct 2014.

Syme, S. L. (2005). The social determinants of disease: Some roots of the movement. *Epidemiologic Perspectives and Innovations, 2,* 2–23.

Tapio, P., & Huutoniemi, K. (Eds.). (2014). *Transdisciplinary sustainability studies: A heuristic approach*. London: Routledge.

Wickson, F., Carew, A. L., & Russell, A. W. (2006). Transdisciplinary research: Characteristics, quandaries and quality. *Futures, 38*(9), 1046–1059.

Wiesmann, U., Hurni, H., Ott, C., & Zingerli, C. (2011). Combining the concepts of transdisciplinarity and partnership in research for sustainable development. In W. Urs & H. Hurni (Eds.), *Perspectives of the Swiss National Centre of Competence in Research (NCCR) North-South* (Vol. 6, pp. 43–70). Bern: University of Bern.

Woolf, S. H. (2008). The meaning of translational research and why it matters. *JAMA, 299*(2), 211–213.

Youngblood, D. (2007). Multidisciplinary, interdisciplinary, and bridging disciplines: A matter of process. *Journal of Research Practice, 3*(2), Article M18. http://jrp.icaap.org/index.php/jrp/article/view/104/101. Accessed May 2014.

Linda Neuhauser DrPH, MPH   is Clinical Professor of Community Health and Human Development at the University of California, Berkeley School of Public Health. Her research, teaching and practice are focused on using transdisciplinary processes co-create research, interventions and policies to improve health. She is especially interested in adapting design methods from engineering, architecture and computer science to improve large-scale health initiatives. She also heads the UC Berkeley Health Research for Action center http://www.healthresearchforaction.org/ that works with diverse groups to co-design, implement and evaluate health programs in the US and globally. She helped transform the Doctor of Public Health program at the UC Berkeley School of Public into a transdisciplinary program that trains students to address important health problems by integrating knowledge from many disciplines and applying it in many societal contexts. She participates in many inter- and transdisciplinary collaboratives.

Christian Pohl   with a PhD in environmental sciences, is co-director of the transdisciplinarity-net (www.transdisciplinarity.ch) of the Swiss Academies of Arts and Sciences and core member of the Transdisciplinarity Lab of the Department of Environmental Systems Science at ETH Zurich (www.tdlab.usys.ethz.ch). He studied environmental sciences, followed by a doctoral thesis on uncertainty in environmental assessments. As a post-doc he moved to the field of science studies and analysed inter- and transdisciplinary research. Over the last decade Christian Pohl has substantially contributed to the advancement of theory and practice of transdisciplinary research, specifically in the field of sustainable development (cf. Principles for Designing Transdisciplinary Research, Handbook of Transdisciplinary Research, Methods for Transdisciplinary Research). Currently he is engaged in developing a compilation of methods for coproducing knowledge and in chairing the Sustainable Development at Universities Programme (2013–2016).

Educational Knowledge in Professional Practice: A transdisciplinary approach

Carol Costley

Introduction

This chapter begins to make the case that transdisciplinarity occurs in programmes of study in universities as well as in the design of research projects. It sets out this proposition by examining educational knowledge used in continuing professional development (CPD) modules and programmes that have proved successful for many people involved in learning in and through professional practice. The case is specifically made through an example of the curriculum area of work-based and professional studies (WBPS), which has been a way of undertaking CPD at all university levels for over 20 years and is particularly prevalent in the UK. Some universities have constructed WBPS programmes as a field of study in its own right.

First, the background of the WBPS field of study is provided so that its epistemological roots can demonstrate that the educational knowledge used in the construction of the field were determined upon wide and generic criteria. The curricula, pedagogical approaches and assessment processes are all based upon knowledge that can be understood as cutting across and going beyond disciplines. WBPS concerns the unity and connectivity of knowledge as well as an approach to self development and to creativity and problem solving in specific contexts. An objective of the WBPS field is to meet the needs of people studying outside the university in places of work, communities and voluntary activities. Such all-embracing knowledge construction necessarily requires new methodological approaches to research projects and to teaching and learning. The principle of the work-placement is not followed here, where disciplinary knowledge is achieved 'by' undertaking work and thus demonstrating that disciplinary learning outcomes have been met. Instead, learning outcomes for WBPS are generic in character and have wider possibilities that are not constrained by a discipline. WBPS is an area that can be thought of as a mode

C. Costley (✉)
Middlesex University, London, UK
e-mail: c.costley@mdx.ac.uk

© Springer International Publishing Switzerland 2015
P. Gibbs (ed.), *Transdisciplinary Professional Learning and Practice,*
DOI 10.1007/978-3-319-11590-0_9

of study but in the case that is made below, it has been constructed as a field of educational knowledge that is mainly transdisciplinary (TD).

Background to Work-Based and Professional Studies in the UK

Work Based Learning Studies (WBL) is a field of study prevalent in the UK that approaches knowledge as TD. It has a TD approach and understanding of knowledge in its curriculum, pedagogy and assessments. Some higher education institutions (HEI) have whole programmes based on this approach whilst others have modules and other elements of programmes that are TD. Several universities across the UK were awarded a grant in the early 1990s, from the then Department for Employment, for the 'Curriculum in the workplace' Project. It was the work of this project, and the development of the Universities Association for Continuing Education network, that launched WBL in higher education in the UK.

At Middlesex University, for example, the development of university accreditation services in 1991, and the influence of the Learning from Experience Trust, underpinned the development of the WBL curriculum, which, at first, became part of the independent learning studies curriculum area (Osborne et al. 1998). WBL started in 1992 with the intention of providing a curriculum model for people at work and to form partnerships with organisations. It started by using the existing 'Independent Learning Studies' but included new WBL modules that were created as part of a review of independent learning. At the same time, the University of Portsmouth had also received a grant, after which it established a Centre for WBL. WBL was soon instituted by many other UK universities.

Independent study can be thought of as a process, a method and a philosophy of education (Forster 1972 cited in Candy 1991). It has its pedagogical roots in Adult Learning (Freire 1972; Knowles 1990; Mezirow 1991). The tradition of Adult Learning has also had a significant influence on the development of WBL. Experiential learning, independent studies and most work roles all involve abilities that cut across the wider curriculum in higher education. In 1995, WBL Studies at Middlesex was validated as a field of study in its own right. Despite this happening just after the *first World Congress of Transdisciplinarity* (1994) where the charter of transdisciplinarity was adopted a TD approach to curriculum was not well known or well understood.

The University of Portsmouth had taken a similar approach but, like other universities such as Humberside and Lincoln, had a central unit for WBL that connected to other subject areas across the university where subject disciplines wanted elements of WBL to be part of their awards. They also developed stand-alone awards in WBL as did the Universities of Teesside and Chester.

Many of the universities that had taken part in the 1992 funded project developed an approach to knowledge in the field that drew upon and developed modules used by independent study—especially learning agreements and negotiated shell modules— and combined them with *Accreditation of Prior and Experiential Learning* (APEL) and WBL research modules.

The WBL movement was also greatly informed by the various approaches to APEL especially as it was informed by the *Learning from Experience Trust* and by the Capability movement (HEA Capability journal archive) which was popularised through the *Royal Society for Arts' Education for Capability* project. There was a growing need for professionals to move beyond discipline-specific expertise and engage with, what Schön (1987, p. 3) terms, the "swampy lowland" of practice.

With the influences of Independent Learning, Adult Learning, APEL and the Capability movement, the pioneers of WBL then also gained experience of working with organisations. They soon developed partnership models (Garnett 2001; Garnett et al. 2001), which included accrediting company courses, developing learning agreements with organisations in every professional area and further development of work-based methodologies and work-based projects. The work of the WBL movement led to further publications in more organisational learning and business areas as well as an 'education' focus. The WBL network continues to straddle these two more general areas in approaches to curriculum and to research. Universities such as Glasgow Caledonian, Middlesex and Teesside have used the same TD approach to WBL whilst other colleagues across the UK, who run programmes of WBL, blend subject discipline areas with the more TD approaches of WBL in a variety of different ways.

The Bachelors and Master in WBL that was developed in many universities across the UK was the basis for the development of the Doctorate in Professional Studies in 1997, a highly successful TD doctorate now practiced by universities in the UK. A TD approach to educational knowledge in work-based and professional studies (WBPS) is therefore practiced at all h.e. levels from Foundation to Doctorate.

However, WBPS did not emerge from a subject discipline; rather, from the outset, it did use methodologies drawn from the Social Sciences and Humanities to guide practitioners in their approach to their research projects. Methodologies have since broadened with a wide range of practitioner–researcher enquiry approaches.

The methodologies used by academics engaged with the learning and teaching in Professional Studies, in relation to their own research, can vary according to the nature of the research (e.g. developing the curriculum, pedagogical research, evaluative research). For these academics who engage mainly in pedagogical research, researching the underlying philosophies and theories supporting the curriculum area and policy-related research, their research is not necessarily TD. Unlike subject disciplines, where the academics are undertaking research interests that are in line with their research students, the WBPS curriculum area does not have such an affiliation.

The tendency for WBPS to follow a TD curriculum has much in common with the international TD research movement. However, WBL has developed a pedagogical approach in these instances rather than a research approach. Examples of where WBPS is defined and discussed as TD include those of Boud (2001); Gibbs and Costley (2006); Costley and Armsby (2007a); Gibbs and Garnett (2007).

WBPS does not stem, from the need to enable large research projects, such as those commissioned by the Organization for Economic Cooperation and Development (OECD). It stems, instead, from developing a curriculum model for people in work contexts that has its roots in Independent Studies, Adult Education, and experiential learning in the early 1990s. Most models of WBPS in higher education entail a pedagogical approach to both curriculum and research, are embedded in practice, and have been designed by educationalists whose main focus has been learning and teaching in h.e.

Having described above the development of educational knowledge in Work Based Learning and Professional Studies, the chapter now moves to defining the content and its relation to TD through Bernstien's message systems as articulated below.

Educational knowledge can be understood through three 'message' systems:

- Curriculum (classification)—Some knowledge is regarded as appropriate, some knowledge is not.
- Pedagogy (framing)—*how* this selection of knowledge is taught
- Assessment—dependent on, or is constrained by, curriculum and pedagogy.

Bernstein (1971)

Bernstein's (1971) message systems about social production and reproduction of knowledge demonstrate how social inequalities in relation to educational knowledge can be passed on. As a validated field of study in many universities, WBPS arose from and were constructed as TD from the outset and the TD approach has meant that knowledge that may not have previously been recognised as worthwhile, higher level knowledge has now been legitimised in the h.e. sector (Armsby et al. 2006). The three message systems articulated below demonstrate how structuring educational knowledge as TD can enable a wider engagement of practitioners in h.e. The educational knowledge that is embraced may have remained hidden but these structures require practitioners to refine a complex area of practice through contemporaneous and retrospective reflection, synthesis and insight that is the result of their experience in practice. Reflection in and action on experience is followed by the composition of an artefact and an exegesis that can bring a powerful and constructive legitimacy to practice contexts.

Work-Based and Professional Studies

Curriculum

WBPS curricular draws upon the knowledge that is appropriate for 'work' (paid and unpaid) in its many contexts and for individuals and groups with their various positionalities. Some tutors of WBPS may not name the way WBPS is classified as TD. For example knowledge claims are sometimes described as generic, inter or multidisciplinary. It is also sometimes the case that the generic or TD elements sit alongside a more subject discipline element of the programmes. For a specific breakdown of curriculum content in WBL, see Helyer (2010).

Some common elements of the WBPS curricula are: accreditation of prior learning, planning and learning contracts and agreements, and practitioner-led enquiry projects.

Accreditation of Prior and Experiential Learning (APEL) and Reflection/Reflexivity

APEL provides opportunities for individuals to progress to h.e. programmes and for the academic credit they have achieved to count towards university qualifications. APEL is most often used to gain specific credit that can be bench-marked against existing university modules; however, general credit can be awarded for almost any range of high level abilities. The process of making a claim for credit usually involves facilitation, discussion and reflection that has a particular purpose when reflecting on the learning achieved from the endeavours involved in gaining general credit. The claim will require evidence, cross referencing, formative review, possible interview and assessment requirements of the specific university with the Qualifications Credit Framework (QCF). Academic credit can be awarded at any university level and these go from Foundation to Doctorate level (levels 3–8).

Examples of areas of general credit that can be claimed are for key or core skills such as 'communication', 'leadership' and 'team-working'. However claims can be made in almost any area where there is learning from significant human endeavour. Examples of the areas of learning that can be claimed are 'Traffic Accident Investigation', 'Community Music', 'Managing Events', 'Bookkeeping', 'Managing Data' and 'Project Planning' but the possibilities are countless because these involve capabilities derived from a variety of professional practices.

General credit enables learners to have all of their learning recognized, even the abilities that do not form an exact match to existing university modules. Learners express their learning in 'areas' rather than modules and the areas are formulations of their own choosing that may not necessarily conform to modules or a specific discipline. These areas of learning can then be used towards self-directed TD programmes of study.

Reflection on learning and a reflexivity in engaging with experience are a key element of WBPS programmes of study and have been acknowledged as fundamental to learning and teaching in the area of professional education if undertaken with due rigour, thoughtfulness and criticality (Bradbury et al. 2010).

Planning and Learning Contract/Agreements

Learning contract or agreements bring ideas and areas of knowledge together related to individuals and groups of individuals in specific contexts. They can be defined as a

> ... means of reconciling the 'imposed' requirements from institutions and society with the learners' need to be self-directing. It enables them to blend these requirements in with their own personal goals and objectives, to choose ways of achieving them and the measure of their own progress toward achieving them. (Knowles 1975, p. 130)

Agreements are an important aspect for learners to engage in an independent decision about their learning and they move responsibility for learning from the tutor to student. Learners build their own programmes in a three-way learning agreement among university, learner and employer or professional field. The bringing together of the parts of the learning that are considered relevant to study engages learners in a self-developmental exercise where a consideration of the *whole of their learning* needs to be taken into consideration. It does not need to involve a disciplinary focus.

Practitioner-Led Enquiry Projects

The practitioner-led research and development projects are the key element of a Work-based and Professional Studies award and are based upon interventions underpinned by research in particular work contexts. The projects chime to some extent with Nicolaou's (ibid) view of TD as methodology in so far as the learners are engaged in solving highly contextualised problems and seek to do this using appropriate practice-oriented methodological approaches.

There is a connection between methodology and the generation of knowledge within academic fields of practice. Methodologies that have been constructed for the purposes of distinct academic disciplines, for knowledge that is codified within the academy, do not necessarily hold effective and appropriate approaches to generate and codify a practice-oriented production of knowledge. Even methodologies that have a local, generalised purpose, approached with rigour and a consideration for values, design of research and a considered and worthwhile outcome, can be problematic, e.g., certain forms of participatory action research with a "mechanical sequence of steps" (Kemmis and Wilkinson 1998, pp. 21–24).

Different methodologies can be employed that avoid the problems of monological research structures that disciplines often impose (Kincheloe 2004) and can focus on knowledge that is grounded in experience and understanding of work practices and values. In this sense, a distinction can be made between methodologies primarily directed towards the production of academic fields themselves and methodologies that are more aligned for practice in professional and community fields of activity. For example, there is a strong sense that practitioner-researchers have much in common with the notion of Levi-Strausse's bricoleur, i.e., the practitioner engaging with what is ready at hand (1966, pp. 16–22). The research is always decentred; the starting point can be, as Berry (2004, p. 108) states, "a point of entry text" that provides the possibility for a number of alternative points of entry. Approaching practitioner-led projects from a variety of perspectives in this way opens up opportunities for different perspectives and appropriate change to practice that is purposeful and creative. Other methodological approaches are beginning to develop and there are related discussions concerning insider research and ethical considerations in practitioner-led research projects (Costley et al. 2010; Costley and Armsby 2007a; Gray 2009).

Pedagogy

The second component of Bernstein's (1971) message systems is pedagogy. Work-based learners do not usually learn in classrooms; indeed, they understand and already have some expertise of practice settings where their tutors often do not have familiarity. Learning and teaching can therefore be more of a facilitative experience, dispersing some of the more traditional power dynamics between teachers and learners. The adviser role is usually a broad one that does not require particular disciplinary knowledge. Candidates who undertake WBPS modules and programmes of study are usually supported by an adviser, have access to library and other resources, often a virtual learning environment, and are provided with guidance materials.

The role of adviser involves good facilitation skills, knowledge that is grounded in experience, an understanding of work practices and values, and a pedagogic approach that is conducive to dealing with informal learning. The abilities of advisers involve a knowledge of work in context, learning consultancy skills, reflexivity and reviewing skills (Boud and Costley 2006). Moreover the adviser takes on the role of the critical teacher:

> the authority of the critical teacher is dialectical: as teachers relinquish the authority of truth providers, they assume the mature authority of facilitators of student inquiry and problem posing. In relation to such teacher authority, students gain their freedom they gain the ability to become self-directed human beings capable of producing their own knowledge. (Kincheloe 2008, p. 17)

Their role requires them to support learners in localizing and specializing their own learning as the subject of study through reflection on experience, conceptualising and describing that learning. They do this in relation to wider contexts through discursive negotiation and engagement with, for example, communities of practice, employers, colleagues, tutors and other learners. Such educational contexts require learners to be self-directed and to resolve their own objectives and progression opportunities. Also, Advisers need knowledge of reflective practice, knowledge of programme planning, APEL and work-based projects. Advisers work alongside Candidates, rather than acting as teacher or instructor, to help them develop themselves, resulting in the Candidate's approaching their work critically and reflexively.

Assessment

The third component of Bernstein's (1971) message systems is assessment. A subject discipline can require students to gain the knowledge of that discipline through workplace experience e.g. on work placements and in sandwich years. In these cases, students would still be assessed on the same body of disciplinary knowledge but their means of attaining that knowledge have been work-based. Subject discipline areas often also require students to gain separately assessed key skills that pertain to being capable in a practice setting. The key skill or graduate skills are likely to be applicable to any subject area but they are theoretically isolated from practice and from the subject discipline by being judged on their own. This is not the case in WBPS as a field. The curriculum itself is practice-led and the assessments are linked to a broad assessment structure that is based upon a whole programme of study making connections that are relevant, useful and creative. Boud's (2001) chapter, in the now classic book on WBL, firmly made the link between WBL as an HE development and cited transdisciplinarity particularly in relation to its assessment. Two key areas of assessment that can be clearly defined as TD are Assessments of APEL claims for general or non-specific credit and the assessment of work-based projects.

Assessments of APEL claims for academic credit aim to evaluate and quantify experiential learning in terms of credit points at a particular level; there are reflective accounts, evidence is required, and the accreditation assessment practice is normally subject to internal moderation and external scrutiny.

General credit does not require bench-marking against learning outcomes of specific modules or other units of learning prescribed by educational institutions. Instead the assessor gauges the learning that has been achieved towards generic level criteria that involves a keen understanding of education levels and quantification of credits (Costley 2014). Experienced advisers judge the level of learning in relation to QCF. Where a particular specialisation or subject discipline expertise cuts across aspects of the area that are claimed, an assessor may seek expert advice, often available amongst other university staff.

Assessing work-based projects requires knowledge of research and development approaches, how to review work-based literature, and understanding of the workplace as a source of knowledge generation (Costley and Armsby 2007a).

Examples of generic assessment criteria used for Work-based and Professional Studies:
- Identification of and appropriate use of sources of knowledge and evidence
- Selection and justification of approaches
- Ethical understanding
- Analysis and synthesis of information and ideas
- Self appraisal and reflection on practice
- Action planning leading to effective and appropriate action
- Evaluation of information and ideas
- Application of learning
- Effective use of resources
- Effective communication
- Working and learning autonomously and with others

The above criteria are expressed differently at different h.e. levels and relate well to the UK quality assurance agency's overarching criteria. The WBPS criteria include subject discipline knowledge only in the way it may be applied within the context of the work and learning being undertaken.

The approach to knowledge in the curriculum and pedagogy is TD in nature as the knowledge claims presented by learners, and the knowledge construction, generation and use of work-based projects, are based upon a comprehensive understanding of an individual or group experience. Their work (or endeavour) takes account of aspects of learning that go beyond the discipline but can include disciplinary knowledge. Assessment approaches are designed to suit the experiential nature of this kind of learning based on the interâŁłrelationship and interâŁłdependency among understanding learning, critical reflection and the identification and development of capability within a WBL context (Brodie and Irving 2007).

Discussion

The two main approaches to transdisciplinarity, as described by McGregor and Volckmann (2011), each have resonance for WBL. One approach has an "exclusive concentration on joint solving of problems pertaining to the science-technology-society triad", and emphasizes societal issues and the notion that practice situations inform the science community (Gibbons et al. 1994; Nowotny et al. 2001, 2003). The other approach views TD as a methodology in its own right (Nicolescu 2002, 2010), with the emphasis on methodology and what the WBL community have interpreted as approaches to practitioner-led research projects. Both of these TD approaches engage in large scale research projects in which they articulate problem solving in the areas of climate change, unsustainability, poverty and these problems have their cause in social–political–technological developments; therefore, a TD research that brings science, politics and technology together can help address the problems. In WBPS, the curriculum was built around the principles of creative interventions, problem solving and self-development through practitioner research and development for 'real world' issues. WBPS and has a perspective that views knowledge from outside of the university rather than through a disciplinary lens. WBPS also engages in practice-based project work and is involved in developing appropriate methodological approaches.

Having constructed the approach to knowledge in WBPS according to Bernstein's (1971) three message systems, it is reasonable to say that WBPS can be and is usually TD in all of its systems. The curriculum starts with APEL claims for general credit, then constructs a learning plan that draws on reflection upon an individual's wholistic view of current learning and the potential practitioner-research in which he or she will engage. The practitioner-research (or enquiry) into their practice is then based upon a project, usually in a 'real world', 'real time' situation and is undertaken by employing a TD approach. The pedagogical approach is more facilitative, drawing alongside the learner and helping the learner to develop a view of knowledge that is relevant to the individual's experience, context and educational purpose. Assessment draws on generic criteria that relate to work-based learning outcomes.

The flexibility in ways of approaching WBL programmes means that a range of models of WBL can be offered. WBL therefore comes in different forms and is

> frequently unplanned, informal, retrospective and serendipitous, though it may also be planned and organised by the individual learner, the employer, or a third party such as an educational institution, professional or trade body....... a substantial proportion.... is concerned with higher-level skills and knowledge and with the development and use of broad, high-level capability (Lester and Costley 2010)

WBPS is not unproblematic especially as it involves the positionality and, related to this, identities of the learners as they usually have specific roles and circumstances relating to their professional situation. To some extent the problematic areas arise from the way structures of power, position learners and learner's position themselves within narratives concerned with the production of knowledge used to develop practices outside the higher education academy. The intertwining of government policy initiatives, universities and workplaces in innovation adds to the complexity of these power relations. Knowledge and experience of policy makers can contrast with the actions taken by practitioner-researchers based on knowledge and experience of localised practices.

Practitioner-research in work situations, and the relations of power in the production, distribution and consumption of practice-based knowledge, provides the basis for work based programmes of study including Professional Doctorates. These programmes provide a locus for examining workplace discourses and discourses in h.e. mediating work-based programmes and the development of WBPS curricula, pedagogies and assessment. WBPS is based in practice contexts but can rarely be interpreted as an applied version of existing subjects. There may be no pre-existing science to apply because transdisciplinarity is more socially accountable and reflexive involving fields of understanding rather than disciplines (Boud 2001).

The WBPS field of study involves a shift in the way knowledge production is understood so that new forms of knowledge have evolved out of a disciplinary matrix and continue to exist alongside the disciplines. The knowledge production in this field is characterised as TD with its distribution in social settings outside of the h.e. environment (Gibbons et al. 1994). WBPS has formulated ways in which h.e. can recognise, accredit, develop and research knowledge production in sites that are not controlled by the academy and do not have specific purposes that are codified by the academy. For Nowotny et al. (2001, p. 15) "the growth of knowledge industries has not only led to the proliferation of the sites of knowledge production but also has tended to erode the traditional demarcation between knowledge and institutions". There is a sense in which WBPS has attempted to bring knowledge production outside of the academy into a new formularisation within the academy that could bring about new classifications and framings that may engender new concerns. This is an area that needs further exploration.

The epistemological basis of WBPS tends to be rooted in a form of pragmatism (in the philosophical sense that emphasises the interdependency of knowing and doing) as articulated by Dewey (1938) among others, coupled with a constructivist, and to some extent phenomenological, perspective in which learners are regarded as autonomous selves making sense of their contexts and roles through active participation. This is reflected in Schön's (1987) notion of constructionism, where knowing and doing coexist in a spiral of activity where knowledge informs practice, which generates further knowledge that in turn leads to changes in practice. Such *epistemologies of practice* have connectivity with a TD approach because knowledge is created outside of academia through a variety of practices in highly context-bound situations. The university has developed a role in theorising these practices and constructing innovative curricular, pedagogies and assessments with TD as a guiding principle.

New epistemologies brought about by a TD approach have significant implications for universities, particularly in developing practices and systems to support work practices that may not be generated nor used in an academic context and this is the case for most WBPS students. WBPS became concerned with knowledge in practice, which is constituted in the reflexive processes of the practitioner, the discursive and material processes of the particular context, and the socio-political setting. This knowledge in practice does not fit easily into disciplines but it is increasingly acknowledged as valuable in work settings.

Conclusion

This chapter has only begun to make the case for a TD field of study that involves TD curricular, pedagogy and assessment. It was more straightforward to make the case for practitioner research because there is already a body of knowledge that relates TD to research. The case being made here is more about learning and teaching through a TD lens and there are significant epistemological issues that still need to be addressed in this area. Even so, a set of principles and practices have emerged that can be regarded as marking out a TD approach to WBPS as a distinct field of activity within universities rather than purely as a mode of learning within disciplinary or professional fields. These are backed by a developing area of scholarship that has begun to theorise WBPS as a field of study in its own right, juxtaposed with the view of it as a mode of learning within an academic or professional discipline. Currently programmes of WBPS are still constrained in many universities by assumptions based on disciplinary structures as well as on modes of operating that are geared to the needs of younger full-time students. A TD approach is able to provide maximum benefit for professionals in the working environment. Both the practice and theorisation of WBPS as a TD field needs to continue to develop for the field to mature. In this way confidence can be gained in integrating learning for the immediate context with learning that develops underlying capacity and development for practitioners whilst building productive knowledge within organisations, social groups and communities.

References

Armsby, P., Costley, C., & Garnett, J. (2006). The legitimisation of knowledge: A work based learning perspective of APEL. *International Journal of Lifelong Learning and Education, 25*(4), 369–383.

Bernstein, B. (1971). On the classification and framing of educational knowledge. In M. F. D. Young (Ed.), *Knowledge and control: New directions for the sociology of education* (pp. 47–69). London: Collier MacMillan.

Berry, K. S. (2004). In J. L. Kincheloe & K. S. Berry (Eds.), *Rigor and complexity in educational research* (2nd ed.). Maidenhead: OU.

Boud, D. (2001). Creating a work-based curriculum. In D. Boud & N. Solomon (Eds.), *Work-based learning: A new higher education?* (pp. 44–58). Milton Keynes: The Society for Research into Higher Education and Open University Press. ISBN 9780335205806.

Boud, D., & Costley, C. (2006). From project supervision to advising: new conceptions of the practice. *Innovations in Education and Teaching International, 44*(2), 119–130.

Bradbury, H., Frost, N., Kilminster, S., & Zukas, M. (2010). *Beyond reflective practice: New approaches to professional lifelong learning*. London: Routledge.

Brodie, P., & Irving, K. (2007). Assessment in work-based learning: Investigating a pedagogical approach to enhance student learning. *Assessment and Evaluation in Higher Education, 32*(1), 11–19.

Candy, P. (1991). *Self-direction for lifelong learning: A comprehensive guide to theory and practice*. San Francisco: Jossey Bass.

Costley, C. (2014). General credit: A recognition of lifewide learning. In N. Jackson & J. Willis (Eds.), *Lifewide learning & education in universities and colleges*. E-book. Lifewide Education. http://www.learninglives.co.uk/e-book.html. Accessed 9 Oct 2014.

Costley, C., & Armsby, P. (2007a). *WBL assessed as a field or a mode of study. Assessment and Evaluation in Higher Education, 32*(1), 21–33.

Costley, C., & Armsby, P. (2007b). Research influences on a professional doctorate. *Research in Post-Compulsory Education, 12*(3), 343–357.

Costley, C., & Armsby, P. (2007c). Methodologies for undergraduates doing practitioner investigations at work. *Journal of Workplace Learning, 19*(3), 131–145.

Costley, C., Elliott, G., & Gibbs, P. (2010). *Doing work based research; Approaches to enquiry for insider-researchers*. London: Sage.

Council for Adult and Experiential Learning. http://www.cael.org/. Accessed 9 Oct 2014.

Dewey, J. (1938). *Experience and education*. New York: Collier.

Freire, P. (1972). *Pedagogy of the oppressed*. Harmondsworth: Penguin.

Garnett, J. (2001). WBL and the intellectual capital of universities and employers. *Learning Organization, 8*(2), 78–81. ISSN 0969-6474.

Garnett, J., Comerford, A., & Webb, N. (2001). Working with partners to promote intellectual capital. In D. Boud & N. Soloman (Eds.), *Work-based learning: A new higher education?* Milton Keynes: The Society for Research into Higher Education and Open University Press. ISBN 9780335205806.

Gibbons, M., Limoges, C., Nowotny, H., Schwartzman, S., Scott, P., & Trow, M. (1994). *The new production of knowledge: The dynamics of science and research in contemporary societies*. London: Sage.

Gibbs, P., & Costley, C. (2006). Work-based learning: Discipline, field or discursive space or what? *Research in Post-Compulsory Education, 11*(3), 341–350. ISSN 1359-6748.

Gibbs, P., & Garnett, J. (2007). Work-based learning as a field of study. *Research in Post-Compulsory Education, 12*(3), 409–421. ISSN 1359-6748.

Gray, D. E. (2009). *Doing research in the real world* (2nd ed.). London: Sage.

Helyer, R. (2010). *The WBL student handbook*. Palgrave: Basingstoke.

Kemmis, S., & Wilkinson, M. (1998). Participatory action research and the study of practice. In B. Atweh, S. Kemmis & P. Weeks (Eds.), *Action research in practice: Partnerships for social justice in education* (pp. 21–36). London: Routledge.

Kincheloe, J. L. (2004). Questions of disciplinarity/interdisciplinarity in a changing world. In J. L. Kincheloe & K. S. Berry (Eds.), *Rigor and complexity in educational research* (2nd ed.). Maidenhead: OU.

Kincheloe, J. L. (2008). *Critical pedagogy*. New York: Peter Lang Publishing.

Knowles, M. S. (1975). *Self-directed learning*. New York: Association.

Knowles, M. S. (1990). *The adult learner: A neglected species* (4th ed.). London: Gulf Publishing.

Lester, S., & Costley, C. (2010). Work-based learning at higher education level: Value, practice and critique. *Studies in Higher Education, 35*(5), 561–575.

Levi Strauss, C. (1966). *The savage mind*. Chicago: University of Chicago Press.

McGregor, S. L. T., & Volckmann, R. (2011). *Transversity*. Tuscan: Integral Publishing.

Mezirow, J. (1991). *Transformative dimensions of adult learning*. San Francisco: Jossey Bass.

Nicolescu, B. (2002). *Manifesto of transdisciplinarity* (trans: K. -C. Voss). New York: SUNY.

Nicolescu, B. (2010). Disciplinary boundaries—What are they and how they can be transgressed? Paper prepared for the international symposium on research across boundaries. Luxembourg: University of Luxembourg. http://basarab.nicolescu.perso.sfr.fr/Basarab/Docs_articles/Disciplinary_Boundaries.htm#_ftn1. Accessed 9 Oct 2014.

Nowotny, H., Scott, P., & Gibbons, M. (2001). *Re-thinking science: Knowledge and the public in an age of uncertainty*. Cambridge: Polity Press.

Nowotny, H., Scott, P., & Gibbons, M. (2003). Mode 2 revisited: The new production of knowledge. *Minerva, 41*(3), 179–194.

Osborne, C., Davies, J., & Garnett, J. (1998). Guiding the student to the centre of the stakeholder curriculum: independent and work-based learning at Middlesex University. In J. Stephenson & M. Yorke (Eds.), *Capability and Quality in Higher Education*. London: Kogan Page. http://www.heacademy.ac.uk/assets/documents/resources/heca/heca_cq_10.pdf. Accessed 9 Oct 2014.

Schön, D. (1987). *Educating the reflective practitioner*. San Francisco: Jossey-Bass.

The Higher Education Capability Journal Archive. Capability. *HEA Archive*. http://www.heacademy.ac.uk/HECA. Accessed 9 Oct 2014.

The Learning from Experience Trust. http://letaplapel.blogspot.co.uk/2013/04/welcome-to-learning-from-experience.html. Accessed 28 March.

World Congress on Transdisciplinarity. (1994). Charter adopted at the First World Congress of Trandisciplinarity, Convento da Arrábida, Portugal, November 2–6. http://marianathieriot.wordpress.com/2014/03/12/charter-of-transdisciplinarity/.

Carol Costley is a Professor of Work and Learning and Head of Research and Research Degrees at the Institute for Work Based Learning, Middlesex University. Her research interests are in examining methodologies and epistemologies in work based learning (WBL) in higher education to professional doctorate level. She has written about WBL pedagogy and the development of WBL as a field of study, especially trans-disciplinarity, equity, ethics and practitioner-researcher issues. Her research profile is at http://www.mdx.ac.uk/aboutus/staffdirectory/carol-costley.aspx.

What's Actually New About Transdisciplinarity? How Scholars from Applied Studies Can Benefit from Cross-disciplinary Learning Processes on Transdisciplinarity

Marianne Penker and Andreas Muhar

The complexity of current problems of society, the high level of uncertainty and the high decision stakes involved call for a new form of transdisciplinary knowledge production that integrates society in research processes (Klein et al. 2001; Hirsch Hadorn et al. 2008; Bammer 2005; Gibbons et al. 1994; Funtowicz and Ravetz 1993). Didn't transdisciplinarity actually exist before this discourse, but under different names? Has transdisciplinarity even worked best in traditional applied fields of science that have just not been labelled before as being transdisciplinary, such as agricultural sciences, development studies, medicine or planning? In these fields, cross-disciplinary knowledge integration and participatory research have had a clear instrumental value long before the current transdisciplinary discourse. Therefore, scholars from such disciplines might challenge the innovativeness and newness of transdisciplinary research and question its benefit. This chapter looks into the merits of researching and teaching transdisciplinarity on top of doing it. International and cross-disciplinary exchange can address crucial questions of group size and group compositions, adequate funding conditions and methods that help to deal with powerful interest groups and thus contribute to high quality, legitimate and societal effective outcomes of transdisciplinary research processes. By publishing and teaching on transdisciplinarity, we make specific concepts and approaches accessible to the critique of others. Thus we can benefit from the academic principle of scepticism that is a key for quality management and effective innovation processes.

Introduction

Applied sciences, such as planning studies, food or agricultural sciences, development or sustainability studies are often confronted with wicked problems (Rittel and Webber 1973), i.e. ambiguous problem definitions or unclear, conflicting and

M. Penker (✉) · A. Muhar
University of Natural Resources and Life Sciences, Vienna, Austria
e-mail: marianne.penker@boku.ac.at

© Springer International Publishing Switzerland 2015
P. Gibbs (ed.), *Transdisciplinary Professional Learning and Practice,*
DOI 10.1007/978-3-319-11590-0_10

dynamically changing goals. If facts are uncertain, values disputed and decision stakes high, the task of designing long-term guidelines for governments, public administration, businesses or civil society will be particularly challenging and research results alone generally not sufficient to provide a clear path for future development.

The high level of uncertainty and the high decision stakes involved call for a new form of transdisciplinary knowledge production (Klein et al. 2001; Hirsch Hadorn et al. 2008; Bammer 2005; McDonald et al. 2009; Pohl and Hirsch Hadorn 2007), also referred to as "mode 2 science" (Gibbons et al. 1994; Nowotny et al. 2001) or "post-normal science" (Funtowicz and Ravetz 1993), characterized by knowledge production, knowledge integration and quality management as co-operative tasks of scientists and society. In fact, this form of transdisciplinarity is frequently referred to as the Swiss or Zürich school, which emerged from an International Transdisciplinary Conference held in Zurich in 2000 (see proceedings at Klein et al. 2001). There are two major motivations to opt for transdisciplinary: the hopes that higher quality research will be produced due to a broader knowledge base (McDonald et al. 2009; Hirsch Hadorn et al. 2008; Enengel et al. 2012; Klein et al. 2001) and that one's research will have a greater impact on society (e.g., Häberli et al. 2001; Bammer 2005; Volkery et al. 2008; Garb et al. 2008; Enengel et al. 2012).

Researchers in various fields have developed, applied and refined different methods to tackle the synthesis of heterogeneous, incomplete and uncertain academic knowledge and expertise from politics, administration, civil society or businesses, however, with little cross-fertilization. Bammer (2005) therefore calls for a new specialization or a discipline of "integration and implementation research", i.e. an intensified cross-disciplinary exchange on interactive group processes of knowledge co-production.

While few applied scientists would describe themselves as transdisciplinary researchers, many have taken on an integrative role in cross-disciplinary research addressing real-world problems for decades. They integrate relevant knowledge, theories and methods from diverse disciplines and involve stakeholders, when it comes to implicit local knowledge, to values, preferences and priorities for future development. Therefore on the one hand, applied researchers may considerably contribute to the methodological and theoretical discourse on transdisciplinarity. On the other hand, they might also challenge the innovativeness and newness of "transdisciplinary research" and the relevance of the associated discourse.

Despite the broadly acknowledged need for knowledge integration across disciplines and between science and society (e.g., EC 2006; UNESCO 1999; OECD 1996; UNCED 1992) and a steadily growing number of publications on principles and case-based implementation of transdisciplinary research, there is little systematically elaborated methodological expertise to assist integration researchers (Defila et al. 2006; McDonald et al. 2009). Many applied researchers have experience in transdisciplinary knowledge production but have rarely contributed to the international academic transdisciplinarity debate. Starting from this lack of theoretical and methodological reflection on transdisciplinarity among applied scholars, this paper looks into the challenges and opportunities of learning processes in applied sciences to contribute to transdisciplinary methods and theories.

This essay is based on our personal involvement in various inter- and transdisciplinary projects in the fields of landscape planning and regional development. Furthermore, we are co-chairing a transdisciplinary doctoral school of sustainable development (Muhar et al. 2013) and teach inter- and transdisciplinary methods and approaches for students interested in natural resource management. This transdisciplinary experience has been reflected in numerous discussions with other applied researchers in agricultural and forest science, nature conservation, environmental and sustainability studies at our university and other research organisations, but also with stakeholders in businesses, public administration or civil society. This article provides the opportunity to reflect on transdisciplinary learning processes in applied studies.

The following section looks into the ontology of transdisciplinary research practices in applied sciences and planning. Then we address the challenges and merits of common learning processes on transdisciplinarity and thus provide an epistemological perspective. The paper concludes with some remarks on how reflections on transdisciplinary practices and associated scientific learning processes can be institutionalized.

Transdisciplinary Traditions and Associated Challenges in Applied Sciences and Planning

Funtowicz and Ravetz (1993) distinguish between Applied 'Normal' Science, Expert-Professional Judgment and Post-Normal Science (see Fig. 1). This terminological distinction is very helpful for reflecting practices and epistemologies in science. What can be distinguished clearly on the terminological level is often very blurred when it comes to actual practices. As we have argued above, many applied scholars would not describe their practices as transdisciplinary, although they integrate different epistemologies from various academic disciplines and local expertise.

In the everyday life of applied researchers the distinction between these different forms of science is less relevant than the boundaries between their work and those of professional consultancy. The next section illustrates that it is actually quite difficult to draw clear boundaries between transdisciplinary research and consulting, as both focus on problem solving and knowledge integration.

Innovation versus Problem Solving

When it comes to the question of distinguishing transdisciplinary research from professional consultancy, the answer is not so clear cut. Criteria that account for good transdisciplinary research are also relevant for good consultancy projects:

- representative involvement of all stakeholder groups affected (not only those targeted by the project sponsor),

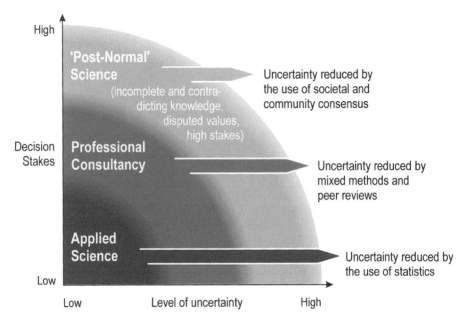

Fig. 1 Terminological distinction between different forms of problem-oriented science. (according to Funtowicz and Ravetz 1993)

- the best available disciplinary knowledge based on adequate and up-to-date methodology,
- the integration of the external academic perspective and the internal perspective of the stakeholders on eye-level,
- a process design that avoids assertive personalities or powerful groups to dominate the process,
- an integrative perspective on the problem and possible solutions, taking into account the whole system, and also long-term, un-intended side-effects,
- openness towards all plausible results and solutions (no predetermined solutions).

One significant difference between research and consultancy is the claim of novelty that is inherent with academic research. While the task of consultancy is to produce solutions to a problem, academic research should also be innovative so that results do not only contribute to problem solving but are also publishable in scientific media. When designing a project, scientists need to keep in mind that their research should not be regarded as routine by the academic community but rather address a "research gap". The problems of stakeholders need not necessarily be compatible with methodological, empirical or theoretical knowledge gaps. We experienced situations where stakeholders proposed project topics that the researchers had to decline as they did not see enough innovative potential in the planned cooperation. Such incidences can of course cause significant irritation amongst stakeholders and do not reflect a mutual understanding of the factors driving the system of science (academic impact) and that of society (societal impact). Communication between the producers and users of research and boundary objects such as participatory scenarios, modelling or assessments help to better understand the other side's knowledge claims or criteria of credibility (Cash et al. 2003).

Transdisciplinary research is expected to produce solutions for real-life problems by providing access to the real-world character of human reasoning and interaction considering the affording and constraining nature of social and material contexts (Horlick-Jones and Sime 2004). When a wide range of both academic and non-academic perspectives are integrated in early phases of the research, they can provide useful feedback throughout the course of the project which helps to avoid unrealistic recommendations. This also facilitates minimization of conflicts and contributes to the legitimacy of the outcomes. However, this "reality check" (see Wickson et al. 2006) can also impede creativity. We postulate—though we have to admit that we do not have a systematic documentation supporting this argument—that results from transdisciplinary projects tend to be rather consensus oriented than visionary. The reality check often leads to a reproduction of existing mind sets; innovative ideas can sound totally unrealistic for case actors in the beginning and may need some isolation from full reality to be elaborated and further developed before being scrutinised for practicability (van Buuren and Lorbach 2009). Consequently, transdisciplinarity must not substitute but should rather complement purpose free, curiosity-driven research.

Identification and Integration of Stakeholders

Stakeholder integration is a focal topic associated with transdisciplinary processes, and many calls for project proposals demand a significant degree of stakeholder integration as precondition for funding. Yet it is rarely defined what types of stakeholders should be integrated and in which particular phases of a project (see Enengel et al. 2012); however, many aspects of stakeholder integration pre-determine the course and the outcome of transdisciplinary processes (EEA 2001; Penker and Wytrzens 2005).

Challenges include an adequate invitation list, certain groups' un-willingness or inability to participate and dominant personalities and interests (e.g., Cheng and Mattor 2006; Diduck and Sinclair 2002; Hodge 2007; Smith 2008). Single groups may hold power over others (Hodge 2007; Ishihara and Pascual 2009), and particular interests pushed by some participants can result in ineffective discussions and missing or poor results (Carlsson and Berkes 2005).

Collins and Evans (2002, p. 270) distinguish "Studies of Expertise and Experience" from democratic decisions in the political sphere involving the whole public or elected representatives. This draws up questions of group composition, representativeness of the different interest groups involved, but also the legitimacy of the process. In this context, we must also be aware that drawing in large or very heterogeneous groups of participants is often considered as a challenge for participatory research projects (Madlener et al. 2007; McDonald et al. 2009). Much more knowledge is needed on ideal group size and group composition, as well as rules for collective choice to guarantee a fair, transparent process resulting in legitimated results.

Apart from group size, group composition and power relations, we see two more challenges. Firstly, transdisciplinary projects under the normative paradigm of sustainability have a tendency to be oriented towards stakeholder groups whose interests and values are in line with those of the researchers. E.g., in the context of agricultural research at our own university, there are much more projects involving organic farmers or alpine pastoralists compared to mainstream conventional or industrial farmers. Similarly in the field of transportation research, there are more transdisciplinary projects designed to involve pedestrians or cyclists compared to SUV-owners or motorbikers. This means that the perspective of groups perceived as "unsustainably behaving" is often missed out as a consequence of the project design, despite the fact that the knowledge that could be gained from cooperation with them would be very relevant for developing solutions for sustainable development (Jauss and Backhaus 2013). One simple explanation for this exclusion is of course the fact that in practice it is much easier to motivate highly valued groups for participation as opposed to unpopular groups.

A second critical aspect is the role of organized (strategic) stakeholders as gatekeepers. Transdisciplinary processes are hardly ever the result of a bottom-up initiative from a local community. Typically, the initiative is with researchers, persons from administration (regional managers) or organized stakeholders such as NGOs or professional interest groups. Even when later in the process also non-organised stakeholders ("regular community members") are being involved, typically the organised stakeholders continue to act as communication nodes and thus also have an influence on the selection of participants. Strategic stakeholders usually have an academic background and therefore speak the same language as researchers, which is very useful in developing project proposals etc. On the other hand, their perspectives and interests can of course sometimes differ from the rest of the non-organised stakeholder community (Pettersen et al. 2009).

Funding Partners, Project Ownership and Project Duration

Virtually all transdisciplinary research projects we conducted in the past decades were third-party funded, as the regular budget of an academic unit hardly ever allows for organizing comprehensive research processes with extensive stakeholder integration. Funding can either come from case actors such as public authorities, local communities and NGOs that all have a certain stake in the project, or from "neutral" research funding organisations. Even when the main funding comes from "neutral" organisations, they often demand some co-funding from the case arena. This creates two different types of stakeholders: the ones with financial power and those without. Challenging stakeholders are funders who not only have a stake in the project, but who also have a predefined idea of the research results. These funders see the project as "their project". It needs considerable skills, power and persistency on the researchers' side to guarantee good scientific practice (e.g., impartiality, innovation and openness to all kind of solutions). Otherwise researchers and their reputation of impartiality and "scientific objectivity" are instrumentalised for individual self-serving interests.

On the other hand, in third-party financed projects funded from research programmes, scientists draft the proposal usually without much involvement of stakeholders. These are generally invited after the successful application, when the problem to be targeted by the project has already been defined by the scientists. At this stage of point, stakeholders see the project as the researchers' project, representing research priorities and interests rather than local stakeholders' needs. This is also an explanation for the difficulty of finding stakeholders willing to participate in many transdisciplinary research projects. The compromise between innovation and practical applicability is difficult to find, needs time, trust and openness, and rarely does research funding provide enough time resources for this phase of matching, problem definition and project development.

Funding programs for scientific research usually predefine the project duration. We hardly ever had the means to conduct a research project over more than three years, including the time for dissemination and implementation. Building up new project relationships, creating trust between stakeholders, achieving working performance and developing results often requires a long run-up phase. The first phase of project definition is therefore very time-consuming (Penker and Wytrzens 2008). This time is then missing in the final phases of the project, and typically, when it comes to the implementation of project results, the researchers have to leave the stage because funding is over.

This causes a remarkable discrepancy: While the principles of transdisciplinarity emphasise the importance of orientation towards real-life issues, the implementation phases of many projects fail to have an impact on the real world. Therefore it would be essential to either have longer project funding cycles or to develop specific means (e.g. implementation facilitators) to secure the implementation of the results in the respective case situation to finally achieve the central goal of empowerment of local stakeholders (Brandt et al. 2013).

Actual implementation of research results into practical solutions will be easier in projects jointly planned by stakeholders and scientists, accompanied by professional facilitation, characterised by shared ownership, win-win solutions (innovation for scientists and practical solutions for stakeholders) and sufficient time for joint learning processes and actual implementation. The "projectification" of research (research is predominately organised in forms of one to three years projects, Felt 2010) is not in line with the need for long-term and continuous transdisciplinary processes. Best science-society collaborations are often found in contexts of long-standing relationships between stakeholder groups and scientists, which have been established in many of the traditional fields of applied research (e.g., the close and long-term relationships between agronomists or veterinaries and "their" farmers, between the planning scholars and planners in public administration and local governments).

Rebranding as an Opportunity for Reflection and Learning Processes

Implicit Knowledge and Skills

Many applied researchers are aware that stakeholder interaction can stimulate social learning and thus positively influence the quality, feasibility and acceptance of the results and the likelihood of their actual implementation. Nevertheless, we experience a growing gap between theorists of transdisciplinarity and the majority of those researchers who are implementing transdisciplinary approaches in their projects, often rather implicitly and without having read and reflected on the theoretical literature. One reason for this could also be the tendency in some of theoretical literature to use a quite sophisticated academic language and discuss theoretical issues that not necessarily provide support for the practical implementation of transdisciplinarity projects. We also found that scholars with an applied natural sciences background have more difficulties (or less motivation) to read such texts as opposed to social scientists.

While few of the scholars in applied science would describe themselves as transdisciplinary researchers, many have taken on a transdisciplinary role for decades. Therefore, they have a vast experiential knowledge of how to set up processes and to interact with stakeholders. Yet, in favour of disciplinary publications, applied researchers reflect very little on their own role in and methods for transdisciplinary knowledge integration. Thus, there is a need to systematically explore and utilise this treasure of practical, yet often implicit knowledge. We hope that a rebranding of applied participatory research as transdisciplinary research opens the door for more reflection and publications on critical aspects affecting the quality, legitimacy and societal effectiveness of the outcomes of transdisciplinary research.

Topics for Learning Processes on Transdisciplinarity

In the preceeding section we discussed challenges of transdisciplinary processes. In this section we reflect on the associated need for learning processes. As discussed above, transdisciplinary processes as participatory approaches are confronted with major challenges pertaining from group dynamics that have to be adequately addressed. Group processes running out of control can seriously endanger transdisciplinary research. The integration of cross-disciplinary and local expert knowledge involves more than just bringing together knowledge in terms of "facts"; it requires appreciation of different epistemologies, as well as different underlying values, interests, paradigms and world views (McDonald et al. 2009). While most academics are trusted to be guided by curiosity and no other personal interests, stakeholders might follow particular strategic interests to influence the results. More reflection is needed on power relations in transdisciplinary projects, on how to make hidden

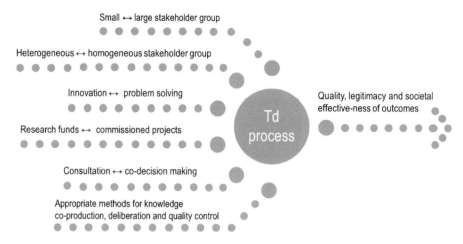

Fig. 2 Topics for learning processes on transdisciplinarity

agendas visible and negotiable in a fair deliberative process. The degree of participation (consultancy versus co-decision making), the source of funding and associated project ownership will shift power relations between science and stakeholders. Some circumstances call for full scientific control over the research process, in other situations clear rules for co-decision making are needed, whereas in transdisciplinary teams of long standing collaboration and mutual trust, the interaction can be more spontaneous and trust based. However, we must not underestimate the fundamental trade-offs between legitimacy, scientific credibility and societal impact, which sometimes require active mediation by boundary organizations bridging science and society (Cash et al. 2003).

As illustrated in Fig. 2, several questions have to be addressed for societally effective, legitimate and high-quality outcomes. Is the participating group large enough, representative and legitimate to be involved into research? Does the group cover all relevant expertise? Do dominant interests steer the process and compromise the quality of results? How do different funding models affect power-relations and ownership among scholars and stakeholders? What is the appropriate level of participation between consultation and co-decision making ? And which research design and methods are helpful to address these challenges while guaranteeing effective knowledge co-production, high scientific quality standards and feasible solutions to societal problems?

An international and cross-disciplinary exchange on these issues can spur application of and innovation in theories and methods for transdisciplinary knowledge generation, knowledge integration and quality management. By publishing on transdisciplinarity, we make specific concepts and approaches accessible to the critique of others. Thus, we can benefit from the academic principle of scepticism, which is key for quality management and effective innovation processes.

The Role of Applied Researchers in Transdisciplinary Reflection

Due to their long-standing experience in cross-disciplinary and participatory research, many applied researchers could contribute to the development of theories
and methods for transdisciplinary research or a "new" specialization in knowledge
integration and implementation (Bammer 2005). However, the recent academic discourse on transdisciplinarity, integration and implementation science, mode 2 and
post-normal science has not much benefited from their experience. Applied studies, instead of striving for becoming a "proper" discipline (e.g. Isard 2001; Maier
et al. 2008), might become more aware of their comparative advantage regarding the
expertise in problem-oriented knowledge integration across different academic epistemologies and between academia, business, politics and planning (see also Bailly
and Gibson 2003).

Conclusions: Need for Institutionalisation of Reflection and Dialogue

We have argued above that cross-disciplinary knowledge integration and participatory research have had a clear instrumental value in many fields of applied
research long before the current discourse on transdisciplinarity. Therefore scholars
in these fields might challenge the innovativeness and newness of transdisciplinary
research and question the benefit of the related discourse. We have further listed
some crucial open questions in transdisciplinary research. The experience of applied researchers—often a tacit knowledge—could contribute important answers to
these questions. Therefore, we see considerable merits in reflecting, researching and
teaching transdisciplinarity on top of doing it.

   We hope that the re-branding of participatory applied research focusing on problem solving into transdisciplinary research spurs an epistemological reflection and
cross-disciplinary learning processes on knowledge co-production between science
and society. We hope that more applied scholars will be motivated to share their
treasure of implicit expertise on transdisciplinary practices with experts in other
disciplines and thus contribute to the development of theoretical and methodological knowledge on how to improve transdisciplinary processes for higher scientific
quality, legitimacy and societal effectiveness.

   The current incentives and evaluation structures in academia do not encourage this
cross-disciplinary reflection on transdisciplinarity. Many of these structures are based
on comparative assessments and reputation within the scholar's narrow discipline
(peer reviews of PhD-theses, project applications, publications, disciplinary confer-
ences, journals and research programmes). Therefore, cross-disciplinary structures
in the form of inter- and transdisciplinary research programs, cross-departmental
platforms and seminars, and publication media are needed for learning processes on
transdisciplinarity. Inclusion of transdisciplinary theories and methods into curricula
of master and PhD-programmes might not only be helpful for future researchers but

also for those graduates working in business, NGOs and public authorities where they also have to deal with different stakeholder groups, their paradigms and mind sets and need to integrate diverse types of knowledge and interests.

References

Bailly, A., & Gibson, L. J. (2003). Regional science: Directions for the future. *Regional Science, 83*(1), 127–138.

Bammer, G. (2005). Integration and implementation sciences: Building a new specialization. *Ecology and Society,* 10(2), 6. [online] http://www.ecologyandsociety.org/vol10/iss2/art6/.

Brandt, P., Ernst, A., Gralle, F., Luederitz, C., Lang, D., Newig, J., Reinert, F., Abson, D., & von Wehrden, H. (2013). Review of transdisciplinary research in sustainability science. *Ecological Economics, 92,* 1–15.

Carlsson, L., & Berkes, F. (2005). Co-management: Concepts and methodological implications. *Journal of Environmental Management, 75,* 65–76.

Cash, D. W., Clark, W. C., Alcock, F., Dickson, N. M., Eckley, N., Guston, D. H., Jäger, J., & Mitchell, R. B. (2003). Knowledge systems for sustainable development. *PNAS, 100*(14), 8086–8091.

Cheng, A. S., & Mattor, K. M. (2006). Why won't they come? Stakeholder perspectives on collaborative national forest planning by participation level. *Environmental Management, 38,* 545–561.

Collins, H. M., & Evans, R. (2002). The third wave of science studies: Studies of expertise and experience. *Social Studies of Science, 32*(2), 235–296.

Defila, R., di Giulio, A., & Scheuermann, M. (2006). *Forschungsverbundmanagement: Handbuch für die Gestaltung inter- und transdisziplinärer Projekte.* Zürich: Hochschulverlag an der ETH Zürich.

Diduck, A., & Sinclair, A. J. (2002). Public involvement in environmental assessment: The case of the nonparticipant. *Environmental Management, 29,* 578–588.

EC. (2006). *Renewed EU sustainable development strategy, as adopted by the European Council on 15/16 June 2006.* European Council DOC 10917/06. http://register.consilium. europa.eu/pdf/en/06/st10/st10917.en06.pdf. Accessed 28 Sept 2014.

EEA. (2001). *Designing effective assessments: The role of participation, science and governance, and focus.* Experts corner by Noelle Eckley, Environmental Issue Report No 26. Copenhagen: European Environmental Agency (EEA).

Enengel, B., Muhar, A., Penker, M., Freyer, B., Drlik, S., & Ritter, F. (2012). Co-production of knowledge in transdisciplinary doctoral theses on landscape development—An analysis of actor roles and knowledge types in different research phases. *Landscape and Urban Planning, 105*(1–2), 106–117.

Felt, U. (2010). Transdisziplinarität als Wissenskultur und Praxis (Transdisciplinarity as culture and practice). *GAIA, 19,* 75–77.

Funtowicz, S. O., & Ravetz, J. R. (1993). Science for the post-normal age. *Futures, 25,* 739–755.

Garb, Y., Pulver, S., & VanDeveer, S. (2008). Scenarios in society, society in scenarios: Toward a social scientific analysis of storyline-driven environmental modeling. *Environmental Research Letters, 3,* 1–8.

Gibbons, M., Limoges, C., Nowotny, H., Schwarztman, S., Scott, P., & Trow, M. (1994). *The new production of knowledge: The dynamics of science and research in contemporary societies.* London: Sage.

Häberli, R., Bill, A., Grossenbacher-Mansuy, W., Klein, J. T., Scholz, R. W., & Welti, M. (2001). Synthesis. In J. T. Klein, W. Grossenbacher-Mansuy, R. Häberli, A. Bill, R. W. Scholz, & M. Welti (Eds.), *Transdisciplinarity: Joint problem solving among science, technology, and society. An effective way for managing complexity* (pp. 6–22). Basel: Birkhäuser.

Hirsch Hadorn, G., Biber-Klemm, S., Grossenbacher-Mansuy, W., Hoffmann-Riem, H., Joye, D., Pohl, C., Wiesmann, U., & Zemp, E. (2008). The emergence of transdisciplinarity as a form of research. In G. Hirsch Hadorn, H. Hoffmann-Riem, S. Biber-Klemm, W. Grossenbacher-Mansuy, D. Joye, C. Pohl, U. Wiesmann, & E. Zemp (Eds.), *Handbook of transdisciplinary research*. New York: Springer.

Hodge, I. (2007). The governance of rural land in a liberalised world. *Journal of Agricultural Economics, 58*, 409–432.

Horlick-Jones, T., & Sime, J. (2004). Living on the border: Knowledge, risk and transdisciplinarity. *Futures, 36*(4), 441–457.

Isard, W. (2001). The future of regional science: Remarks prompted by professors Alonso and Teitz. *International Regional Science Review, 24*(3), 415–423.

Ishihara, H., & Pascual, U. (2009). Social capital in community level environmental governance: A critique. *Ecological Economics, 68*, 1549–1562.

Jauss, A., & Backhaus, N. (2013). Motorcycling over the Ofenpass: Perception of the Swiss National Park and the Ofenpass from the perspective of motorcyclists. *eco.mont, 5*, 19–26. doi:10.1553/eco.mont-5-1s19.

Klein, J.-T., Grossenbacher-Mansuy, W., Häberli, R., Bill, A., Scholz, R., & Welti, M. (Eds.). (2001). *Transdisciplinarity: Joint problem solving among science, technology, and society. An effective way for managing complexity*. Basel: Birkhäuser.

Madlener, R., Kowalski, K., & Stagl, S. (2007). New ways for the integrated appraisal of national energy scenarios: The case of renewable energy use in Austria. *Energy Policy, 35*, 6060–6074.

Maier, G., Kaufmann, A., & Vyborny, M. (2008). Is regional science a scientific discipline? Answers from a citation based social network analysis. *SRE—Discussion papers, 2008/02*. Institute for the Environment and Regional Development, WU Vienna University of Economics and Business: Vienna. http://epub.wu.ac.at/1226/. Accessed 28 Sept 2014.

McDonald, D., Bammer, G., & Deane, P. (2009). *Research integration using dialogue methods*. Canberra: The Australian National University E Press.

Muhar, A., Visser, J., & van Breda, J. (2013). Experiences from establishing structured inter- and transdisciplinary doctoral programs in sustainability: A comparison of two cases in South Africa and Austria. *Journal of Cleaner Production, 61*, 122–129.

Nowotny, H., Scott, P., & Gibbons, M. (2001). *Re-thinking science. Knowledge and the public in an age of uncertainty*. Cambridge: Polity Press.

OECD. (1996). *The knowledge-based economy*. Paris: OECD (Organization for Economic Co-operation and Development).

Penker, M., & Wytrzens, H. K. (2005). Scenarios for the Austrian food chain in 2020 and its landscape impacts. *Landscape and Urban Planning, 71*(2/4), 175–189.

Penker, M., & Wytrzens, H. K. (2008). Evaluating landscape governance: A tool for legal-ecological assessments. In G. Hirsch Hadorn, H. Hoffmann-Riem, S. Biber-Klemm, W. Grossenbacher-Mansuy, D. Joye, C. Pohl, U. Wiesmann, & E. Zemp (Eds.), *Handbook of transdisciplinary research* (pp. 245–258). New York: Springer.

Pettersen, A. R., Moland, E., Olsen, E. M., & Knutsen, J. A. (2009). Lobster reserves in coastal Skagerrak—An integrated analysis of the implementation process. In E. Dahl, E. Moksness, & J. Støttrup (Eds.), *Integrated coastal zone management* (pp. 178–188). London: Wiley-Blackwell.

Pohl, C., & Hirsch Hadorn, G. (2007). *Principles for designing transdisciplinary research— Proposed by the Swiss Academies of Arts and Sciences*. Munich: oekom.

Rittel, H. W. J., & Webber, M. M. (1973). Dilemmas in a general theory of planning. *Policy Sciences, 4*, 155–169.

Smith, J. L. (2008). A critical appreciation of the "bottom-up" approach to sustainable water management: Embracing complexity rather than desirability. *Local Environment, 13*, 353–366.

UNCED. (1992). Agenda 21. UNCED online text. http://sustainabledevelopment.un.org/index.php?page=view&nr=23&type=400&menu=35. Accessed 28 Sept 2014.

UNESCO. (1999). Introductory note to the UNESCO world conference on science. Science for the 21st century: A new commitment. Budapest: UNESCO (United Nations Educational, Scientific and Cultural Organization).

Van Buuren, A., & Loorbach, D. (2009). Policy innovation in isolation? Conditions for policy renewal by transition arenas and pilot projects. *Public Management Review, 11,* 375–392.

Volkery, A., Ribeiro, T., Henrichs, T., & Hoogeveen, Y. (2008). Your vision or my model? Lessons from participatory land use scenario development on a European scale. *Systemic Practice and Action Research, 21,* 459–477.

Wickson, F., Carew, A., & Russell, A. (2006). Transdisciplinary research: Characteristics, quandaries and quality. *Futures, 38,* 1046–1059.

Marianne Penker is associate professor of regional development at the BOKU University of Natural Resources and Life Sciences in Vienna, Institute for Sustainable Economic Development. She is an experienced leader and participant of inter- and transdisciplinary research projects. Her publications focus on sustainable local development, landscape governance, collective action in rural areas, sustainable food systems, and on transdisciplinary knowledge co-production between science and society. Concepts and methods of transdisciplinary research also play a role in her teaching. She is deputy head of the Doctoral School Sustainable Development and the Institute for Sustainable Economic Development and member of the National Committee Man and Biosphere at the Austrian Academy of Sciences.

Andreas Muhar PhD is associate professor and head of the Institute of Landscape Development, Recreation and Conservation Planning, as well as of the Doctoral School of Sustainable Development at BOKU University of Natural Resources and Life Sciences Vienna, Austria. Previous career stages were at the Faculty of Architecture and Planning, University of Technology, Vienna, and at the Faculty of Environmental Sciences, Griffith University, Brisbane, Australia. His original disciplinary background is landscape planning and biology, the research focus evolved from natural science-oriented approaches to environmental protection towards integrative approaches to landscape development and landscape-based tourism with an emphasis on transdisciplinary knowledge co-production and knowledge integration for sustainable development.

Part III
Section Three

Transdisciplinarity as Epistemology, Ontology or Principles of Practical Judgement

Paul Gibbs

> *(N)ow, that the matter of no new truth can come from induction or from deduction, we have seen. It can only come from abduction; and abduction is, after all, nothing but guessing. We are therefore bound to hope that, although the possible explanations of our facts may be strictly innumerable, yet our mind will be able, in some finite number of guesses, to guess the sole true explanation of them.*
>
> (Peirce, *The Essential Peirce*, p. 107, 1901/1998a)

Transdisciplinary Problems

Professional practices occur in workplaces, social systems that confound simple analysis, where things change and turn messy. There are many disciplinary approaches to take (e.g. anthropological, psychological and sociological) but, I propose, attempts to determine what and why things happen within professional practice prove difficult from any single disciplinary and epistemological perspective. I take these transdisciplinary problems to be issues that are complex and involve societal concerns, which lose their very nature when deconstructed to simple disciplinary interventions and, indeed, confound such mono-disciplinary interventions. These issues need to be taken at their face value, informed by a range of knowledges and resolved within the constraints of the socio-political context that, in many cases, created them.

Transdisciplinary issues require professional engagement in a wide range of professional contexts. Mitrany and Stokols (2005) point to the sectors of urban planning, public policy and environmental management that, they state:

> long have understood that complex problems such as community violence, environmental degradation, transit-related injuries, sustainable development and urban change are unlikely to be resolved in the absence of efforts to integrate knowledge drawn from several different disciplines. (2005, p. 437)

P. Gibbs (✉)
Middlesex University, London, UK
e-mail: paul.gibbs@mdx.ac.uk

© Springer International Publishing Switzerland 2015

P. Gibbs (ed.), *Transdisciplinary Professional Learning and Practice*,
DOI 10.1007/978-3-319-11590-0_11

They propose a research training programme to support such professional engagement. King et al. (2009) see similar requirements in childcare, Bellamy et al. (2013) in social work, Clark (2013) in nursing, and (Gibbs 2013) in business services. I first consider the nebulous notion of transdisciplinarity, ascribing a third form of logical inference to how we can reason solutions to transdisciplinary problems, and then consider how critical realism offers an epistemological grounding for researching transdisciplinary professional problems.

What is Transdisciplinarity?

The emergence of transdisciplinarity has been in response to often-failed attempts of closed system, discipline-based approaches to solve complex social problems (various reports and definitions can be found within projects reported by the Organisation for Economic Co-operation and Development (OECD), the United Nations Educational, Scientific and Cultural Organization, (UNESCO) and the European Union (EU). These failures are often contingent upon disaggregated notions of epistemology and the compounding failures of ontological incongruities evident in discipline-based approaches. Such approaches are not confined to large, seemingly insurmountable social problems, but apply equally well to issues within workplaces, which seemingly defy traditional managerial approaches of human resource management, operations management and marketing.

Boundary-spanning transdisciplinarity emerges from the examination of such value-laden issues as childcare, the policing of communities and environmental issues. These issues are recognized by the impact they have on society and on the power society offers its 'experts' to lead the political and economic discussions around their solutions. Application of solutions to problems have to be paid for and prioritized in forms that influence democratic society and demand judgement on the practical alternatives affecting others, and thus confront those who have merely studied, simultaneously or in sequence, several areas of knowledge without making any connections between them (Max-Neef 2005, p. 6). Because of its nature, it is not surprising that a variety of interpretations of transdisciplinarity abound; finding an all-embracing definition represents Deleuzian multiplicity in its difficulty (see Pohl and Hadorn 2007; Lawrence 2010; Nicolescu 2010; and Klein 2010, the most quoted authorities). Nevertheless, rather than a delineation of the approaches offered, analysis of these contributions points to commonality among those problems that benefit from the transdisciplinary perspective. The problems tend towards the complex and heterogeneous; specific, local and uncertain. Epistemologically they seek satisfying explanation that enables, warrants and improves our ability to seize opportunities; and involvement of practical action for the good of, and through, others.

Pohl and Hadorn define transdisciplinary research as an approach when:

> knowledge about a societal relevant problem field is uncertain, when the concrete nature of the problem is disputed and when there is a great deal at stake for those concerned by problems and those involved in dealing with them. (2007, p. 20)

This characterization is clear; yet, the methodological approaches to resolve the problems are epistemologically closed and warrant a coherent ontological explanation. For Pohl and Hadorn (2007), transdisciplinary research needs to come to terms with the complexity of the problem, be aware of its diversity, develop practice-based solutions and direct the results to the common good. According to Wiesmann et al. (2008), this involves ideas on the scope, process and outcomes of transdisciplinary research. Specifically, it involves a debate with society at large through scientific principles. This debate transgresses disciplinary boundaries and includes deliberations about facts, practices *and* values. It requires a recursive research design where problems are defined cooperatively. Solutions combine knowledge forms (systems, target and transformative) in an integrated fashion. Its results are related to societal settings and the results are valid in *that* environment. It has its own form, but is based on sound disciplinary contributions.

Later in the chapter, this transdisciplinary approach will be contrasted directly with, and finds a re-conceptualized home within, a critical realism approach.

Phronetic Method

How then might we understand, or at least effectively act in, such complexity? These concerns are too important to be hampered by the constraints put on practical knowledge in specific disciplines and professional hegemonies. What can be taken as the practice-based knowledge in the solution (expertise) is pragmatic, utilitarian and open to a transdisciplinary interpretation (with *trans* meaning across, through and beyond disciplinary boundaries). That is, it is creation of new and imaginative understanding built upon and from the available and presenting causality-predicated epistemologies of the professional attending the problem within a closed system of the presenting problem.

To seek such insights often requires collaboration, contextualization and reflection leading to reasoning that is a collective, ethical, problem-based 'explanatory' engagement. Such rich understanding aligns itself with a case-by-case approach. As Yin states, case studies provide a process of 'enquiry that investigates a contemporary phenomenon within its real-life context, especially when the boundaries between phenomenon and context are not clearly evident' (2003, p. 13).[1] In this sense, the case study works to provide the specific context within which resemblance of one case study to another can first be spotted and then used to structure examination of another situation, without the need to abstract guiding principles or formalistic domains of principles, such as defining a discipline or profession.

---

[1] Although, as a research strategy, case studies are not uncontested (see Verschuren 2003; or Diefenbach 2009).

Such a case-by-case approach is advocated by Flyvbjerg (1998) in what he calls the *phronetic* method, using 'thick' analysis of the details of a phenomenon from which more general insights can be gained. Moreover, *phronetic* social science:

> explores historic circumstances and current practices to find avenues for praxis. The task of *phronetic* social science is to clarify and deliberate about the problems and risks we face and to outline how things may be done differently, in full knowledge that we cannot find ultimate answers to these questions or even a single version of what the questions are. (2001, p. 140)

This approach, and Flyvbjerg et al.'s (2012) extension, articulate a contemporary recognition of *phronēsis* in case study analysis, and this is carried forward throughout the argument made in this paper. Importantly, Flyvbjerg's interpretation of *phronēsis* in his *phronetic* approach gives research an ontological purpose—one that asks why the research is being undertaken, whether it is desirable and whether it should be done.

Epistemologically, the *phronetic* approach embraces mixed methodology and the array of methods that can be called upon. As Schram states, 'mixed-method projects are entirely consistent with phronetic social science' (2012, p. 200). Importantly, this approach of openness to solutions, without rejecting what is taken as truth, avoids a relative stance on what can be taken as truth. This openness is embedded in the specific problem being addressed; the prejudicial discipline approach is suspended in a process of social realism, where the presenting problems and its consequences are the focus, not the definition of the problem, so as to justify certain approaches.

A *phronetic* approach is not bound by a disciplinary prejudice, but is reliant on judgement. The wider the importance of that judgement on the specific case, the higher is the likelihood that the resolution of the case will be successful. This is transdisciplinary in that it requires skills and epistemic perspectives that are both ranged between disciplines and transcend them, seeking method and knowledge from within the problem. Such *problem-generated knowledge* and its validation are nestled within the problem, and the application of the phronetic method allows a solution to be revealed from it. It is similar to the approach of diagnosis undertaken by medical doctors, but not to a particular solution—Western versus Chinese medics, for instance. Crudely, the second sees symptoms; makes judgements on the reason/cause of the malady; and, based on the whole circumstances as presented, not just the physically embodied, proposes an action designed to resolve the problem. Different solutions to the way in which the problem is perceived and conceived determine the resources at hand serve to solve the problem. In Western cultures, seeking just a medical approach is often not sufficiently comprehensive to cure a fever in someone in poor housing, as it will not resolve the underlying cause—the housing—despite taking account of it in the proposed remedy. However, as a political rather than a palliative force, medicine can indeed achieve this, yet demands wider transdisciplinary skills.

Arguing case-by-case thus emerges as an independent mode of proof or rational persuasion that performance, based on a practical judgement, can offer. It offers insights into how each case's consequences create transdisciplinary solutions. The ability to make those practical judgements is based on deliberation, experience and practical reasoning, mediated through experience and a discernment of the decision situation. The choice is an act of *phronetic* insight designed to effect change in others through communication, compelling or persuading them through the use of case studies.

However, how do we approach problems when the discipline approach is invalid and the epistemological justifications upon which they are based are suspended? The approach advocated here is based on the expansion of logical forms of argument initially found in the work of Peirce and his revision of the basis of logical argument. Rather than relying on an explanation as a static starting point or proposition, he investigates how we might recognize a problem as something that needs resolution. Neither induction nor deduction do this; they work from premise to causation, or from cause to theory, in paradigms of previous knowledge. Clearly, such a new position may hide fallacious arguments of necessary-ness that deduction may guard against; yet, given the uncertainty of the subject matter, the soundness of the argument has to work harder to support its validity and avoid relativism (a criticism leveled at transdisciplinarity itself). Peirce introduces us to abduction and retroduction, which I discuss next.

Peirce and Pragmatic Reasoning

Peirce did not claim to have discovered abduction but to have revealed it as the third form of logic originally proposed alongside deduction and induction by Aristotle. Peirce reveals abduction through a tighter reading and concludes that, as the third form, it was present within Aristotle's structure of reason, attributing its lack of presence to a longstanding failure in translation of the *Prior Analytics* (Aristotle 1995, Book 2, Chap. 25, concerning the commonality of forms of reductions). For Peirce, good abduction is established on the basis of 'whether it fulfills its ends' (1903/1998b, p. 250). In the philosophy of science, and within epistemology, abduction is often discussed as 'inference to the best explanation'. Thus, recent discussions of abduction are contextualized within 'a context of justification', whereas Peirce's work addresses abduction within 'the context of discovery'. For Peirce, abduction is a form of reasoning to discover new theories and propositions. He supports the central aspects of Aristotelian reasoning once, so to speak, we are started on a problem, but questions how we might suspect that a problem exists in our world view. He argues that we become aware of a discontinuity in the harmony of our way of being, disrupted or ruptured, by our observation that what we see does not match the reality of what we know, and for which we cannot find adequate meaning to resolve the discontinuity that disturbed our previously tranquility. Magic is a familiar phenomenon that seems to confound logic, leaving us in disbelief at how we ordinarily form judgements.

Peirce terms the rupture of our everyday acceptance 'abduction': 'that is to say, by the spontaneous conjectures of instinctive reason; and neither deduction nor induction contributes to a single new concept' (1901/1998a, p. 443). This retroduction makes possible a research process characterized by the linking of evidence, which produces general conclusions based on a set of limited observation. This process is abduction and is the basis upon which we can *begin* to argue deductively and inferentially. However, because of its uncertain beginning, inductive argument is always open to counter-examples and deduction has to be an active, continually evolving, dynamic process. Starting with abduction (Peirce refers to 'informed guessing'), the dualism between pure inductive and deductive research processes is seen as a continuous process, ebbing and flowing, seeking to find the best way of understanding and reconceptualizing a reality in order to master it (see Scott 2005, 2010). The linking continuum for the three forms of reasoning is 'necessity'. Valid deductive arguments are necessarily true, because the conclusion follows from the premise. The truth of the premise guarantees the truth of the conclusion that, as based on inductive reasoning of reality, is theorized through an abductive insight. Einstein's reconceptualization of Newtonian laws in physics, Freud's identification of the unconscious, Galileo's central placement of the sun and Kuhn's concepts of epistemological change are examples of abductive reasoning.

Peirce explores abduction's logical form as a questioning of what has previously been taken as true. This allows us to wonder about an observation as it relates to our systematic understanding of what is taken as known.[2] To illustrate the logical form of abduction, Richardson and Kramer (2006, p. 500) use a Peirce example as follows:

Result   [We have the experience that] the beans are white [but this experience lacks any real meaning for us].

Rule   [The claim that] all the beans from this bag are white [is meaningful in this setting].

Case   [Therefore, it is both plausible and meaningful to hypothesize that] these beans are from this bag.

Richardson and Kramer's explanation is that 'a new idea or a hypothesis (these beans are from this bag) is added to two "givens" (the rule and the result)' (2006, p. 500). Further, and in a more contemporary form, Hammersley considers abduction as an expansion of our understanding. It provides:

> the development of an explanatory or theoretical idea which often results from close exam-
> ination of particular cases. The process of inference involved here is not a matter of strict
> logic it is not deductive nor does it follow some 'inductive logic', it is ampliative, in the
> sense that the conclusion is not already present in the premises. (2005, p. 5)

For Peirce, abduction comes to us 'like a flash. It is an act of insight, although a very fallible one' (1998c, p. 227). It works, according to Peirce, when a *surprising* observation is surprising because of the nature of that which had been taken as truth, and that cannot now explain the new observation. Such inquisitiveness to examine the

---

[2] Knowledge is taken as a social interpretation of the reality external to the observer. Thus there is an external reality, but how we construct the meaning of that reality is social influenced. This is discussed further in the next section, but is critical in determining our ontological and epistemological positions.

new observation may be restricted by a world view looking for similarity rather than difference. Moreover, it is the search for this form of insight, when the disciplined solution is inadequate, that leads to the pragmatic *phronetic* understanding of complex situations in order to act in a specific, morally justified way; to solve a problem without recourse to a single theoretical paradigm. It is about making judgements of practice and producing practical knowledge that can challenge power, in ways that inform real efforts to produce change (Schram 2012, p. 20). Bybee suggests that 'abduction allows us to infer new information, it also enables us to use it as evidence to justify a conclusion. In other words, abduction has a rhetorical as well as logical forces' (1991, pp. 293/294), moreover its ability to persuade 'depends on how readily its audience can think of a conclusion different from the one the argument advances to account for the initial conditions' (ibid, p. 296).

This approach is warranted as the abductive information is not safe from fallacies. These fallacies can be managed in the specific abductive case study if more attributes can be revealed. For example, the moon looking like green cheese is insufficient for the proposal to gain any credibility.

The suggested approach in the case study mode of investigation is to use abductive reasoning to formulate understanding, which leads to persuasive resolution of problems by utilizing, but not presuming, a discipline-based solution. It is thus not pitted against disciplines, but privileges the reasoning of the abductive case study above a body of knowledge and its associated epistemology. It is plausible as an approach to building a research approach to solve real and complex problems within our world space. It provides an engagement that allows a reasoning that is not merely an end in itself, but rather a means to regain unity beyond the boundaries and plurality of disciplines. Yet, it may still lack a formal layered structure to the reality it investigates. This layering can be found in in an exploration, for example in critical realism. The proposal, then, is to retain the value-laden principles of *phronetic* analysis but frame the analysis in a way that connects the cases to the real world through networks of transdisciplinary insight at work in the flux of social reality revealed through critical realism. This is clearly not the only approach that might be used for transdisciplinary knowledge. Scholz and Tietje (2002) wisely advocate caution and, especially, Stauffacher et al. (2006) provide a 'learning framework based on what we call functional socio-cultural constructivism and project-based learning' (p. 253). Critical realism offers a phronetic framework for considering transdisciplinary problems that combines the desire to find causal explanation in order to act but without the positivist desire to create general laws. In this aspect, realism has the same genius as pragmatism and links well with the notion of realism developed by Peirce and, indeed, with deliberative intentionality of Aristotle. As Gorski proposes, critical realism provides the 'best available starting point for anyone interested in a post-positivist and post-structuralist vision of the social sciences' (2013, p. 668). The system offers rich opportunities for the development of methodologies as developed by Danermark et al. (2002, see below) and Olsen (2010). In contrast with pragmatism, critical realism does not discard a reality outside one's being but argues that it is knowable, both epistemologically and ontologically. Although humans are rarely able to experience more than a subset of the tendencies generated by the complex interplay between causal powers, it is possible to advance *contingently stable*, or context-bound, knowledge claims while recognizing that these are always potentially fallible (Modell 2009, p. 212).

This approach assumes that reality is an open system, not enframed by the disciplinary forces and social conventions that structure our understanding. Valuable as this notion might be for everyday practices, it fails when we encounter problems beyond simple disciplinary description. It follows both that an open system needs to remain open under investigation and that the contingent circumstances for a particular explanation are likely to prevail. Easton suggests that '(C)ritical realists accept that there are differences between the empirical, the actual and the real, and that data are collected from people as well as from, and about, material things. As a result they accept that any explanations are necessarily fundamentally interpretivist in character' (ibid, p. 124).

An Abductive Approach

I turn now to how critical realism provides the reality structure for an abductive reasoning that transcends the closure of systems imposed by disciplinary knowledge. In so doing, I will consider how the use of abductive logic helps in developing an approach to transdisciplinary problem-solving through what might be called the abductive case study. The central claim here is that abduction is an inference where a recontextualizing (and I propose that transdisciplinary has this essence of reconceptualization) is central and that the need for any new conceptualization is revealed through insight.

Danermark et al. (2002, pp. 109–111) offer a basis of a critical realism approach to research in six stages and, based on this, the following model is proposed. It begins with a process of description from which flows the second stage of identifying the key components. Stages three and four of the model cover abduction's retroduction phase, where inter- and transdisciplinary theoretical re-description take place, and consider the theoretical nature of the entities involved in the case with the ways they act and the verity of mechanism through which causal powers influence the entities. This is undertaken in the domain of the real. The fifth stage, that of abduction, spans the real and the actual and reviews how the structural components of the mechanisms are identified and how these interact and are contextualized. The components may be social, physical and technological, and according to the problem classified into people, technology, organization and tasks. Moreover, it is at this stage that explanations of the phenomena of emergence arise. It may be how the market mechanism operates, which stands behind how things are but denies direct investigation. The final stages are in the domain of the empirical, where theory development, the abstraction and contextualization, and action are undertaken. There is some blurring of these stages in actual research practice and it is its imaginative approach to re-description and interpretation prior to theory that sets this approach apart.

In comparing this approach with the transdisciplinary model offered by Pohl and Hadorn (2007), what emerges is a clear ontological difference through the use of domain of reality. Pohl and Hadorn's transdisciplinary research model is recursive, intending to reduce the complexity of the problem and effect its solution by creating a closed system for analysis. Danermark's approach, however, allows for the openness of the social problem and provides a layered richness that Pohl and Hadorn's approach struggles to provide, since its epistemological stance is not founded on any coherent ontological basis but is methodologically driven. This is not to put each in tension with one another but to show that, although the identification of elements and structures is relevant to the problem, the transdisciplinary approach of Pohl and Hadorn falls into Bhaskar's 'epistemic fallacy' (Bhaskar 1989, p. 18). It does so by premising the solution as causal within one domain of reality, in that:

> various sciences as attempting to understand things and structures in themselves at their own level of being, without making reference to the diverse conditions under which they exist and act, and as making causal claims which are specific to the events and individuals concerned. (Bhaskar 1978, p. 78)

Professionals' Application of Transidisciplinary Practice

Clearly, not all problems lend themselves to the transdisciplinary research approach outlined above, and the choice of the appropriate methodology is critical. Following Ockham's razor, the simpler the approach to solving a problem the better; but some problems resist deconstruction or are too important to be neglected on the basis of disciplinary barriers. Professional issues such as child protection, peace studies, empathy for distant others and happiness are critical. Abductive reasoning can provide insights into these and other problems that engage professionals. Wise and often brave professional teams move 'towards the "*exemplary knowledge*" of abduction and phronesis' (Thomas 2010, p. 578). Such approaches are in evidence, especially in the collected works of transdisciplinary case studies edited by Brown et al. (2010).

To put into practice a transdisciplinary research approach effectively, the project itself needs to find its own transdisciplinarity as a distinct form of personal agency, an agency that is motivational and that acts systematically and openly. More importantly, it has to have its own rationality and, where the agent is not reducible to the individual, it has to have an ontological commitment to the group project management as if it were an agency in its own right. When such an agency is created, it liberates individuals from their prior form of evaluation and allows for the building of a consensus. This represents a convergence of judgement of shared intention that leads to reliability and predictability within the team as a precursor to planning, which is then based on principles adopted by the new agent and not on the specifics of the participating (likely disciplinary-bound) individuals. This separation of agency from structure formulates a notion that both agency and structure have independent powers, even if they work on each other (Archer 2000).

The adoption of an abductive approach ought to offer space unencumbered by disciplined thought. This is thought that is judged only against the feasibility of finding an end solution, not its epistemological relatedness to prior forms of knowledge or to their associated disciplines—and a good place to start seems to be guessing, which is persuasive, value-laden, motivational and credible. To be clear, the preliminary 'guessing' of solutions must involve those for whom the solution is pertinent. The approach advocated is not a disciplinary expert one. On the contrary, it involves as many participants as possible: all those who have an interest in resolving a specific problem and for whom the outcome is particularly impactful.

Having strengthened this argument, the chapter has explored the advantages of seeking good practical judgement through transdisciplinary inquiry rather than closed system theory. For Fleetwood, this means that disparate insights from different disciplines are revealed in the combination of insights without contradiction, and the use of research techniques, methodology, epistemology and ontology in such a way that knowledge is consistent with how the social world is thought to be. He summarizes it thus: 'the meta-theoretical apparatus of critical realism furnishes us with a clear idea of what a theory, model or account can and should do: it can, and should, *explain*' (Fleetwood 2006, p. 81). This approach coheres with Easton (2010) and provides a framework for critical theory to provide a platform for transdisciplinary enquiry under the guidance of *phronetic* judgement.

Is there any evidence of the *phronetic* abductive approached succeeding? Or is problem-based investigation into professional or work-based learning being used in work-based studies? Given Boud and Solomon's (2001) desire to develop transdisciplinary research approaches to work-based studies, the results seem disappointing. Costley and Armsby (2007) failed to find sufficient evidence in their limited study of undergraduate work-based study students. Workman (2007) identified a lack of appreciation of structure in her study of (insider workplace) researchers and suggested an approach not dissimilar to that advocated here. In a more recent work from Middlesex University, yet to be published, Maguire investigated 50 professional doctoral reports from one institution. She found their methodologies revealing, as candidates were predominately informed by social constructivism, phenomenology, hermeneutics and mixed methodologies; the dependence upon qualitative approaches shows a lack of appreciation of the complexity of the contexts and of a realist epistemological stance. Maguire's preliminary analysis points to difficulties in understanding the open system and social structures of the workplace, and frequent reliance on approaches that fail to capture the richness of the problems. The methodologies in use tend to close the system and are not innovative in the sense required by Boud and Solomon; there is little evidence of reconceptualization and plenty of struggle to reveal worthwhile and impactful conclusions and recommendations. Indeed, the research shows a conflation of recommendation and conclusion that, it may be speculated, has its cause in the failure to apply the tripartite analysis of critical realism or other such approach (transcendental, scientific or social realism, for instance) that could account for the emergence of understanding.

Based on this small, but likely to be indicative, sample of work-based study research methods, little has been achieved in answering the call for transdisciplinary tools to assist the understanding of professional practices in the workplace. The abductive approach might be one contribution, albeit limited. The onus is on those involved not to look for the simple but the complex. The search for these tools ought not to be undertaken by adopting the existing components of closed system research, but by recognizing the distinctive emergence of social causal powers in an ontologically stratified social reality, through the relational ordering of their underlying components. The sustainability of these entities is thus relationally determined. Although these stratified social causal powers have life beyond their underpinning elements, ignoring them misses the problematic messy issues and the significance of their emergence. Their emergence is the transdisciplinarity of the reality, and to understand the openness requires the creativity of abduction and retroduction along with the phronetic process.

In this respect, the Danermark et al. model offers some insights, and Meyer and Lunnay (2013) have used it to effect in studying trust. However, the advantage of more general application of the model to work-based studies is not evident.

Concluding Comments

Thomas justifies the validity of this approach by arguing 'through the connections and insights it offers between another's experience and one's own. The essence comes in understandability emerging from *phronēsis*—in other words, from the connection to one's own situation' (2010, p. 579). The insights of transdisciplinary action are also based on readiness to see the *layered reality* within a problem, perhaps concealed when viewing it through a single disciplinary lens. Through abductively harnessing prudent judgements (i.e., best guesses), through the medium of transdisciplinarity, an imaginative and creative reconceptionalization of problems can be facilitated. This is not to argue that abduction has only one purpose but that, according to Krohn (2008), the space reserved for the abductive approach is between nomothetic explanation and ideographic understanding manifest in reflective practical judgement. This encourages experts to 'expand their capacity to properly judge the next case. They become more prudent' (2008, p. 376).

These moments of vision are the origin of the abductive process; a process of creativity and imagination. Insight is identified within the *phronetic* abductive study proposed in this chapter. Thomas (2010) justifies such an approach as a process of empathy, of understanding the other person's perceptual horizon, and advocates an 'anatomy of narrative' approach.

For transdisciplinary research, it means investigating disciplines' relationship with knowledge and how these analyses are reviewed creatively. The structure of the problem, in terms of agency and structure, form the open system of which the problem is an irruption. These processes cannot be dictated, for the revealing of the relationship itself will offer up approaches to forms of understanding, but it is sufficient to suggest that they may flow from the empirical to the poetic. Beyond this chapter but found in a Heideggerian claim that '(p)oetry wells up only from devoted thought thinking back, recollecting' (Heidegger 1993, p. 376) it points to an approach that warrants future attention. Poetry liberates us imaginatively from the closed functioning of language, so we might think anew. As Rosenberg (2000) describes it, poetic transdisciplinary research is *rhizomatic* in nature: it sets out roots and shoots that break and reform, reproduce and transform in the space between substantiation and deviation.

References

Archer, M. (2000). *Being human: The problem of agency*. Cambridge: Cambridge University Press.

Aristotle. (1995). In J. Barnes (Ed.), *The complete works of Aristotle*. Princeton: Princeton University Press.

Bellamy, J. L., Mullen, E. J., Satterfield, J. M., Newhouse, R. P., Ferguson, M., Brownson R. C., & Spring, B. (2013). Implementing evidence-based practice education in social work: A transdisciplinary approach. *Research on social work practice, 23*(4), 246–256.

Bhaskar, R. (1978). *A realist theory of science*. Hassocks: Harvester.

Bhaskar, R. (1989). *Reclaiming reality: A critical introduction to contemporary philosophy*. London: Verso.

Boud, D., & Solomon, N. (2001). Future directions for work-based learning: Reconfiguring higher education. In D. Boud & N. Solomon (Eds.), *Work-based learning: A new higher education?* Buckingham: SRHE and Open University Press.

Brown, V. A., Harris, J. A., & Russell, J. Y. (Eds.). (2010). *Tackling wicked problems through the transdisciplinary imagination*. Washington: Earthscan.

Bybee, M. D. (Ed.). (1991). Abduction and rhetorical theory. *Philosophy and Rhetoric, 24*(4), 281–300.

Clark, C. S. (2013). Resistance to change in the nursing profession: Creative transdisciplinary solutions. *Creative Nursing, 19*(2), 70–76.

Costley, C., & Armsby, P. (2007). Methodologies for undergraduates doing practitioner investigations at work. *Journal of Workplace Learning, 19*(3), 131–145.

Danermark, B., Ekstrom, M., Jakobsen, L., & Karlsson, J. (2002). *Explaining society: Critical realism in the social sciences*. London: Routledge.

Diefenbach, T. (2009). Are case studies more than sophisticated storytelling? Methodological problems of qualitative empirical research mainly based on semi-structured interview. *Quality and Quantity, 43*, 875–894.

Easton, G. (2010). Critical realism in case study research. *Industrial Marketing Management, 39*(1), 118–128.

Fleetwood, S. (2006). Re-thinking labour markets: A critical realist-socioeconomic perspective. *Capital & Class, 89*, 59–89.

Flyvbjerg, B. (1998). *Rationality and power democracy in practice*. Chicago: University of Chicago.

Flyvbjerg, B., Landman, T., & Schram, S. (Eds.). (2012). *Real social science: Applied phronesis*. Cambridge: Cambridge University Press.

Gibbs, P. (2013). *Multidisciplinary practice*. Hong Kong: BMA.

Gorski, P. S. (2013). What is critical realism? And why should you care? *Contemporary Sociology: A Journal of Reviews, 42*, 658.

Hammersley, M. (2005). Assessing quality in qualitative research. http://www.birmingham.ac.uk/ Documents/college-social-sciences/education/projects/esrc-2005-seminarseries4.pdf. Accessed 29 Sept 2014.

Heidegger, M. (1993). What calls for thinking. In D. F. Krell (Ed.), *Basic writings* (pp. 365–392). London: Routledge.

King, G., Strachan, D., Tucker, M., Duwyn, B., Desserud, S., & Shillington, M. (2009). The application of a transdisciplinary model for early intervention services. *Infants and Young Children, 22*, 211–223.

Klein, J. T. (2010). A taxonomy of interdisciplinary knowledge. In R. Frodeman, J. T. Klein, & C. Mitcham (Eds.), *The Oxford handbook of interdisciplinary knowledge* (pp. 15–30). Oxford: Oxford University Press.

Krohn, W. (2008). Learning from case studies. In G. H. Hadorn, H. HoffmanRiem, S. Biber-Klemm, W. Grossenbacher-Mansury, D. Joye, C. Pohl, U. Wiesmann, & E. Zemp (Eds.), *Handbook of transdisciplinary research* (pp. 369–354). Dordrecht: Springer.

Lawrence, R. J. (2010). Beyond disciplinary confinement to imaginative transdisciplinarity. In V. A. Brown, J. A. Harris, & J. Y. Russell (Eds.), *Tackling wicked problems* (pp. 16–30). Washington: Earthscan.

Max-Neef, M. A. (2005). Foundations of transdisciplinarity. *Ecological Economics, 53*(1), 5–16.

Meyer, S. B., & Lunnay, B. (2013). The application of abductive and retroductive inference for the design and analysis of theory-driven sociological research. *Sociological Research Online, 18*(1), 12. http://www.socresonline.org.uk/18/1/contents.html. Accessed 8 March 2013.

Mitrany, M., & Stokols, D. (2005). Gauging the transdisciplinary qualities and outcomes of doctoral training programs. *Journal of Planning Education and Research, 24*, 437–440.

Modell, S. (2009). In defence of triangulation: A critical realist approach to mixed methods research in management accounting. *Management Accounting Research, 20*, 208–221.

Nicolescu, B. (2010). Methodology of transdisciplinarity—Levels of reality, logic of the included middle and complexity. *Transdisciplinary Journal of Engineering & Science, 1*(1), 19–38.

Olsen, W. (2010). *Realist methods, Volume II*. London: Sage.

Peirce, C. S. (1901/1998a). On the logic of drawing history from ancient documents, especially from testimonies. In *The essential Peirce* (pp. 75–114). Indiana: Indiana University.

Peirce, C. S. (1903/1998b). What makes a reasoning sound. In *The essential Peirce* (pp. 242–257). Indiana: Indiana University.

Peirce, C. S. (1903/1998c). Pragmatism as the logic of abduction. In *The essential Peirce* (pp. 226–241). Indiana: Indiana University.

Pohl, C., & Hadorn, G. H. (2007). *Principles for designing transdisciplinary research* (trans: A. B. Zimmerman). Munich: OEKOM.

Richardson R. R., & Kramer, E. H. (2006). Abduction as the type of inference that characterizes the development of a grounded theory. *Qualitative Research, 6*, 497–513.

Rosenberg, T. (2000). 'The reservoir': Towards a poetic model of research in design. *Working papers in art and design, 1*. http://sitem.herts.ac.uk/artdes_research/papers/wpades/vol1/rosenberg2.html. Accessed 12 March 2013.

Schram, S. (2012). Phronetic social science: An idea whose time has come. In B. Flyvbjerg, T. Landman, & S. Schram (Eds.), *Real social science: Applied phronesis* (pp. 15–26). Cambridge: Cambridge University Press.

Scholz, R. W., & Tietje, O. (2002). *Embedded case study methods: Integrating quantitative and qualitative knowledge*. London: Sage.

Scott, D. (2005). Critical realism and empirical research methods in education. *Journal of Philosophy of Education, 39*(4), 633–646.

Scott, D. (2010). *Education, epistemology and critical realism*. London: Routledge.

Stauffacher, M., Walter, A. I., Lang, D. J., Wiek, A., & Scholz, R. W. (2006). Learning to research environmental problems from a functional socio-cultural constructivism perspective: The transdisciplinary case study approach. *International Journal of Sustainability in Higher Education, 7*(3), 252–275.

Thomas, G. (2010). Doing case study: Abduction not induction, phronesis not theory. *Qualitative Inquiry, 16*, 575–582.

Verschuren, P. (2003). Case study as a research strategy: Some ambiguities and opportunities. *International Journal of Social Research Methodology, 6*(2), 121–139.

Wiesmann, U., Biber-Klemm, S., Grossenbacher-Mansuy, W., Hadorn, G., HoffmanRiem, H., Joye, D., Pohl, C., & Zemp, E. (2008). Enhancing transdisciplinary research: A synthesis in

15 propositions. In G. Hirsch Hadorn, H. HoffmannRiem, S. Biber-Klemm, W. Grossenbacher-Mansuy, D. Joye, C. Pohl, U. Wiesmann, & E. Zemp (Eds.), *Handbook of transdisciplinary research*, Chap. 29 (pp. 433–432). Dordrecht: Springer.

Workman, B. (2007). 'Casing the joint': Explorations by the insider-researcher preparing for work-based projects. *Journal of Workplace Learning, 19*(3), 146–160.

Yin, R. K. (2003). *Case study research. Design and method* (3rd edn.). Thousand Oaks: Sage.

Paul Gibbs is Professor of Education at Middlesex University. His interests and publications span higher education marketing, philosophy, professional practice and time. He is Series Editor of *Educational Thinker* for Springer, holds positions on a number the editorial board of a number of international journal and has participated in a number of European projects. His elective interests find a conceptual home in transdisciplinarity.

Transdisciplinarity as Translation

Kate Maguire

In doctoral level professional studies and work based learning, we are in a constant and intensified mode of 'trans-lating' across different realms of experience, domains of practice, epistemological paradigms, objects of knowledge, learning and relational styles, values and purposes. The intensification is propelled by survival in a globalised, post modern, technological world of multiple truths, multiple voices, limited resources and indeed limited time. This set of conditions has rekindled interest, or rather an imperative, to regenerate Thoth/Hermes, progenitor of hermeneutics and his outstanding skills in the art of trans-lation which negotiated across difference respecting all sides and holding them in communicative balance so that the 'knowing' on each side could be trans-formed by the 'knowing' of the other. If we are to avoid a paradigmatic colonialism that converts or dominates to arrive at homogeneity, we need to develop higher level skills in negotiating 'between' to co-create knowledge and trans-form how we think and what we do to meet the challenges of the future. Trans-disciplinarity seeks to move forward in this way. This chapter looks at the role of trans-lation and at the leading edge thinking of such fields as environmental sciences and contemporary translation studies to formulate a contribution to explicating and operationalising trans-disciplinarity to arrive at 'metanoia', another way of knowing. This is of interest to those who are planning to undertake collaborative research using a transdisciplinary approach and those involved in supervising doctoral research.

Metanoia is a term that has been used in a number of ways including 'repentance' which is its original Greek meaning in theology and 'another way of knowing'. It is in the sense of 'another way of knowing' that it is used in this chapter.

K. Maguire (✉)
Middlesex University, London, UK
e-mail: k.maguire@mdx.ac.uk

© Springer International Publishing Switzerland 2015
P. Gibbs (ed.), *Transdisciplinary Professional Learning and Practice,*
DOI 10.1007/978-3-319-11590-0_12

A good place to start is to look at transdisciplinarity's most common loci, purposes and drivers. In the field of professional doctoral research[1], issues have been raised about needing to clarify what it is in order to draw up some guidance as to how to teach, evaluate and assess doctoral level research that purports to be transdisciplinary or whose purpose may benefit from a transdisciplinary approach. In professional doctorates it is both. My knowledge culture is social anthropology, psychotherapy and doctoral level professional studies. In each of these loci, practitioners know what transdisciplinarity is in practice, they experience it, they work with and through it, and they promote it. My purpose in this undertaking is to seek to articulate transdisciplinarity more coherently as an appropriate response to an increasingly complex world where not only discipline/domain/sector islands are increasingly more connected but those connections are also to the public at large as having stakeholdership in solutions for the future. That coherence involves understanding what transdisciplinary refers to so that we might be more able to guide the facilitation and assessment of it regardless of whether it is an approach to knowledge, to research or to the individual's professional practice. Transdiscipinarity is about boundary or border crossing to arrive at knowledge co-creation and co-production but in order to do that it has to challenge existing hegemonies and not become one itself. Nicolescu's vision of transdisciplinarity (1998) is of interconnecting 'bridges', a vision of transdisciplinarity which Klein (2004, p. 516) cites as 'transcultural, transnational and encompasses ethics, spirituality and creativity.'

What is emerging from the literature, with significant contributions from environmental sciences, philosophy, humanities and translation studies, is that transdisciplinarity can be seen as a conceptual framework for research that provides a comprehensive response to increasing social, political and economic complexity in which traditional boundaries have to be crossed to arrive at new thinking and approaches to find solutions at local, regional and global levels to a range of problems from life improvement to human survival. Individual case studies are cited and retrospectives are taking place to find theoretical underpinnings and to refine such a conceptual framework through which to articulate the nature and achievement of knowledge formation and how to attain optimisation of application that is useful to the widest number of stakeholders. One such example to draw on for such purposes is critical theory (Bronner 2011, p. 114)

> Critical theory was originally intended as an interdisciplinary enterprise to which each might bring his or her unique disciplinary talent and expertise. Its representatives highlighted the relationship between philosophy and politics, society and psychology, culture and liberation...The Frankfurt School called outworn concepts into question...They also intimated the need for a new understanding of the relation between theory and practice... Democracy remains unfinished; cosmopolitanism is challenged by identity; socialism requires a new definition...The cultural inheritance of the past has still not been reclaimed... and the ability of audiences to learn still requires criteria concerning what needs to be taught....Engaging in these matters requires an interdisciplinary outlook formed by liberating norms.

---

[1] For the purposes of this chapter, the nomenclature 'professional doctorate' will be used as inclusive of practice based doctorates.

Here there is a clear declaration of the social action element in a coming together of knowledges with the purpose of liberating thinking to deal with new contingencies. However one could go much further back, say, to Confucius and his ideas on education (Ryu 2010, p. 20).

> Education in the Confucian tradition has been considered the most valuable activity in life and a tool for self cultivation of humanity... the whole focus of Confucian education is the development of whole persons rather than narrowly trained specialists.

In this example from an applied philosopher who lived two and a half thousand years ago, the advance in a humanity focused world starts with education which needs to be on the development of the self of the child. This idea of self is inextricably linked to community and for the child to become an informed and 'virtuous' human being requires an openness to all kinds of knowledge.

Historically there are many examples in research and in literature of what we can now position as transdisciplinary approaches and individuals as transdisciplinary practitioners, so many in fact that it would seem that our perception of discipline islands that has dominated knowledge in the West for so long is to some extent a false construct. There has traditionally been interdisciplinary exchange within certain clusters of disciplines such as branches of science and social science. It is when the islands have been culturally more distant from each other, such as natural sciences and social sciences, that the differences and preciousness have come into play with language reflecting the perceived nature of relationship at a distance: terms such as *heretical, borrowing, raiding, plundering* to refer to what is now acknowledged as *fruitful knowledge exchange*, and *subjective, objective* as distinct criticisms and faults rather than *complementarities*. There was always a plurality of voices, what has shifted is the exponential growth of the plurality and the increased interconnectivity and interdependency of those islands. According to Ruano (2011, p. 44) talking about interdisciplinarity in translation studies

> The key to progress is largely thought to lie in *consensus* rather than disparity, in *integration* rather than dispersion of theories or perspectives, in affirmation of a *shared ground*... rather than in the scrutiny of discrepancies; in short... in *conciliation* rather than in variety, let alone conflict, of viewpoints, disciplines and paradigms

But then goes on to add a warning (Ruano 2011, p. 47) :

> The current effort at finding a common theoretical basis may result not in strengthening the discipline but in hampering its progress, to the extent that the marginalisation of dissenting voices might prevent it from engaging in self-critical reflection and from being aware of its limitations.... claiming absolute comprehensiveness implies denying the complexity of the phenomenon under study, a stance blatantly in contradiction with the trend towards "problematizing" objects of research in the current intellectual climate (Baker 2002, pp. 50–53).

This should not be the aim of transdisciplinarity, to establish a comprehensive and thereby exclusive theoretical and practice framework which, although based on consensus, integration and shared ground, would nevertheless silence dissenting voices. It is rather to do the opposite. It recognises both the need for and value of discipline islands and the flexibility and fluidity of an approach to research that responds to the realties, discontinuities and contingencies that are in a constant state of flux as location in temporality overtakes geographical location in what Augé (2009) calls a culture of supermodernity.

Osborne (2011, p. 15) pinpoints the concept of transdisciplinarity in the 'post philosophical' theoretical heritage of twentieth century European philosophy and being: "a universalizing conceptual movement that recognizes... that the idea of philosophy can only be realised outside the idea of philosophy itself" thereby opening it up to other discourses to engage in it. He proposes that

> The notion of transdisciplinarity is an advance, formally, in denoting a movement across existing fields (as opposed to a thinking *between* them or a *multiplication of* them); and it is an advance in terms of theoretical content, in so far as it locates the source of transdisciplinary dynamics pragmatically in a process of problem-solving related, ultimately, to problems of experience in everyday life... transdisciplinarity is not the conceptual product of addressing problems defined as policy challenge ... but rather of addressing problems that are *culturally and politically* defined in such a way as to be amenable to theoretical reformulation (ibid).

Klein (2004) and many contemporary commentators and researchers concur that transdisciplinarity is not a single form of knowledge but a dialogue of forms. Such a dialogue is between disciplines, systems and languages, as well as between our different ways of knowing, the plurality of epistemes which include perceiving, sensing, understanding, conceptualising, explaining causality and meaning making. To approach local and global sticky problems requires an engagement with difference across cultural, social and cognitive contexts and across prefigurative and sense making views, in other words, an engagement with the purpose and relevance of any action for a range of stakeholders. Pohl and Hirsch Hadorn (2007), of the Swiss Federal Institute of Technology, working on research and sustainability, have offered three different types of knowledge that can be used to characterise transdisciplinary research: systems, target and transformation, as well as the challenges embedded within them: reflecting on and dealing with uncertainties through real world experiments; clarification and priority setting of various values in relation to the common good as a regulatory principle, and learning how to make existing technologies, regulations, practices and power relations more flexible. As Edgar Morin (2001, p. 5), the French philosopher, points out

> One of the greatest problems we face today is how to adjust our way of thinking to meet the challenge of an increasingly complex, rapidly changing, unpredictable world. We must rethink our way of organising knowledge.

To achieve these transversals or border crossings or interweavings of the 'metissage' (Nouss 2005) that might reorganise and interconnect knowledge for the future, sophisticated bridges of existing knowledge exchange are required to produce new learnings and syntheses sustained by skilled translation between these different realms of knowledge, experience and practice. In such a scenario, researchers are key pollinators and change agents fundamental to the change/solution being sought. Although there are different emphases rather than perspectives on transdisciplinarity, it is the properties, purposes and advantages of transdisciplinarity as embodied in practitioners, the innovation and problematisng which they are dealing with in the complexities of their sectors/domains of practice as well as attention to other stakeholders, that is of interest in this chapter. Through such a focus, the skills

and attributes of a transdisciplinary research supervisor/facilitator or, in this changing knowledge landscape, the translator or navigator of the transversals, may be
revealed or indicated.

The field of translational studies, like professional studies, has progressed rapidly
in the last twenty years. Its current discourses have relevance to transdisciplinarity
and therefore to the research undertaken in professional doctorates which interweave
theory and practice and different sectors and domains: it has refined debates on conceptual frameworks for responding to complexity using spatial metaphors to define
relationships between the different discipline islands—interdisciplinary, multidisciplinary, transdisciplinary; it contributes to emerging pedagogy which underpins
professional doctoral level study that goes beyond interdisciplinarity and multidisciplinarity into the co-creation of new knowledge and concepts; and it offers us
language in which to 'translate' what we do more efficiently and effectively (Duarte
et al. 2006). This chapter will not over concern itself with the differences between inter, multi and trans but rather concentrate on the emergent field of transdisciplinarity
where professional studies is increasingly situated.

Transdisciplinarity can be said to be, like translation, an *area of knowledge,* as
stated by Nouss cited in Duarte et al. (2006, p. 3),

> After 'consciousness' in the nineteenth century and 'language' in the twentieth, 'translation'
> can be considered to define the contemporary ethos. As an area of knowledge, it calls for an
> innovative, transversal and metis [interweaving] epistemology (2005, p. 228).

an *approach to knowledge and research* which is participatory with the non academic
as argued by Cronin (2008, p. 2) in her support of the views of Hirsch Hadorn et al.
(2008):

> Transdisciplinary research [TDR] is a new field of research emerging in the 'knowledge
> society', which links science and policy to address issues such as environmental degradation,
> new technologies public health and social change. Through transdisciplinary approaches
> researchers from a wide range of disciplines work with each other and external stakeholders
> to address real world issues

the approach to knowledge creation for the future according to Russell et al. (2008,
p. 2) involving three areas:

> problem focus (research originates from and is contextualized in 'real-world' problems),
> evolving methodology (the research involves iterative, reflective processes that are responsive
> to the particular questions, settings, and research groupings) and collaboration (including
> collaboration between transdisciplinarity researchers, disciplinary researchers and external
> actors with interests in the research

and, the pursuit of coherence, not unity, within paradoxes of different realities as
proposed by Ramadier (2004) from his work in urban studies which involves the
input of several disciplines and the constant negotiation of concrete and abstract
spatial boundaries.

> ... the notion of unity becomes obsolete, and this is true even at the level of the studied
> object... This, when a given entity changes, it is not only part of the object that changes,
> but the object itself. For example, each city has a history, a transport infrastructure, and a
> heterogeneous social make up. However, each city is different owing to the precise nature

and interrelations between all the components. In other words, there is no such thing as "the city", there are only "cities" (2004, p. 452)… Thus, transdisciplinarity is based on controlled conflict generated by paradoxes. (2004, p. 434)

Klein (2004) who has written extensively on transdisciplinarity reminds us of the significant contribution of Nicolescu (2008) and his founding of CIRET (International Centre for Transdisciplinary Research) in 1996 which shifted notions of knowledge from the one dimensionality of classical thought to a multidimensional frame, 'a scientific and cultural approach'. In the Manifesto, and the essay "New Vision of the World", Nicolescu identified three pillars of transdisciplinarity: complexity, multiple levels of reality, and the logic of the included middle (2004, p. 515).

To further differentiate it, it could be said that interdisciplinarity and multidisciplinarity are terms which usually imply a process of cooperation or collaboration between two or more disciplines which are either logical because they are linked in such as in neuroscience and psychotherapy and may bring about changes in both, or because they come together to solve a problem which requires different inputs, for example, a multidisciplinary approach to mental health. This cooperation does not primarily seek to change the individual discipline's epistemology, methodology or content. Transdisciplinarity, on the other hand, can imply a qualitatively different relationship between disciplines and practices. It is not so much a process of co-operation or collaboration which defines it but an intentional approach to transcend boundaries of disciplines and practices to create a new knowledge synthesis within the individual or domain of practice and indeed in society. As Cronin (2008, p. 2) and others would argue, its aim is *to overcome the gap between knowledge production on the one hand and the demand for knowledge to contribute to the solution of social problems on the other.* In professional studies doctorates this may be the medical devices inventor who, in order to 'translate' his/her invention from bench to the clinic to save lives, needs to visit and learn from the other domains such as regulation; public health policies; insurance; monopolies; media that facilitate or block progress to achieve a creative solution; or it may be the senior non academic practitioner whose intentional engagement with academia changes both domains. Such change agents act as pollinators between the different domains causing new thinking, applications, solutions and practices to emerge.

Key components of transdisciplinarity include stakeholders' views; real world problem solving; change agency; knowledge production; new synthesis; exchange between disciplines and practices with the intention of achieving action that influences the disciplines and practices themselves; mapping and remapping; academic and non academic participation and social responsibility. This author supports social action/responsibility as a key element but recognises that this aspect of transdisciplinarity, while considered by some as the core element that makes transdisciplinarity the most appropriate response to complexity, 'problematising and political' (Osborne 2011, p. 16), it is thought of by others as the unnecessary inclusion of a moral dimension to an approach to knowledge.

These core elements of transdisciplinarity can lead to what can be called *metanoia*, another way of knowing; a knowing 'beyond' which is creative and transformative. This poses challenges for transdisciplinary approaches at doctoral level about the skills and attributes required of those who have the task of facilitating and negotiating this understanding between different realms of experience, thinking and cultures so that a *metanoia* can take place that supports the arriving at a change or response that is of benefit to the largest number of stakeholders. This involves not only the role of academics but the roles of the public in various forms such as the workplace senior practitioner; the spokesperson for a public health charity; the CEO of a major energy company; the people in a location where major change is being researched which will affect their lives and livelihoods; governments and international institutions tasked with protecting human rights and global sustainability through policies, guidelines and regulations.

Formulating and Predications

Transdisciplinarity is, according to Klein (2004, p. 521), simultaneously an attitude and a form of action. A key consideration is how to conceptualise transdisciplinary research in a way that reveals what is needed to develop, evaluate and assess it. For these purposes I suggest formulating transdisciplinary research as i) that carried out by an individual for the purposes of attending to a challenge or a problem resulting in innovative and impactful outcomes in a local context through critical reflexivity relating to context and practices including their own with attention to the complexity of the 'situation', the ethics of participation and the implications of intended/consequential change ii) that carried out by a group, group being anything more than one, who come together to solve a problem and in doing that new knowledge is created and new thinking emerges of value to all the participants. The first part of the formulation is predicated on the premise that all modern practitioners and prospective practitioners are by definition transdisciplinary to varying degrees: the engineer who runs a business; the banker who takes courses in human resource management; the technologist who develops academic programmes; the teacher who in practice is a counsellor; the small town engineer who believes he or she has something to offer a multinational enterprise; the aspiring graduate seeking membership or fellowship of a professional body. The research that such senior professionals in sectors or communities of practice, or prospective professionals undertake is most likely to be an individual enterprise in the domain of epistemic plurality and border crossing with intended impact on the context locality in which the research activity is grounded—the real everyday world. The second part of the formulation is predicated on the notion that researchers from academic and practice discipline islands are coming together to contribute to resolving challenges of the macrocosm even if they are working at the microcosmic level by global standards, each willing to set aside or be flexible about the structures, beliefs and practices which are the pillars of their individual island cultures and all intending to engage in some way with a range of stakeholders who are part of the 'context', from members of the public to government bodies. Klein (2004, p. 517) citing Nowotny et al. (2001) captures this aspect of the formulation as the extension of

> The concept of Mode 2 in the idea of "contextualisation", moving from the strict realm of application to the *agora* of public debate

The transdisciplinary group enters, in a sense, a virtual world, a helicopter view, of not only problem solving but problem choosing, suspending post figurative hierarchies of the epistemes and practices of their discipline or sector cultures to trade or transform old lamps into new ones that will evolve knowledge in a way that optimises inclusion in an equitable future related to sustainability of resources and optimal distribution. In other words, to achieve what Klein (2004, p. 519) has distilled from other transdisciplinary proponents, the concept of a 'genuinely human science', releasing a knowledge genie from the lamp more appropriate to our accelerated world.

I would suggest that enabling a transdisciplinary approach to research and knowledge in an individual or group requires something different from the traditional role of supervisor whose expertise in the discipline is privileged over any relational, reflexive, observational, enabling, coaching, interpretative, 'trans' skills that have come to be the attributes of the transdisciplinary adviser[2] in professional doctorates. I would also suggest that to be a successful transdisciplinary adviser is not predicated solely on mastering disciplines but mastering how to facilitate connections and communications in a way that results in creative and practical change agency transforming of not only the researcher, their professional environment and society but of the adviser and their evolving pedagogy and of the trandisciplinary group and their evolving epistemologies in a process of mutual learning. The individual and the group approaches to transdisciplinary research are both figurations of applied research that go beyond application to new theories and approaches that need to involve other constituents beyond the researchers and their sponsors.

Mobjörk (2010, p. 866) raises this issue of the roles of the various actors and conceptualises the transdisciplinary framework as involving a range of actors in consultative roles and in participatory researcher roles.

> Transdisciplinarity is currently perceived as an extended knowledge production including a variety of actors and with an open perception of the relevance of different forms of scientific and lay knowledge. By stressing scope of collaboration, a clearer distinction can be established between interdisciplinarity and transdisciplinarity than was possible with the former focus on degree of integration. However, integration is still an essential feature of transdisciplinarity and in emphasising the need to acknowledge the different roles actors can play in knowledge production a distinction can be identified between two different forms of transdisciplinarity; consulting versus participatory transdisciplinarity.

Mobjörk (2010, p. 869) is also making a case for clearer articulation as this has implications for funders of research, clearly delineated areas of responsibility and ownership and criteria for evaluating the research and its outcomes. He confirms that on the subject of methodology, which has always been a required skill in research supervisors, that it is not a specific methodological approach that is needed but a focus on the context. Such a focus will yield the questions that need to be asked and define the methods most appropriate to extract the data.

---

[2] Nomenclature: in some professional doctorates involving doctorates undertaken by senior practitioners, the doctoral supervisor or director of studies is referred to as the 'adviser' in recognition of the collaborative, dialogic and knowledge exchange elements of the relationship.

Regarding methodology, the prevailing consensus within the literature on transdisciplinarity is that there is no single methodology or set of methodologies that can be used to distinguish transdisciplinarity from other research practices. Instead, the focus lies on describing the features common to appropriate methods for transdisciplinary research. An essential consideration within these descriptions is the concept of reflexivity, i.e. transdisciplinary research needs to respond and reflect the problem and context under investigation. As Wickson et al. note, transdisciplinarity is 'characterised by an interpretation of epistemologies in the development of methodology' and thus presents profound epistemological challenges and calls for a pluralistic approach to methodology.... it must be able to grasp complexity. Hence, transdisciplinarity needs approaches that can deal with uncertainty and take into account the diversity of perceptions from various actors. Suitable methods for conducting transdisciplinary research must therefore support these requirements and one way of describing this is by using 'context-dependence'. If knowledge is considered context-dependent, the different interests, methods and goals of those producing knowledge must be considered.

Nicolescu (1998) does not propose 'specialists' in transdisciplinarity, Ruona warns against a new transdisciplinarity being an exclusive system of consensus, Klein (2004) makes a case for fluidity and flexibility, Mobjörk (2010) gives a reasoned argument on evolving methodologies and Ramadier (2004) talks of coherence not unity. Such contributions to the development of a conceptual framework for transdisciplinarity have not yet produced the skills and attributes required of a transdisciplinary research supervisor but they do indicate some loose formulation. I suggest, based on existing discourses, that the research supervision nomenclature shift to research facilitation and that the facilitation is not conducted in a hierarchical relationship of apprentice and master or science over humanities or academic over professional or worker but in a collaborative enterprise in which various expertises are made available for exchange and synthesising. The facilitating teams for the individual and for the group would be constituted differently but with shared attributes and values, the values being a commitment to outcomes that contribute to a wider distribution of benefits and inclusion and a perception of knowledge as neither the privilege of the elite or paradigm bound. The suggestions are predicated on the conceptualisation of our world as having the characteristics of the superorganism, an archipelago of islands with their own cultures interconnected through a complex system of networks, what Laplantine and Nouss (2008) refer to as the 'metissage'. Every researcher needs to take into consideration that they cannot nor should be unplugged from the complexity and that exclusion of any part of that complexity in any research activity should not result in marginalisation or exclusivity. There are those who will research on and for the sustainability of the islands, those who research on the exchange between them to keep the connections open and high functioning and those who research the survival of the whole organism. These are different but interconnected areas for research focus. In this scenario there can be 'no final vocabulary' (Rorty 1989, p. 73) but rather a contribution to an emerging metanoic language that captures commonalities and introduces new terms or a new and appropriate application of existing ones. Ramadier (2004, p. 432) continuing on his notion of seeking coherence within paradoxes not unity, places 'articulation' as a key component of transdisciplinarity if it is to achieve its goals.

articulation is what enables us to seek coherence within paradoxes, and not unity. The notion of "articulation", as we have defined it, allows us to perform a transition between the different levels of reality that can generate paradoxes. Thus, the difficulty of transdisciplinarity lies in going beyond the superpositions of realities, through articulation. Indeed, we are often tempted to be satisfied with superposition, in order to avoid paradox.

The superpositions are also sustained by language. Language can inhibit cultural growth or enrich it. Language can facilitate new conceptualisations of knowledge to enhance public as well as discipline or academic understanding. Examples would be Deleuze and Guattari's (1980) use of 'rhizome' the botanical term for mass roots to denote multiplicity and interconnections in non hierarchical structures between all aspects of society, and 'metissage', the interweaving of connections, cultures, ideas (Laplantine and Nouss 2008). Articulating transdisciplinarity as a knowledge approach for the future is inclusive of reflexivity, respect for plural epistemes, knowledge exchange not transfer, social responsibility, which as coda could be described as humanising principles

The advantages of transdisciplinarity vary from large scale to small scale but in the metaphor of the superorganism it is the proverbial butterfly wings; small and large are no longer the most appropriate adjectives for such activities, rather something that describes the context eg local or regional; both can have significant impact or unanticipated outcomes including barely any impact at all or unwanted outcomes. Transdisciplinary notions can contribute to the epistemological implications for our theories of pedagogic practices when universities are facing pressure to feed employability demands and it offers greater opportunity to engage in discourses with researchers, veteran and new, on social responsibility, moral dilemmas and value driven agendas.

Lawrence and Després (2004, p. 403) describe transdisciplinarity in a way that underlines the role of the researcher but which gives indication of what may then be required of the person or people who take a facilitating role in the research choice and undertaking.

> ... transdisciplinarity has become the actor oriented negotiation of knowledge or what Julie Thompson Klein calls "generative form of communicative action that is context- specific".

At a fundamental level, a transdisciplinary facilitator then needs the observational and record keeping skills of the ethnographer, the listening and reflexive skills of a coach or counsellor and the translation skills of a hermenuet—that is one who seeks to facilitate the multiple directional flows of information across different realms of experience prepared to use tricks such a metaphors and frameworks to rapidly conceptualise complex issues and their solutions against a backdrop of fast moving time in which long term reflecting and planning can be surpassed by technologies and changing political landscapes. However drawing on Mobjörk's thinking (2010) around consultative and participatory transdisciplinarity, it would be important to make a further distinction when thinking about transdisciplinary research facilitation and that is whether the researcher is an individual 'de facto' transdisciplinary practitioner intent on making an impact on practice and context or a group of individuals who come from different sectors, disciplines, domains and experiences to

Table 1 Facilitating a transdisciplinary approach

TD doctoral research	Individual	Group	Attributes
Research facilitator	Researcher is primary facilitator of their own research, the leader and manager of the research undertaking with a value system related to social action and distributed benefits eg research motivation is to improve context conditions to optimise benefits for all constituents	Facilitates team communication, providing the optimum conditions for working together and facilitating choice of problem, knowledge exchange, syntheses and creation towards practical outcomes. Part of the context is social action or 'for the common good'	Project Planning Communication Distilling Translating Coaching Mediation Ethical awareness
Subject expert	Works closely with TD expert and/or work/sector specialist to support the researcher through collaborative and dialogic engagement that is context specific	Subject experts are the researchers and their exchanges are facilitated but not controlled by the research facilitator	Subject knowledge expertise but joining the project with the intention of openness to ideas from outside of own knowledge and practice culture
TD expert	One skilled in discourses on border crossings and the interfaces of difference drawing on generic skills from previous successful doctoral candidates, mentors theories of praxis etc	Embodied in the research facilitator	Ability to conceptualise and map complexity and navigate it. Flexibility, imagination, ethical awareness of border crossing and implications of change
Work/sector based specialist effectively a member of the 'context public'—consultative or part of the research activity/evaluation/ assessment	Experienced in work/sector environments of relevance to the research project	Consultant to or part of the TD team	Awareness of ethical dilemmas, regulatory tensions, political and social dimensions of work/sector environments and cultures
Complexity expert	Embodied in the researcher, the TD expert and the subject expert	Manages the practical aspects of the project based on expertise in complexity	Technological expertise impact implications, risk assessment, budgets, feasibility, IP, patents

Table 2 Further features of TD (drawn from literature) which can inform attitudes and attributes of current and potential researchers and practitioners

Sensitizing concept	Generalised capacity
Reflexivity	Suprascientific search for meaning
Reflection on consequences of action	Development of attributes begins at school education level
Deliberative practitioner	Human science
Interdeterminancy	Intuitive judgement

work together on a project. The following table is an attempt, far from exhaustive, to pull together the various strands of conceptualising a transdisciplinary facilitation framework and what may be required to facilitate its successful execution (Tables 1 and 2).

Transdisciplinarity in professional studies doctorates aims to go beyond the 'strait-jacket' (Osborne 2011) of mere problem solving into an era that does not negate disciplines and dilute them into some kind of epistemological soup but rather creates the conditions for more metanoic solutions to managing complexity and the liberating of thinking and action from hegemonic island paradigms. These may be disciplined bound in higher education but in the world of markets, resources and political manoeuvring in which profit and power are synonymous, the hegemonic islands are global companies and super-institutions with vested interests and therefore have more power to exclude, marginalise or reduce the share in the future of large sections of the inhabitants of the planet. A transdisciplinary approach can do in the new hegemonic islands what it has started to do in research education and practice.

> Transdisciplinarity was once one of many terms. It has become a major imperative across all sectors of society and knowledge domains, making it more than a fad or fashion. It has become an essential mode of thought and action Klein (2004, p. 524)

References

Augé, M. (2009). *Non-places: Introduction to an anthropology of supermodernity*. London: Verso.
Baker, M. (2002). Aspectos pragmaticos del contacto intercultural y falsas dicotomias en los estudios de traduccion. In R. Alvarez (ed) *Cartografias de la traduccion: del post-estructuralismo al multiculturalismo* (pp. 43–58, Trans. R. Martib Ruan & Torres del Rey). Salamanca: Ediciones Colegio de Espana.
Bronner, S. E. (2011). *Critical theory: A very short introduction*. Oxford University Press.
Cronin, K. (2008). Transdisciplinary Research (TDR) and sustainability. Report for the Ministry of Research, Science and Technology (MoRST New Zealand). http://learningforsustainability.net/pubs/Transdisciplinary_Research_and_Sustainability.pdf. Accessed 12 May 2013.
Deleuze, G., & Guattari, F. (1980). *A thousand plateaus* (trans: Brian Massumi). London: Continuum.
Duarte, J. F., Rosa, A. A., & Seruya, T. (Eds.). (2006). *Translation studies at the interface of disciplines* (Vol. 68). Benjamins Translation Library.

Hirsch Hadorn, G., Hoffman-Riem, H., Biber-Klemm, S., Grossenbacher-Mansuy, W., Joye, D., Pohl, C., Wiesmann, U., & Zemp, E. (Eds.). (2008). *Handbook of transdisciplinary research.* Springer.

Klein, J. T. (2004). Prospects for transdisciplinarity. In R. Lawrence & C. Després (Eds.), *Special Issue, Transdisciplinarity, futures 36*(4), 397–526. Elsevier.

Laplantine, F., & Nouss, A. (2008). *Le métissage: Un exposé pour comprendre, un essai pour réfléchir.* Teraedre.

Lawrence, R., & Després, C. (Eds.). (2004). Futures of transdisciplinarity. *Futures, 36*(4), 397–526

Mobjörk, M. (2010). Consulting versus participatory transdisciplinarity: A refined classification of transdisciplinary research. *Futures, 42*(8), 777–900. (Elsevier).

Morin, E. (2001). *Seven complex lesson in education for the future.* Paris: UNESCO.

Nicolescu, B. (1998). The transdisciplinary evolution of the university condition for sustainable development CIRET. Bulletin Interactif du Centre International de Recherches et Études transdisciplinaires n° 12 - Février 1998.

Nicolescu, B. (2008). *Transdisciplinarity: Theory and practice.* Hampton Press.

Nouss, A. (2005). *Plaidoyer pour un monde metis.* Textuel.

Nowotny, H., Scott, P., & Gibbons, M. (2001). *Re-thinking science: Knowledge and the public in an age of uncertainty.* Polity.

Osborne, P. (2011). From structure to rhizome: Transdisciplinarity in French thought (1). In radical philosophy 165 Jan/Feb 2011.

Pohl, C., & Hirsch Hadorn, G. (2007). *Principles for designing transdisciplinary research.* Oekom Verlag GmbH.

Ramadier, T. (2004). Transdicsiplinarity and its challenges: The case of urban studies. In R. Lawrence & C. Després (Eds.), *Transdisciplinarity, futures* (Vol. 36, Issue 4). Elsevier.

Rorty, R. (1989). *Contingency, irony, and solidarity.* Cambridge University Press.

Ruano, M. R. M. (2011). Conciliation of disciplines and paradigms: A challenge and a for future direction in translation studies. In J. F. Duarte, A. A. Rosa, & T. Seruya (Eds.), *Translation studies at the interface of disciplines* (Vol. 68). Benjamins.

Russell, A. W., Wickson, F., & Carew, A. L. (2008). Transdisciplinarity: Context, contradictions and capacity. *Futures, 40*(5), 460–472. (Elsevier).

Ryu, K. (2010). The teachings of confucius: Reviving a humanistic adult education perspective. *International Journal of Continuing Education and Lifelong Learning, 2*(2), 11–28.

Kate Maguire is part of the core team for the transdisciplinary doctorate in professional studies at Middlesex University and leads on the doctorate by public works and on the doctoral supervisor training for the programmes. She came into professional studies through her role as head of the post qualifying doctorate in psychotherapy at the renowned Metanoia Institute. Her background is in social anthropology of the Middle East, trauma psychotherapy and authority dynamics. Her career spans leading human rights projects in the Middle East, broadcasting and production and consulting in the private and public sectors. She is holder of a Beacon award for services to the voluntary sector. She was drawn to professional studies at Middlesex University for its stance on the contribution of practice to knowledge and its role in creating the conditions for more a equitable share in decision making processes to improve the societies in which we live. She has published on a range of subjects related to professional practice in different fields. Her forthcoming book (Springer 2014) is on the anthropologist Margaret Mead's contributions to contemporary education.

The Emergence of the Collective Mind

Valerie A. Brown and John A. Harris

Pattern

Context: With the emergence of human responsibility for a human-dominated planet that marks the era of the Anthropocene, there is a resulting need to extend human understanding of uncertainty and complexity and harness the full capacity of the collective mind.

Issues: Collision courses among the compartmentalized constructions of knowledge inherited from the scientific Enlightenment impede the whole-of-knowledge reach of the collective mind.

Resolution: Collective learning reframes opposites as relationships and extends empirical inquiries into asking the full suite of physical, social, ethical, aesthetic, interpersonal, personal and reflective questions.

Examples: steps in individual and group collective thinking.

Context: The Anthropocene and the Collective Mind

Changes in the construction of knowledge are a regular feature of the human condition (Clark 1971). The 2 million year history of human impact on the planet has been traditionally been described through the human creative use of resources, such as the Stone Age, Bronze Age and Iron Age.[1] The theme of this chapter, the emergence of a collective mind, is a sufficiently significant step forward in the human creative use of social and physical resources to be representative of the present era of the

---

[1] See http://en.wikipedia.org/wiki/Prehistory [accessed 26.3.14].

V. A. Brown (✉) · J. A. Harris
Fenner School of Environment and Society, Australian National University,
Canberra, Australia
e-mail: val.brown@anu.edu.au

© Springer International Publishing Switzerland 2015
P. Gibbs (ed.), *Transdisciplinary Professional Learning and Practice*,
DOI 10.1007/978-3-319-11590-0_13

Anthropocene. The Anthropocene is the label being given to this time in human history when the entire planet is being affected by the power and range of Anthropos, human actions spurred by human ideas (Steffen et al. 2011). This is not to say that humans are in control of the future. Far from it. The future holds an uncertain outcome as a result of the transformative effects of human interaction with the rest of the living and non-living systems of the planet.

In the twenty-first century, transformational changes in thinking are being generated by global flows of information, finance, resources, and people, bringing together diverse ideas (Falk 1999). The Anthropocene itself is the latest stage in a series of modes of governance. In Western societies, these were the Greek and then the Roman Empires, the Middle Ages, the Renaissance and most recently the scientific Enlightenment. Each era has developed its own basis for the construction of knowledge (Clark 1971). These can be loosely recognized as humanist, administrative, god-given, creative and empirical justifications for evidence. The most recent, the empirical justification applied during the scientific Enlightenment, is losing its long dominance due to its inability to provide adequate answers to the questions raised by the transformational changes taking place around the world (Brown and Harris 2014).

Global changes are generating issues of food security, urbanization, global warming, and spot-fire wars, often described as 'wicked problems' (Rittel and Webber 1973). These are problems that are wickedly difficult to resolve because they are an inherent part of the society that seeks to resolve them (Brown et al. 2010). Since their resolution requires changes in an already-changing human society and the living and non-living systems that contain them, the resolution of wicked problems goes beyond the reach of the formal academic disciplines created during the Enlightenment. Any such resolution will need to go even further and embrace all the human ways of knowing. Every human being has access to the personal, physical, social, ethical, aesthetic and interpersonal forms of understanding, combining that understanding in answers to the reflective question "What does it all mean?"

Recognition of a collective mode of construction of knowledge that does embrace all these ways of knowing is gathering pace. In the 1950s mammalian archeologist Pierre Teilhard de Chardin predicted that the next step in the evolution of the human mind would be a collective mind, a mind of minds, with all minds informing each other, without borders or barriers (Teilhard de Chardin 1955/1975, 1966). It is essential here not to confuse a collective mind with a mass mind that thinks as a single whole. Each collective mind gains strength from being free to develop to its own greatest extent as well as contributing to a richer whole.

During the 1970s, a host of ideas emerged for incorporating paths to the construction of knowledge drawn from beyond the academic disciplines. Pathfinders such as Thomas Kuhn, Silvio Funtowicz, Jerome Ravetz and Gregory Bateson questioned the dominance of empirical science, not only within the disciplines, but as a prototype for all knowledge (Kuhn 1962/1970; Funtowicz and Ravetz 1993; Bateson 1973, 1979). This capacity for a collective mind was being developed long before the arrival of a practical linking mechanism, the Internet in the 1980s. A second wave of fresh thinking appeared at the turn of this century. Helga Nowotny opening up the idea of an open construction of knowledge (Nowotny and Plaice 1994; Gibbons et al. 1994), while Julie Thompson Klein and Christian Pohlin in this volume linked the academic disciplines to the new direction (Klein 1996, 2010). For this second wave, there was digital technology extending the face-to-face human communication of these new ideas into a global electronic web. For those wishing to scope this emerging knowledge landscapes, there is now almost a double literature: on the one hand following classical science and on the other pursuing the new knowledge landscape being laid out by collective minds.

Issue: The Academic Disciplines and the Collective Mind

Disciplines in general continue to follow the framework developed during the scientific Enlightenment, seeking to reduce complexity and rely on objective observations, while training their apprentices in the same mode. However, this approach separates an issue from its changing social and physical context and privileges academic thinking over personal, community, creative and ethical experience. During the last part of the twentieth century, there were increasing efforts to find ways for the academic disciplines to combine in order to better understand rapidly changing and interconnected events (Brown et al. 2010). At first, the focus remained within the disciplinary domains in inter- and multi-disciplinary inquiry. Then the move to transdisciplinarity went further, maintaining the importance of the academic disciplines while accepting forms of knowledge from outside the disciplines.

This shift in thinking began when Thomas Kuhn differentiated between normal standardised empirical science and open-ended revolutionary science (Kuhn 1962/1970). Recognizing the need for creative thinking and an open approach to knowledge in revolutionary science, Funtowicz and Ravetz developed a widely applied Post-Normal Science (Ravetz 1999, 2005). Post Normal Science accepted that revolutionary science had become normal under conditions where, as they said, facts are uncertain, values in dispute, stakes high and decisions urgent. Their proposition was that revolutionary conditions had become normal in times of transformational change and so revolutionary science with its open-endedness and imagination had become the new normal science. Other initiatives which carry revolutionary thinking into mainstream practice have been spreading rapidly. Educational institutions at all levels have increasingly included applied and integrated courses. Popular writing has introduced the theoretical ideas of the social and physical sciences into every-day knowledge and vice versa. Science fiction in text and film is another avenue for expanding the public knowledge base through connecting the physical, the social and the creative.

Increasingly, frameworks for a collective mind have become vehicles for moving to realize the full scope of human potential. Helga Nowotny and colleagues extended transdisciplinarity to include the idea of type 2 knowledge with six characteristics. Their new construction of knowledge is grounded in experience, welcomes diversity, goes beyond the disciplines, and is transgressive in that it violates traditional rules

(Nowotny et al. 2001). It is also accountable and rigorous in its tests for validity. Building on the same foundation, versions of the individual collective mind have emerged in multiple fields. Case studies of an unbounded mind that is both transgressive and goes beyond disciplines demonstrate inventiveness in the business world (Mitroff and Linstone 1993). A pragmatic and democratic mind is able to draw on learning from the whole of human experience (Ansell 2011). A participatory mind is totally immersed in the complex world of human relationships (Skolimowski 1994).

For minds linked to other minds in groups of any size, a range of authors have suggested dynamic frameworks that can harness the diversity in a collective mind, and join together parts and wholes. Bateson's *ecology of mind* draws on the interconnected rhythms of natural systems (Bateson 1973, 1979). Alexander's *pattern language* incorporates the inherent energy of all life-giving systems when they can be captured in participatory planning and design (Alexander et al. 1977). The present authors' proposition for a *transformation science* extends the normal science of the Enlightenment to address the conditions of the Anthropocene (Brown and Harris 2014).[2]

The strong currents towards both individual and group collective thinking confirm Pierre Teilhard de Chardin's prophecy of collective thinking as the next step in human evolution (Teilhard de Chardin 1955/1975).[3] The Ostroms, Elinor and Vincent, restructure natural resource management as governance of collective common pool resources (Ostrom 1990) and Elinor gains a Nobel Prize.[4] The Mindells, Arnold and Amy, rethink democracy as each individual's collective thinking joining together, leading to a deeper democracy (Mindell 1992, 2002). Christopher Alexander gives us a pattern language which leads to revolutionary collective thinking in town planning, engineering design and the software design for social media (Alexander et al. 1977). The boundaries erected within cultures, genders, ages and capacities are becoming permeable. The world is entering a new era of thought. Whether it survives as the mainstream, or is blocked by compartmentalized thinking, or generates yet another dimension of thought is as yet unknown.

This wave of new thinking about how we can best think should be no surprise. The human mind has access to the capacities of introspection and reflection, and of physical, social, ethical, aesthetic, and sympathetic interpretations of the world as its birthright (Brown and Harris 2014). The practice of collective thinking is available to everyone, and access to collective learning is already part of lifelong formal and informal education, at least to some degree (Brown and Lambert 2013). Nor is the idea of a collective mind with an innate capacity for collective thinking a new idea. Following on from the time of the Renaissance, mathematician Rene Descartes, known as the father of the Enlightenment, wrote (Descartes 1637/1946, p. iv):

---

[2] Chapter 8. Transformation science: A science of change.
[3] Teilhard de Chardin predicted a new phase of human evolution, the noosphere, literally a sphere of thought that surrounds the globe.
[4] See http://en.wikipedia.org/wiki/Elinor_Ostrom [accessed 27.3.14].

> the diversity of our opinions does not arise from some being endowed with a greater share of reason than others. . . To be possessed of a vigorous mind is not enough; the prime requisite is rightly to apply it. (Rene Descartes 1647)

And in another message from the seventeenth century:

> No man is an island,
> entire of itself,
> . . . Any man's death diminishes me,
> because I am involved in mankind,
> And therefore never send to know for whom the bell tolls;
> It tolls for thee. (John Donne 1607)[5]

And more recently:

> I am large. I contain multitudes . . . .
> Missing me in one place, search in another,
> I stop somewhere waiting for you. (Walt Whitman 1986) [6]

The collective mind moves beyond the individual to the community, national and international scene. Pressures have been rising for political agreements to be formulated through collective rather than polarised thinking. National centres for dialogue in Sweden, Canada and Australia have been purpose-built for round-table negotiations rather than as theatres for formal debates. Major global dilemmas are being addressed through international think tanks rather than established structures, as for example the annual *Davos World Economic Forum*, the *Global Social Forum* and the *Copenhagen Climate Change Convention*. Global social movements based on collective thinking at the local scale are making a difference through programs such as *Transition Towns, Healthy Cities* and *Common Ground*.[7]

The one direct action program endorsed by the inaugural United Nations Conference on Environment and Development in Rio de Janeiro in 1992 called for a collective mind. The program was Local Agenda 21. The aim was specified as "*shared governance for a given locality which incorporates the goals of all stakeholders in that community, and balances social, economic and environmental resources*" an aim requiring the application of a collective mind, individually and as a group (Local Agenda 21, Chap. 28, 1992).[8] Over the two decades 1992–2012 the Local Sustainability Project based at the Australian National University, Canberra, worked towards the aims of Local Agenda 21 with over 300 collective action projects in seven countries (Brown and Lambert 2013).

This experience of conducting the Local Sustainability Project in partnership with local communities produced a collective learning framework, four reframed paradoxes and a set of seven questions which together were found to encapsulate the workings of a collective mind (Brown and Harris 2014). An early insight was that

---

[5] John Donne, Devotions upon Emergent Occasions, Meditation 17, 1624.

[6] Walt Whitman, *Song of Myself*, 1855, p. 14.

[7] Web search engines have comprehensive accounts of each of these significant examples given in this paragraph of the collective mind at work.

[8] See http://en.wikipedia.org/wiki/Earth_Summit [accessed 25.3.14].

taking part in any significant transformational change involved two separate learning spirals: collective learning within *individuals* and collective learning among a *group*. Collective learning in each case tapped into the human capacity to combine all ways of knowing: the intra-personal, the physical, the social, the ethical, the aesthetic, the inter-personal and the reflective. The two applications of collective thinking, individual and group, are described in practice in the examples below.

A second insight was the recognition of the need to welcome paradox, examples of two things that cannot both be true, rather than to try to resolve them. A paradox proved to be a signal that here was a potential catalyst for change. The Local Sustainability Project found that moving a paradox from its basis in opposing positions to a dynamic relationship facilitated transformational change. For instance, there is conflict between advocates of early prevention and post hoc treatment for the impacts of climate change, when it would seem sensible for them to pool their skills to pursue both.

This renegotiation from opposites to relationships was particularly effective for exploring some of the basic issues of the Anthropocene. Parts and wholes, stability and change, individuals and society, and rational and creative thinking are routinely represented as separate entities, often in opposition to one another. Gregory Bateson[9] points out that such division can lead to a schizophrenic understanding of each of those dimensions (Bateson 1958, 1973). Such divisions make trying to service both components a disruptive double bind, unless there was some bridging position.

Take the concept of gender for instance. Bateson described the ways in which the more polarised the gender relations, the more a community develops formal ways of negotiating relationships between male and female, from marriage to parenting. Where a third more tolerant position exists, the less tension surrounding that issue. For instance, Aboriginal Australia has a complex pattern of behaviour between the sexes that is firmly reinforced. Sisters and brothers, mothers-in-law and sons-in-law may not look at each other much less speak. Non-aboriginal Australia has legislated for marriage within and between the sexes, and marriage itself has become optional, with heterosexual marriages dropping below 50 % of the population.

In the Local Sustainability Project, the conclusion that paradoxes can cover dynamic relationships led to ways to negotiate viable alternatives to extreme positions. The relationships between each pair could be radically reconfigured for a community to accept transformational change. This was particularly fruitful with the four dimensions of transformational thinking identified above. In working with parts and wholes, synergy among the parts allows the emergence of a radically new whole. Rhythms of stability and change can create adjustments through developing a self-organising system. Allowing interactions among the diversity of individuals within a society generates a strong shared community ethos to develop. Collective learning arises from the fusion of inductive and deductive logic in abductive reasoning, which makes use of both, allowing rational and creative thinking to create leaps forward in the one enterprise. However, these changes from paradox to relationships represent

---

[9] Part 11: Form and pathology in relationship.

large changes in the current normal pattern of Anthropocene thought. Each will require compensatory action, a bridging position to help people make the changes that includes "but" and "or" by "both" and "and".

Resolution: Accepting Paradoxes and Framing Collective Questions

A third insight from the Local Sustainability Project studies provided a practical pathway to respond to the challenges of the other two insights. In the case of both individuals and groups, drawing on the full capacities of the participants in a shared area of concern required answers to a suite of seven questions. In each case, two questions were posed internally by the individual thinkers (intrapersonal and reflective questions) and five questions explore a full understanding of the context (physical, social, ethical, aesthetic, and inter-personal). The five questions of the context of the issue generalised from the field studies were:

With the hope of living in a peaceful, just and creative society:

- Is it physically possible for this society to support humans in their diverse chosen lifestyles?
- Is it socially a rule that all members of this society contribute their full potential to their hoped for future?
- Are there ethical principles that hold that all members of this society should respect each other and their supporting environment?
- Are there aesthetically satisfying ways for all members, no matter what culture or creed, to live in harmonious relationships with their social and natural environments?
- Is there a sympathetic understanding between the diverse interests in the same society and among different interests in other societies?

Expanding on the two inward and five outward-directed questions:

Introspective questions are best asked at the beginning of a collective learning spiral, before exploring the issue itself. Each of the diverse participants will have their own position on each of the answers to the outward-directed questions. For the individual, reflection is internal and lies within the more-than-conscious as well as the conscious mind. The cycle of this reflection is described as the final step of the process. Sources of insights into this process include Michael Polanyi, Jerome Bruner and Howard Gardner (Polanyi 1958; Bruner 1986, 1990, 1996; Gardner 1983, 1993).

Physical questions explore the material world. This is the world we can see, touch, count, measure, and invent highly creative tools to extend our own capacity to investigate and describe. Telescopes and microscopes, the abacus and the computer are all extensions of the human mind. The language of the physical world includes observations, numbers, descriptions, algorithms, systems, probabilities and diagrams. Seminal writer on scientific methods include Carl Popper, James Watson,

Helga Nowotny, Peter Scott and Michael Gibbons (Popper 1963, 1972; Watson 1968; Nowotny and Plaice 1994; Gibbons et al. 1994; Nowotny et al. 2001).

Social questions address the way every human being is reared in a community through social learning which develops their way to talk, cook food, count, build shelter, make artefacts, store resources, rear children and take part in the community's own way of constructing reality (Mead 1928, 1978). This is as true of the smallest village as the most powerful nation. The language is modelling, symbols, icons, metaphors, artefacts, patterns, and narratives. Influential writers include Michel Foucault, Roland Barthes and Pierre Bordieu (Foucault 1969/2002; Barthes 1957/1972, 1975; Bourdieu 1984, 1990).

Ethical Questions   Ethical questions take the form of what should be? How should we live? How should we treat each other? How should we share resources, help others in need, live up to our own ideals? All human societies construct reference points intended to keep intact this complex network of rules for living together, some as icons, some as gods, and some as patterns of ideals. Ethics are not necessarily consistent or positive. For instance adultery is not legislated against in Western countries, although it may be regarded as immoral; in other cultures it brings a death sentence. There are reviews of ethical principles for human responsibility for other humans, other living things and the state of the material world by John Passmore, Thomas Berry, David Suzuki and all the religions (Passmore 1974/1980; Berry 1999; Suzuki et al. 1997/2007).

Aesthetic Questions   Societies differ widely in their choice of aesthetic expression. In all cultures, aesthetic expression is a heightening of the emotions released by the patterning of ideas, sound, movement, visuals and language. Scientists express their sense of the aesthetic by describing their work as 'a beautiful experiment', 'an elegant solution'. Every community has some shared ideas about acceptable disorder. Interpretations of aesthetic responses come from literary and artistic reviews of the time. A seminal work is Roland Barthes *Image, Music, Text*, and other writers are Arthur Koestler and Mary Midgley (Barthes 1977; Koestler 1964/1989, 1967, 1978).[10]

Sympathetic Questions   There are many patterns of sympathetic understanding that form within and between groups of people: the young and the old, within a family and among siblings, within communities of practice and instantaneously between one human being and another. In many cultures this form of understanding is expressed through a language of "thou" relationships. Sympathetic communication within inter-personal relationships is always partly non-verbal. Classic writing deep understanding between humans is Martin Buber's " I and thou", and Arnold Mindell on Deep democracy (Buber 1975; Mindell 1992).

Reflective questions are answered by considering the answers to the introspective questions and the outward directed inquiries as a whole. To ask and answer reflexive

---

[10] See http://en.wikipedia.org/wiki/Mary_Midgley [accessed 30.4.14].

questions is the greatest challenge of all in forming a collective mind, individually and as a group. Reflective questions ask for skills such as imagination, creativity, and intuition. Traditional ways of bringing the answers together include the Gestalt, a creative leap, hypotheses, collage, a symphony, meditation, prayer, and poetry. The results of reflective thinking are appearing from the digital world in data visualisations, videos, face book, and twitter patterns. This is the domain of the philosopher Isaiah Berlin (1959/1990, 1998). Others influential writers are Pierre Teilhard de Chardin, Gregory Bateson, and Stephen J. Gould (1977, 2002, 2004).

While the order above appeared to be the optimum order to ask the questions, in practice, in the range of case studies of transformational change, the sequence can be entered into at any point. There is no hard and fast rule. The fixed points are that all the questions are asked, answered by the appropriate form of evidence and by the full range of key interests and the process concludes with the reflection on the whole.

Example 1. Asking the Collective Questions of Oneself

The first step for each individual in a collective learning spiral is to consider their position on the four re-oriented paradoxes (parts and wholes, stability and change, individual and society, and rational and creative), and to ask the seven collective questions of themselves in relation to the issue of concern. Since the dominant approach to the four paradoxes during the scientific era has been to place them in opposition to one another, collective thinking here may require a cognitive shift in one's own thinking. For those already perceiving each paradox as a dynamic connection, as synergistic, stochastic, developmental, and holistic respectively, they will need to appreciate that others will still be considering them as poles apart. For those involved in transformational change, changing the content makes very little difference to the system, while changing the relationships between the parts of the system in this way generates major differences (Capra 1996).

Introspective questions involve the individual in establishing pathways from their conscious to their more-than conscious mind. Recent neuroscience has identified 95 % of an individual's use of their brain as taking place within their so-called unconscious mind (Lackoff and Johnson 1999). Asking questions on the physical domain asks that you realistically assess your own experience in the field. Social questions are asked from within the questioner's and answered from within the respondent's own social profile. Where the two profiles match there is a risk of too narrow an understanding. Where the social profiles differ there is a risk of misunderstanding.

Ethical questions are not always acknowledged, shared or even recognized as ethical principles at all. Yet every human being is guided by ethical principles which determine their relationships with others and their decision-making. Aesthetic questions may be in the eye of the questioner; they are also preset by cultural expectations of beauty and ugliness, naivety and elegance, boredom and excitement. Sympathetic questions of oneself about one's own relationships with places, living and non-living things and human beings are already part of your identity. There can be a difference between people and places that social rules say you ought to identify with and the ones you actually do.

Reflective questions bring together the questions asked and answers found in the other six avenues of thinking and this requires the choice of an integrative pathway. By adulthood everyone has arrived at a personal style of bringing diverse ideas together in their everyday decision-making. Depending on the particular field, you may be accustomed to using reflective processes of reaching a gestalt, seeking synergies, making creative leaps, building collages, saying a prayer, meditating, finding a synthesis and using your intuition.

For each individual, the extent to which they are prepared to spend time on the seven questions will vary considerably according to priorities. For anyone designing, supervising, evaluating or writing up a collective inquiry or collective learning program, this first step is essential. For the participants in the project, the priority will be determined by the designer. In the example which follows, the core members were asked to share their answers to the interpersonal questions.

Example 2. Taking Part in a Collective Learning Inquiry

Both Brown and Lambert 2013 and Brown and Harris 2014 contain many examples of the collective mind in action. In the example that follows, the focus issue is the management of regenerative agriculture, with the aim of achieving optimum landscape and social health. This issue involves transformational change that affects the entire living and non-living planet; impacts on every different locality; calls on all interests in a community or nation; affects all cultural traditions; crosses all disciplinary boundaries; and calls on all seven ways of understanding the issue. This makes the issue a complex and wicked problem, suitable for taking as an example of applying a collective mind.

The relationship between regenerative agriculture and social health generates several wholes. The whole of the population of interest can be taken to be the dominant production agriculture, with high levels of fertiliser, pollution and mechanical treatment of soil; or it can be the indigenous population who managed the whole Australian continent sustainably and productively for 40,000 years. Or it can be the regenerative landscape management which calls on a mixture of organic farming and efficient mechanical practices, informed by the landscape's indigenous history. Each of those wholes has different sets of parts, and answers every one of the seven questions quite differently. Production agriculture is driven by profit-taking, giant chemical organisations, agronomy, and often absentee landlords. Aboriginal peoples worked to a land ethic in which the land determined their human as well as their land management relations. People were responsible for the land on which they were born. Regenerative farmers formed a sympathetic community of practice, aware that they needed mutual support and to learn from each other.

Exploring the other three paradoxes gives similar depth to an understanding of transformational change. The relationships between stability and change affect each of the potential wholes. The Australian continent is old and depleted of fertile soil. Each of the wholes has a community which seeks to establish a stable future. This is in a highly unstable climate marked for its floods and droughts; and in a resource-dependent country that is highly vulnerable to overseas markets. Thus change is inevitable and will affect each of the stable states in a different way. The outcome will be determined by the system of people, land and the zeitgeist that makes up any particular whole.

In seeking to advance regenerative landscape management in the service of land-scape and social health the relationship between individuals and their community is more important than either separately. So is the importance of giving rational thinking and creative thinking equal emphasis in making decisions based on the interpretation of the other paradoxes.

Collective Learning Step 1. Starting Out: Scoping the Field

The collective learning spiral starts with establishing the shared concern for the problem among all the interests in an issue. For regenerative agriculture and social health the breadth of the interests can make this seem almost impossible if they are asked to agree on the cause or the solution. However, they can readily agree that the connections between the two are a shared concern. Moreover, since all those involved will be making their decisions based on the evidence, the seven collective questions form a common language and the answers provide a shared understanding that allows everyone to make their own full contribution.

In this project a shared understanding of the common concern was developed from 30 founding members with interests in farming, research, management, conservation, sustainable development and design. With later consultation on email, and a day-long workshop, the scoping they developed on the core issue was:

> Regenerative agriculture is a collective enterprise designed to realize an emergent capacity to improve landscape health and with it individual and societal health. It seeks to do this by harnessing the minds and experience of all with an influence in land and in society in regenerative landscape management.
> Important in this process will be knowledge and practice of although not limited to, indigenous people, agriculturalists and other land managers, education and research institutions, government bodies, the health professions, food industries, town planners, neighbourhood groups, those involved in social movements such as healthy urban food systems, healthy soils, and Landcare and community self-sufficiency.

Collective Learning Step 2. Sharing Ideals: Aims for the Program

The original 30 met again to map out a possible course of action, beginning with shar-ing their ideals. The main interests present were farmers, environmental scientists, economists and collective and action researchers. The group were invited to respond to share their own individual answers to the seven collective questions. The aim was not to agree or prioritise; it was to become familiar with each other's positions.

In summary, some of the individual answers covered the seven questions as follows.

Our aims for the outcomes:

- A change in the trajectory of thought, practice and health from degrading to improving with multiple benefits at all levels: social, landscape, health, economies (an ethical question);
- Support human well-being by and with supporting more sustainable production systems (a biophysical question)
- Realising the dream so it can readily change people, landscapes, thinking, working, paradigms (an aesthetic question)
- Realisation of capacity of the social-ecological system, inclusion of commu-nity/environment as a whole (a reflective question)
- Personal fulfilment, advocacy across landscapes, participatory land management (a reflective question)
- Achieve something for society and not just for ourselves (social)
- Seeing a network of people with the same objectives actually making a difference as distinct from tinkering round the edges (sympathetic)
- A shining mind-change recruiting program that Australians can relate to—like the Opera House, Uluru and Bondi Beach (aesthetic)

Collective Learning Step 3. Collecting Facts: Descriptions of Supporting and Impeding Factors

Extensive information on the physical status of landscape production on the one hand and regenerative agriculture on the other proved to be readily available. However, the participants' priorities for collecting the data required differed widely, even dramat-ically. Data collection (1) a detailed profile of physical risks to agriculture, to health and to society from the current agricultural tradition (biophysical evidence). Data collection (2) an almost lyrical account of the emotional and social benefits from a collective regenerative agriculture (social, aesthetic and sympathetic evidence). Data collection (3) an in-depth study of the different lifestyles and practices of pro-duction and generative farmers (social and biophysical evidence). Data collection (4) the research traditions and disciplines of different approaches to agriculture and social health (social and sympathetic evidence). Data collection (5) the community of successful regenerative practitioners (sympathetic evidence). Data collection (6) principles driving production and regenerative farmers (ethical evidence).

The aims of the project made it clear that all approaches are welcome and can contribute to each other, and that there was no incompatibility between the data collections. Yet the authors of several of the collections saw them as taking the project in different directions, and for some, these would be in opposite directions, generating considerable conflict. That conflict led to one resignation from the program.

Collective Learning Step 4. Generating Ideas: Tapping in to the Potential for Transformational Change

Following the original meeting a transformational change strategy developed among the group, designed to meet the goals outlined in the vision. The elements of the strategy covered all dimensions of social change. There was a division between those who say the emergent and developmental nature of the program ideas as sufficient and inspiring, and those who saw it as failure to develop an effective organization.

Collective Learning Step 5. Moving to Action: Initiatives in Progress

By 12 months after the original meeting, the following activities were taking place:

- Alliances had been formed with parallel organisations such as *Soils for Life*, *Safe Food Alliance*, *SEE* (Society, Economics, Environment) *Change*, *International Association of EcoHealth* and *Innovative Farmers*.
- A writing group was established in the Fenner School, Australian National University for mutual support for the writers of seven books on the project theme who had publishing contracts.
- Members were attending international meetings on project themes.
- A website was established, with a blog and a contact point for allied interests.
- A consultancy file and a reference file on community of practice of collective minds were being established as a public resource.

Collective Learning Step 6. Following On

As the program developed it became time to think of how the project could become established for the long term as a permanent catalyst for the desired transformational change. Canvassing members generated alternative options which included a formal structure and an open network, an information base and a dialogue hub, a separate organisation and a series of partnerships, and a unique set of ideas and a shared vision.

Following collective learning principles, the project coordinating team decided that these options were not in conflict. They were all valuable and collaborative steps forward, as the actions in Step 5 demonstrate. The project continues; the outcomes are still uncertain.

Conclusion

This volume documents the increasing spread of transdisciplinary thinking into the fields of education, research, science, workplaces, politics, the arts, social planning and personal decision-making. This chapter has recorded a move to go beyond transdisciplinarity to collective thinking. Transdisciplinary thinking maintains the disciplines as a take-off point for including a wider range of evidence on an issue. In doing so it inevitably continues to remain grounded in the university and research tradition, and in formal administration, with their inheritance of the scientific Enlightenment and the dominance of empirical thought.

Collective thinking offers the opportunity to access the full potential of human thought, no longer restricted to fragmented constructions of knowledge and the limitations of purely quantitative evidence. Field studies found that collective thinking at the personal and at the group level asks for reframing opposites as dynamic relationships, and moving from the limited access to understanding offered by empirical evidence to include asking introspective, physical, social, ethical, aesthetic, sympathetic and reflective questions. One argument for bringing the collective mind into the mainstream is that it is required in order to interpret and influence the transformational changes of the Anthropocene. Another is that human thought has reached an era in which it can expand in unprecedented directions serviced by a digital revolution.

Acknowledgement of the contributions to this article of reader and commentator, Wendy Rainbird.

References

Alexander, C., Ishikawa, S., Silverstein, M., Jacobson, M., Fiksdahl-King, I., & Angel, S. (1977). *A pattern language: Towns, buildings and constructions*. New York: Oxford University Press.

Ansell, C. K. (2011). *Pragmatist democracy: Evolutionary learning as public philosophy*. New York: Oxford University Press.

Barthes, R. (1957/1972). *Mythologies* (trans: A. Lavers). London: Jonathon Cape.

Barthes, R. (1975). *The pleasure of the text* (trans: R. Miller). New York: Hill and Wang.

Barthes, R. (1977). *Image—Music—Text* (trans: S. Heath). New York: Hill and Wang.

Bateson, G. (1958). *Naven: A survey of the problems suggested by a composite picture of the culture of a New Guinea Tribe drawn from three points of view* (2nd edn.). Stanford: Stanford University Press.

Bateson, G. (1973). *Steps to an ecology of mind: Collected essays in anthropology, psychiatry, evolution and epistemology*. St. Albans: Paladin.

Bateson, G. (1979). *Mind and nature: A necessary unity*. London: Wildwood House.

Berlin, I. (1959/1990). The decline of Utopian ideas in the West. In H. Hardy (Ed.), *The crooked timber of humanity: Chapters in the history of ideas*. Princeton: New Jersey Press.

Berlin, I. (1998). *The proper study of mankind: An anthology of essays*. London: Pimlico.

Berry, T. (1999). *The great work: Our way into the future*. New York: Bell Tower.

Bourdieu, P. (1984). *Distinction: A social critique of the judgment of taste* (trans: R. Nice). Cambridge: Harvard University Press.

Bourdieu, P. (1990). *The logic of practice* (trans: R. Nice). Stanford: Stanford University Press.

Buber, M. (1958/2000). *I and Thou* (trans: Ronald Gregor Smith) (2nd edn.). New York: Scribner Classics.

Brown V. A., & Harris, J. A. (2014). *The human capacity for transformational change: Harnessing the collective mind*. London: Routledge.

Brown, V. A., & Lambert, J. A. (2013). *Collective learning for transformational change: A guide to collaborative action*. London: Routledge.

Brown, V. A., Harris, J. A., & Russell, J. Y. (Eds.). (2010). *Tackling wicked problems: Through the transdisciplinary imagination*. London: Earthscan.

Bruner, J. (1986). *Actual minds, possible worlds*. Cambridge: Harvard University Press.

Bruner, J. (1990). *Acts of meaning*. Cambridge: Harvard University Press.

Bruner, J. (1996). *The culture of education*. Cambridge: Harvard University Press.

Capra, F. (1996). *The web of life: A new scientific understanding of living systems*. UK: HarperCollins.

Clark, K. (1971). *Civilization: A personal view*. London: BBC and John Murray.

Descartes, R. (1637/1946). *A discourse on the method of rightly conducting one's reason* (p. 570) (trans: J. Veitch). London: Everyman's Library.

Falk, R. (1999). *Predatory globalization: A critique*. Cambridge: Polity Press.

Foucault, M. (1969/2002). *The archaeology of knowledge* (trans: A. M. Sheridan Smith). London: Routledge.

Funtowicz, S. O., & Ravetz, J. R. (1993). Science for the post-normal age. *Futures, 25*(7), 739–755.

Gardner, H. (1983). *Frames of mind: The theory of multiple intelligences*. New York: Basic Books.

Gardner, H. (1993). *Multiple intelligences: The theory and practice*. New York: Basic Books.

Gibbons, M., Limoges, C., Nowotny, H., Schwartzman, S., Scott, P., & Trow, M. (1994). *The new production of knowledge: The dynamics of science and research in contemporary societies*. New York: SAGE.

Gould, S. J. (1977). *Ever since Darwin: Reflections in natural history*. New York: Norton.

Gould, S. J. (2002). *The structure of evolutionary theory*. Cambridge: Belknap Press.

Gould, S. J. (2004). *The Hedgehog, The Fox and the Magister's pox: Mending and minding the misconceived gap between science and the humanities*. London: Vintage.

Klein, J. T. (1996). *Crossing boundaries: Knowledge, disciplinarities, and interdisciplinarities*. Charlottesville: University of Virginia Press.

Klein, J. T. (2010). *Creating interdisciplinary campus cultures: A model of strength and sustainability*. San Francisco: Jossey-Bass.

Koestler, A. (1964/1989). *The act of creation*. London: Arkana.

Koestler, A. (1967). *The ghost in the machine*. London: Arkana.

Koestler, A. (1978). *Janus: A summing up*. Victoria: Hutchinson of Australia.

Kuhn, T. (1962/1970). *The structure of scientific revolutions*. Chicago: University of Chicago Press.

Lackoff, G., & Johnson, M. (1999). *Philosophy in the flesh: The embodied mind and its challenge to western thought*. New York: Basic Books.

Mead, M. (1928). *Coming of age in Samoa: A psychological study of primitive youth for western society*. New York: William Morrow and Company.

Mead, M. (1978). *Culture and commitment: The new relationships between the generations in the 1970s*. New York: Columbia University Press.

Mindell, A. (1992). *The leader as martial artist: An introduction to deep democracy. Techniques and strategies for resolving conflict and creating community*. San Francisco: HarperCollins.

Mindell, A. (2002). *The deep democracy of open forums: How to transform organizations into communities: Practical steps to conflict prevention and resolution for family, workplace and world*. Charlottesville: Hampton Roads.

Mitroff, I. I., & Linstone, H. A. (1993). *The unbounded mind: Breaking the chains of traditional business thinking*. New York: Oxford University Press.

Nowotny, H. (1994) *Time: The modern and postmodern experience* (trans: N. Plaice). Cambridge: Blackwell and Polity Press.

Nowotny, H., Scott, P., & Gibbons, M. (2001). *Re-thinking science: Knowledge and the public in an age of uncertainty*. MA: Blackwell and Polity Press.

Ostrom, E. (1990). *Governing the commons: The evolution of institutions for collective action*. Cambridge: Cambridge University Press.

Passmore, J. (1974/1980). *Man's responsibility for nature: Ecological problems and western traditions*. London: Duckworth.

Polanyi, M. (1958). *Personal knowledge: Towards a post-critical philosophy*. Chicago: University of Chicago Press.

Popper, K. (1963). *Conjectures and refutations: The growth of scientific knowledge*. London: Harper & Row.

Popper, K. (1972). *Objective knowledge: An evolutionary approach*. Oxford: Oxford University Press.

Ravetz, J. (1999). What is post-normal science? *Futures, 31*(7): 647–653.

Ravetz, J. (2005). *A no-nonsense guide to science*. UK: New Internationalist.

Rittle, H., & Webber, M. (1973). Dilemmas in a general theory of planning. *Policy sciences, 4*, 155–169.

Skolimowski, H. (1994). *The participatory mind: A new theory of knowledge and of the universe*. London: Arkana.

Steffen, W., Grinevald, J., Crutzen P., & Mc Neill, J. (2011). The anthropocene: Conceptual and historical perspectives. *Philosophical Transactions of the Royal Society A, 369*(1938), 842–867.

Suzuki, D., McConnell, A., & Mason, A. (1997/2007). *The sacred balance: Rediscovering our place in nature*. Vancouver: Greystone Books. Teilhard de Chardin, P. (1966). *Man's place in nature* (trans: R. Hague) St James's Place. London: Collins.

Teilhard de Chardin, P. (1966). *Man's place in nature* (trans: R. Hague) St James's Place. London: Collins.

Teilhard de Chardin, P. (1955/1975). *The phenomenon of man* (trans: B. Wall). New York: Harper & Row.

Watson, J. (1968). *The double helix: A personal account of the discovery of the structure of DNA*. Harmondsworth: Penguin.

Whitman, W. (1986). In F. Murphy (Ed.), *Walt Whitman: The complete poems*. London: Penguin Classics.

Valerie Brown Emeritus Professor Valerie A. Brown AO, BSc MEd PhD is currently Director, Local Sustainability Project, Fenner School of Environment and Society, Australian National University. She is Emeritus Professor of the University of Western Sydney after being its Foundation Chair of Environmental Health 1996–2002. Local Sustainability Project is a collective action research program working with organisations, local government and communities on whole-of-community change in Australia, Europe, Fiji, Malaysia, Hong Kong and Nepal, 1989–2014. Her recent books with John Harris are The human capacity for transformational change. Harnessing the collective mind Routledge 2014; and Tackling wicked problems through the transdisciplinary imagination. Earthscan 2010; with Judy Lambert Collective learning and transformational change Routledge 2013; with John Grootjans, Jan Richie et al Sustainability and health: supporting global integrity in public health. Allen and Unwin 2005; With Meg Keen and Robert Dyball Social learning and environmental management: towards a sustainable future. Earthscan 2005. website www.valeriebrown.com.au

John A. Harris is a Visiting Fellow and collective action researcher with the Local Sustainability Project based in the Fenner School of Society and Environment at the Australian National University and the international Alliance for Regenerative Landscapes and Social Health (ARLASH). His academic interests relate to the human understanding of complex social and environmental systems, with emphasis on finding ways for progressing understanding into practice. John's background is in scientific research in ecological systems in Australia, Papua New Guinea and USA and in the teaching and design of university undergraduate and postgraduate curricula in socio-ecological systems at the University of Canberra 1972–1999 Recent books include The Human Capacity for Transformational Change: Harnessing the Collective Mind (co-authored with V. A. Brown) and Earthscan and Routledge 2014 Tackling Wicked Problems Through the Transdisciplinary Imagination (co-edited with V. A. Brown and J. Y. Russell) London: Earthscan 2010

Coda

Paul Gibbs

In this personal review of the important and independent contributions to this book, I want to consider the timing of their development and how it might be possible to draw some of the main ideas together. To do so, I have chosen the ideas of periodicity and rhizomes. A recognition of the real world as a place in which we live and flourish is not new in the ontological literature. How we deal with our being in this world, both personally and as members of communities, has been a central issue for thinkers from ancient times to the present. Many paradigms have been used to create understanding and have worked well in their time—from the seven days of creation to evolution—and given both structure and meaning to our existence. They have forged what we value into part of the way in which humanity regards itself through the advocacy of rights and obligations. The periodization of our self-knowledge and that of our existence in a world of other entities is represented in the practical applications and artefacts that flow from these separate identifiable epochs of time, epochs that are not universal but culturally constructed. I will speak of the Enlightenment and the Renaissance, which have resonance in Europe but little in China or Africa, countries that have their own equally compelling periodization.

The very nature of time is historical and developmental. In contemporary society, commentators refer to a shifting landscape of knowledge production; but what is new is not the shift but the rapidity and busy-ness of change and the temptation to conflate this change with a notion of progress. Changes include different roles for knowledge institutions in a global 'knowledge economy'; increasing demands for knowledge production to address growing national, international and global perspectives that both connect and alienate communities, with some enjoying unimaginable abundance while many people still starve.

Time might be in flux, but how it is temporalized has differed in its flow. Historians have recognized this through discussions of the periodization of time, and we want briefly to locate our discussions of time and the role of our current universities and

P. Gibbs (✉)
Middlesex University, London, UK
e-mail: paul.gibbs@mdx.ac.uk

© Springer International Publishing Switzerland 2015
P. Gibbs (ed.), *Transdisciplinary Professional Learning and Practice,*
DOI 10.1007/978-3-319-11590-0_14

professionals in changing and challenging epochs. The temporality of the history of the university can be found in the interlocking notion of this historical time and our intellectual history. Each shapes higher education institutions and professions by sustaining, permitting, changing and organizing them within it.

Tracing a periodization of intellectual life and time emerging from the Middle Ages, a new type of present could be detected, distinct from that of the ancients, one not determined by past ways but beginning to see a discontinuity between the past and the present. This discontinuity was more evident in the Renaissance, when modern ideas were seen in opposition to those of the Middle Ages. Yet time remained tied to a past, to a tradition not of the immediate past but to the achievement of the Ancients. Aristotelian physics, politics and metaphysics were the benchmarks of Western cultural development. They formed the basis for the power of the Catholic religion and social structures.

The Enlightenment that followed changed this in two major related respects. First came the idea that time was abstract and not God-given, and second, as a consequence of escaping from the eschatology of Church teaching, the idea was entertained that there was a future, empty to be shaped (rather than predestined) that could be intended and filled by humanity for its own purpose. The appearance of time and temporality in opposition to tradition was the beginning of what might be termed modernity and the growth of secular self-determination. It saw not just the understanding of given phenomena but the realization of a power to change things—all things—through acquired knowledge. The threads to understanding the natural world through perceiving what can be taken to be existence was central to the views of thinkers such as Descartes, Kant, Bacon and Hume. These positivists argued that verification can only be through experience or through reasoning. Their most celebrated engagement with the social sciences is found, perhaps, in Hempel's discussion in Logical Positivism and the Social Science (2001). In this essay, Hempel (2001) contended that 'there is no fundamental difference in subject matter between the natural sciences and the psychological and sociological disciplines' (2001, p. 255), a view echoed by fellow logical positivist, Carnap, who claimed that 'all laws of nature, including those that hold for organisms, human beings, and human societies, are logical consequences of the physical laws' (cited in Hempel 2001, p. 267). This position sets itself the task of transposing knowledge that is imperfect and pre-scientific in respect of its scope and constancy into perfect knowledge, perfect to the extent is it causally understandable. It ignores both 'big pictures' and complexity to find ways of unravelling of complexity through the manipulation of variables. It creates sterile, deterministic spaces for humanity and sections knowledge into disciplines to 'aid' understanding, but also to make knowledge that the powerful in society control—academics, scientists and engineers, and those for whom it will bring benefit.

The post-Enlightenment period, that of modernity, nurtured social change and revolution. In addition, time itself became reflexive and broke from the ever-recurring present and now offered new ways of being. It is this epoch of difference, when change occurs and then continues to contribute to change with its own moving vortex, that concerns us here. It valorizes the present over the past and opens up an indeterminate future. It creates a desire for the new and leads to the idea of progress and development. It recognizes, mainly thanks to the work of Husserl (1983), the essence of an experience in a wide range of forms, either indirectly, as others might perceive it, or directly, to uncover the intent behind the experience. Intent is what we intend, or perceive, as a purpose. It is an ordered relationship where we perceive things: a knife for cutting; a code of conduct for reference to acceptable professional conduct; an exciting read for a train journey. It is a world where the messiness of the world cannot easily, if at all, be resolved through Aristotelian categories and prescribed Baconain methodologies; it is a world where problems are highly complex and where contingency is meaningless because of uncertainty. It is a place of encounters, where practices will need to dominate, and are structured around a complexity that has no definable beginning nor end, where our understanding is local, at best, and where the unforeseeable future ought to dominate ways of being. This is the world of the 'rhizome', as developed by Deleuze and Guattari (1987) in *A Thousand Plateaus,* mentioned by a number of authors in this book and used later in this chapter to assist in bringing collective meaning to the contribution of this book.

However, before turning to a discussion of how transdisciplinary research into the practice of professionals is rhizomatic in nature, I offer here a brief outline of what this might mean then make suggestions for how this idea is evident in almost all the chapters in the book, moving to argue that transdisciplinarity is rhizomatic and of 'our time' in nature and period. I finally conclude with the direction of travel that the content of this book has indicated.

Deleuze and Guattari, in their attempt to offer a metaphor for the way in which meaning might be constructed of our world, select the subterranean idea of 'rhizomes' to provide metaphor. This has an ideal imagery of connectivity, albeit potentially accidental to the way we exist and function in the real world. Deleuze and Guattari (1987) summarize the principal characteristics of a rhizome in this important and extensive quote:

> unlike trees or their roots, the rhizome connects any point to any other point, and its traits are not necessarily linked to traits of the same nature; it brings into play very different regimes of signs, and even nonsign states. The rhizome is reducible neither to the One nor the multiple.... The rhizome operates by variation, expansion, conquest, capture, offshoots. Unlike the graphic arts, drawing, or photography, unlike tracings, the rhizome pertains to a map that must be produced, constructed, a map that is always detachable, connectable, reversible, modifiable, and has multiple entryways and exits and its own lines of flight. It is tracings that must be put on the map, not the opposite. In contrast to centered (even polycentric) systems with hierarchical modes of communication and pre-established paths, the rhizome is an acentered, non-hierarchical, non-signifying system without a General and without an organizing memory or central automaton, defined solely by a circulation of states. (1987, p. 21)

Moreover, when applied to our social world, a 'rhizome ceaselessly establishes connections between semiotic chains, organizations of power, and circumstances relative to the arts, sciences, and social struggles' (ibid, p. 8).

This metaphor works well in recognizing both the openness of the way in which events are connected and the problems encountered when research attempts to resolve problem in defined, structurally arborescent ways. The interconnectivity of the encounters rather than causal contingencies makes attempts to deconstruct problems into their constituent parts problematic, as might be found in disciplinary approaches to problems. The metaphor helps us also to discriminate between the notions of the form of multi-, inter- and trans-disciplinarity, commented upon by Gibbs in this volume. To conceive of a problem as an open network, without either a discernible starting place, a time from which a solution may be planned or a point of final resolution, counters the Enlightenment faith in ultimate management. It creates the intellectual space for solutions that employ new, innovative ways of thinking, ways that define our current complex, uncertain and messy epoch.

This book highlights the intellectual debt owed to a small but deeply important group of thinkers who developed the transdisciplinary idea. This includes a number of authors contributing to this book, standing alongside the pioneers who feature in most of the chapters; Nicolescau, Kockelmans and Klein. All have shaped transdisciplinary thinking and all have augmented, illuminated and enhanced the subject. Each has contributed from a different starting point in what might be called rhizomatic transdisciplinarity thinking. Their views and starting places have established the rationale for transdisciplinarity, and benefit from there being no attempt to match them thematically but an acceptance of the different perspectives, often disciplinary and scientific, on solving major issues from the stance of principle. These principles enrich the fertile context of a rhizome of transdisciplinary thinking, nurtured by the values of, and encounters with, those previously excluded from problem solving that dignify the contribution of all stakeholders to solutions.

Rhizomatic Criticality, Learning, Thinking, Networking and Temporality

From these intellectual endeavours the emergent themes appearing within these pages are the different epistemological and ontological stances that the authors take. Perhaps the clearest realization of this is in the recurrent theme of the constraints that disciplinary knowledge places on recognizing problems and what warrants their resolution. In many of the chapters it is not the recognition of wider knowledge networks that is surprising but the difficulty the disciplines have in working together. They need to unshackle themselves of what defined their identify and find a way of being within the problem that satisfies themselves as well as the processes, power and political issues called forth to answer the problem. In the interwoven reality of this book I have identified five significant, if not exclusive, themes. They may not be the most important in terms of attention but they form a way of interpreting a structure to the contributions. I have suggested they might be called; *rhizomatic criticality, learning, thinking, networking* and *temporality*.

Rhizomatic criticality helps explore criteria for decisions, producing an approach that is neither simple nor prescriptive. It threatens the tradition of knowledge creation, the hegemony of those who sanction it and notions of truth that sustain it by replacing certainty with warranted belief. The use of a notion such as rhizomatic criticality would illuminate the super-complexity of encounters rather than engagements and would see an investigator more as a navigator of passages with no firm basis of contingency to guide her and only temporary local mapping for help (I am thinking here of the short-terming of disciplinary knowledge). Indeed, such guidance might not be of much use in a multiple process of understanding complex problems.

The notion of rhizomatic criticality clearly has encounters with a second theme, that of *rhizomatic learning*. Mentioned in many of the chapters is the role of professional education and the importance of formal education and its application to develop skills and mastery. Most of the focus is on the need for wider-ranging appreciation of situations and an ability to translate, moving from one centre for encounter, from one node to another, to see the semiotic where previously only the literal was envisioned. Rhizomatic learning requires the creation of a context within which the curriculum and knowledge are constructed by contributions made by members of the learning community, and which can be reshaped and reconstructed in a dynamic manner in response to environmental conditions. The learning experience itself may build on formal propositional knowledge and also on social, conversational processes, as well as on a personal knowledge-creation process, through the creation of large, unrestrained personal learning networks that may incorporate formal and informal social media. A leading proponent of rhizomatic learning, Cormier, defines the rhizomatic model of learning as where the:

> curriculum is not driven by predefined inputs from experts; it is constructed and negotiated in real time by the contributions of those engaged in the learning process. This community acts as the curriculum, spontaneously shaping, constructing, and reconstructing itself and the subject of its learning in the same way that the rhizome responds to changing environmental conditions. (2008)

Rhizomatic learning requires *rhizomatic thinking*. Indeed, Le Grange, in Deleuze and Guattari (1987), distinguishes between arborescent and rhizomatic thinking. The former refers to conceptions of knowledge as hierarchically articulated branches of a central stem or trunk rooted in firm foundations; a tree, in their instance, which they treat with the same distain as Sartre with the chestnut tree in his *Nausea* (2000).

A significant feature of the content of this book is networking and a notion of rhizomatic network does, I feel, add substance to this idea. *Rhizomatic networking* recognizes the this totalizing of the network in which we live but offers a new opportunity to revive democracy, potentially bypassing barriers of class and ethnicity, provided access is made available. Yet unlike tradition networks the rhizomatic networking is anarchic, for it recognizes no unifying connectivity principles. As Coyne describes it, a 'rhizomic system is dynamic and unresolved, growing and anarchic, in the manner of a rich and open-ended conversation' (2008, p. 553). To achieve such an account, which has explanatory significance for a wide range of methodological approaches to system networks, it assumes underlying relationships and feedback loops and favours other metaphors. It is, of course, necessary to uncover this organizational relationship and, having this information, an abductive approach that is wisely discursive would be more likely to reveal something worthwhile than the imposition of external framing through an implicit closed system model. It enables creative and imaginative thinking about socio-environmental problems. In this sense the rhizomatic network is more of discursive interpretation of the complexity of our world than a network that adheres to systems theory.

The last of many hidden themes in the engagement is the complexity of our periodicity. This time the theme is revealed in a number of interesting ways and argues against a fixed time and, as a consequence, place for the understanding of complex problems, their research and satisfactory resolution. Linking with the above transdisciplinarity has a temporality of it own: *a rhizomatic temporality*. If the links in time are not linear, if time cannot be considered solely to flow in one directions and validity is no longer always underpinned by rationality and logic, then the sequence that gives time its means is disrupted. Time's unfolding becomes more embodied, less abstract, and becomes the homogenizing temporality of known alternativeness, giving way to new and creative possibilities. The future takes no shape from the present and collective thinking liberating rather than entrapping.

Transdisciplinary Research as Poetic

Transdisciplinary research investigates the relationships of knowledge creation in its pragmatic state of problem solution, and how discipline knowledge can help through an analysis that creatively reconstitutes them, not in terms of the disciplines but in terms of the presenting problem. It is a diffractive response to the 'generalising, decontextualising and reductionist' approach that has traditionally characterized disciplinary approaches to knowledge generation. Wickson et al. (2006) have identified a number of challenges for transdisciplinary researchers and these include 'the different dimensions of integration required, the potential for two levels of reflection and the creative conceptual developments demanded by the presence of paradox' (2006, p. 1055). I should like to go one step further and suggest that, for the transdisciplinary researcher, the structure of the problem lies in terms of agency and the open system form of which the problem has irruption properties. These properties are rhizomatic and cannot be dictated, for the revealing of the relationship itself will offer up approaches to forms of understanding, but it may be sufficient to suggest they may flow from the empirical to the poetic.

Heidegger's (1993) claim that poetry has its own temporality has already been referred to in this book but the techno-poetry of rhizomatic combines encounters with different modes of expression and meaning to produce imaginative ways of knowing. The techno-poetic form facilitates connectivity of any point to any other point of knowledge sets offered by problem solvers, researched through situationally defined navigation. It follows no prescript or plan but the encounters the problem presents. The approach seeks to explore states of meaning via the operative environment or the problem. The non-closed nature of the system means it is not reducible to one solution but to a rich understanding of the issues pre-defined by disciplinary knowledge but revealed in the process of investigation. Its importance does not lie in the identification of specific nodes of revelation alone but in the directions of motion and configuration that give rise to an emergent series of readings and interpretations of the problem.

Deleuze and Guattari's rhizomes and rhizomatic ideas, presented as an interpretation in the pages of this book, offer a radical commentary on institutional structures of the professions and their difficulties in working in a transdisciplinary fashion. The pages have shown that where professions present coherent and authoritative knowledge structures they contain within themselves uncertainties and strange, unaccountable practices, especially at the margins of their domains. Rhizomatic analysis within the rubric of transdisciplinary investigation presents a challenge to many of the principles of professionalism that will need to be resolved if the problems of today render the future of others bereft of options.

Future Considerations

Wickson et al. (2006) suggest that, in our shifting landscape, 'knowledge generation in contemporary societies suggests a bright future for transdisciplinary (TD) research'. Interestingly, however, there is currently no clear consensus on what transdisciplinarity is or how its quality can be evaluated (2006, p. 1046). This is echoed by the position of UNESCO (ISSC 2013), among others. The World Social Science Report 2013, Changing Global Environments, represents a comprehensive overview of the field, gathering the thoughts and expertise of hundreds of social scientists from around the world, where transformation and transdisciplinarity are at the fore in devising ways that the social sciences might help confront climate and broader processes of environmental change. The intertwining within it of the human condition, as well as shaping the environment, is not readily dealt with by categorization derived from abstract rationality. It moves us into a new epoch, that of the Anthropocene (see Brown and Harris, this volume). This will see change in the university and its contribution to the identity of the profession. Universities will need to prepare professionals for a transdisciplinary epoch through developing capacity for transdisciplinarity. This will require facing up to the potential tensions between consolidation and interconnection, and between knowledge commodification and mutual learning (Russell et al. 2008). It will require professions to change and to realign and reinterpret within their supporting societies. This demands new thinking and a wider appreciation of what progress, developing personal dignity and humanity mean. A case for this change has been made, I think, by those who have contributed to this book.

References

Cormier, D. (2008). Rhizomatic education: Community as curriculum. *Innovate: Journal of Online Education, 4*(5), 6. http://www.editlib.org/j/ISSN-1552-3233/v/4/n/5/. Accessed 5 Nov 2014.
Coyne, R. (2008). The net effect: Design, the rhizome, and complex philosophy. *Futures, 40*(6), 552–561.
Deleuze, G., & Guattari, F. (1987). *A thousand plateaus: Capitalism and schizophrenia*. Minnesota: University of Minnesota Press.

Heidegger, M. (1993). What calls for thinking. In D. F. Krell (Ed.), *Basic writings* (pp. 365–392). London: Routledge.

Hempel, C. G. (2001). Logistical positivism and social sciences. In *The philosophy of Carl G. Hempel: Studies in science, explanation, and rationality* (pp. 253–274). New York: Oxford University Press.

Husserl, E. (1983). *Ideas pertaining to a pure phenomenology and phenomenological philosophy, 1st book: General introduction to pure phenomenology* (trans: F. Kerston). Dordrecht: Kluwer.

ISSC/UNESCO. (2013). *World social science report 2013: Changing global environments*. Paris: OECD/UNESCO.

Russell, A. W., Wickson, F., & Carew, A. L. (2008). Transdisciplinarity: Context, contradictions and capacity. *Futures, 40,* 460–472.

Sartre, J.-P. (2000). *Nausea* (trans.: R. Baldock). London: Penguin Classics.

Wickson, F., Carew, A. L., & Russell, A. W. (2006). Transdisciplinary research: Characteristics, quandaries and quality. *Futures, 38*(9), 1046–1059.

Paul Gibbs is Professor of Education at Middlesex University. His interests and publications span higher education marketing, philosophy, professional practice and time. He is Series Editor of Educational Thinker for Springer, holds positions on a number the editorial board of a number of international journal and has participated in a number of European projects. His elective interests find a conceptual home in transdisciplinarity.

Index

© Springer International Publishing Switzerland 2015
P. Gibbs (ed.), *Transdisciplinary Professional Learning and Practice,*
DOI 10.1007/978-3-319-11590-0

205

Printed by Printforce, the Netherlands